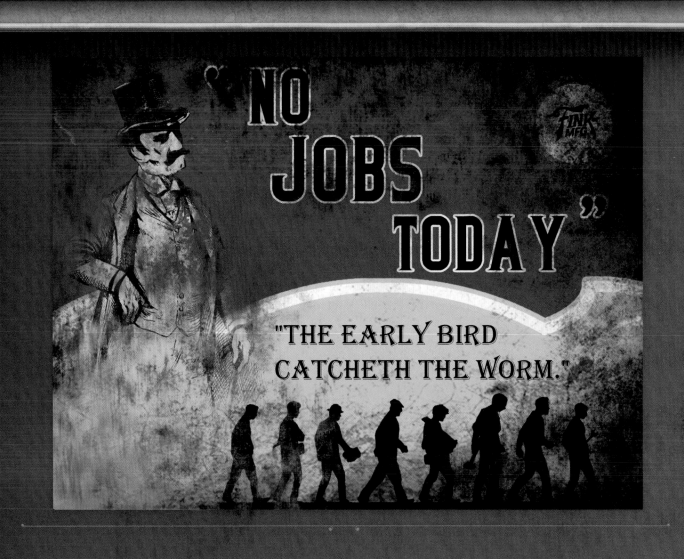

TABLE OF CONTENTS

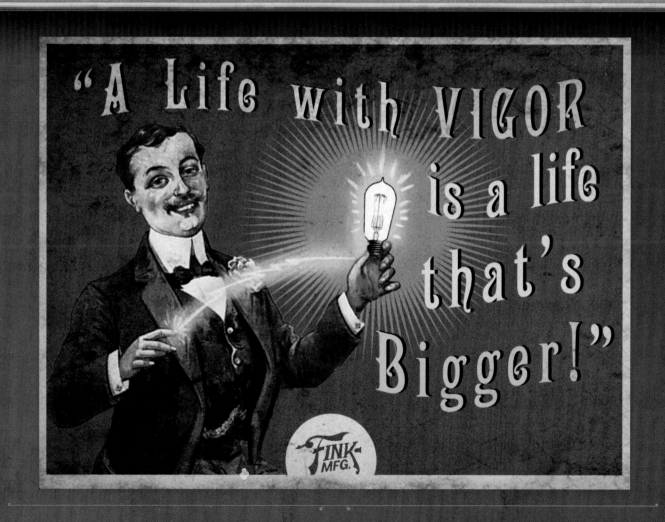

FOREWORD
BY KEN LEVINE

I like strategy guides. Always have. I like poring over data. I like the concept art, the dev team commentary. I like having another part of a game I love that I can put on my shelf.

I've been carrying a strategy guide for a 3DS game in my backpack for months as I travel on press tours and other Irrational business. I find it comforting to know: *I am equipped. I have knowledge.*

Here's a shameful confession: I especially love strategy guides that cover our games. Vain? Sure. But if I'm being honest, it always amazes me how much the guide makers seem to know about a game that I don't know. I get so distracted with the million things going on that sometimes I'm so focused on the part of the game I'm working on that other parts momentarily slip out of memory. The guide is the game, encapsulated, organized. It's a BioShock Infinite encyclopedia, just like the ones I used to pore over in the library in grade school.

Except this one has robots, and skylines and one beautiful, plucky, smart, and potentially dangerous woman. Which beats articles about rice production in ancient Mongolia. (Which, actually, while I write it sounds kind of cool. Note to self: Wikipedia rice production in ancient Mongolia).

That's my long winded way to introduce you to BradyGames' *Official BioShock Infinite Strategy Guide.* It's a true insider's look at the game, to explore the city of Columbia with a packet of information that Booker DeWitt would have killed for. It's packed full of exclusive details and artwork never shared outside our studio.

In order to help the writers and artists responsible for the guide research the game thoroughly, we invited them out to Irrational Games during BioShock Infinite's final hours to play it like crazy and meet with the staff. The crew from Brady not only fashioned a complete walkthrough of the entire game (including looks into all its secret areas and side-quests), they created detailed level maps, breakdowns of the enemies and loot, and bios of the cast that you won't find anywhere else.

To further aid in the making of the guide, we asked our team to share their own personal strategies for playing BioShock Infinite. They fired back with advanced techniques for taking down "heavy hitter" enemies like the Motorized Patriot and Handyman, recommendations for outfitting your character with Gear upgrades that reflect your favorite play-style, weapons and Vigor combo attacks to help you survive the most challenging battles, tips for how to best employ Elizabeth's powers and the high-flying Sky-Line in battle, and more.

That's advice straight from the horse's mouth, as it were… From the combat designers who set up BioShock Infinite's toughest encounters, systems designers who tuned the game's weapons and Vigors, and testers who spent countless hours poring over every inch of the game.

I know I speak for the entire team at Irrational Games when I say we all hope you really enjoy playing BioShock Infinite. You'll soon learn that Columbia is a city teeming with mystery. Who is Booker, and what is the debt that drives him to the city? What are Elizabeth's powers and why has she been locked up since she was a child? Why does Booker have the letters "AD" branded into his right hand? And what, in God's name, is the Songbird?

It will help guide you in your darkest hours. It will be your confidante and your best friend. It will save your butt. We spent nearly five years creating Columbia. Now we pass the creation to you. And that's really where the fun begins.

WELCOME TO THE WORLD OF

BIOSHOCK
INFINITE

Set in 1912, the player assumes the role of former Pinkerton agent Booker DeWitt, sent to the flying city of Columbia on a rescue mission. His target? Elizabeth, imprisoned since childhood. During their daring escape, Booker and Elizabeth form a powerful bond—one that lets Booker augment his own abilities with her world-altering control over the environment. Together, they fight from high-speed Sky-Lines, in the streets and houses of Columbia, on giant zeppelins, and in the clouds, all while learning to harness an expanding arsenal of weapons and abilities.

Forget what you think you know about the *BioShock* name, as your journey to Columbia will be unlike anything you've experienced. *BioShock Infinite* doesn't just deliver you to a city in the sky: it makes you fly once you get there. Everything in Columbia is faster and more intense than what you've seen before. From combat to exploration, the city of Columbia, led by its Prophet Zachary Hale Comstock, will challenge you at every turn. Elizabeth, the girl you've been sent to retrieve, helps you accomplish your mission. This guide will assist you every step of the way.

The *Official BioShock Infinite Strategy Guide* is the culmination of repeat trips and extensive time on-site at Irrational Games. Its authors played through the game numerous times, turned it inside out, interviewed key members of the development staff, and packed everything they could into this guide. Here is just a sample of what you can expect:

DETECTIVE TRAINING: An extensive discussion of every gameplay mechanic present in the game, with a focus on advanced combat techniques, player growth, and difficulty modifiers.

GUNS OF LIBERTY: A detailed analysis of both Founder and Vox Populi arsenals, including all available weapon and damage statistics, tactical advice, and tips for upgrading each weapon through the ubiquitous Minuteman's Armory machines.

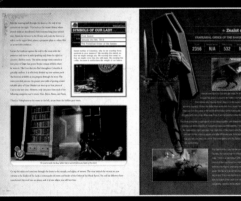

BOOKER'S CAMPAIGN: This in-depth walkthrough guides you every step of the way through the game, highlighting each collectible as you progress. This is presented in a spoiler-free format that simply alerts players to situations in which they have a choice, but leaves the outcomes to be discovered later. Foolproof combat advice and navigational strategies serve to ensure you won't get stuck along the way.

ENEMIES OF THE PEOPLE: Whether a foe is Founder or Vox, you can be sure Booker will ultimately wind up crossing paths with them. This section details enemy behavior and tactics for dispatching them, and it also includes all available enemy health and damage data.

2668-1

...**AND MUCH, MUCH MORE**: Inside this strategy guide, you'll also find transcriptions of all 80 Voxophones, Vigor and Gear strategies, a guide to unlocking all 50 Achievements/ Trophies, and a tremendous collection of beautiful *BioShock Infinite* art you can't see anywhere else.

GRAPHY INC.

DETECTIVE TRAINING

Welcome to Columbia! While it seems like a pleasant place, you'll soon find out that the skies are filled with danger. In this chapter, you'll learn the ins and outs of living in Columbia, as well as how to defeat your enemies with the tools you're provided!

★ CONTROLS ★

BioShock Infinite controls from a first-person perspective, which should be familiar if you're experienced with the genre.

Function	Xbox 360	PlayStation 3	PC
Move/Strafe	L	L	W,A,S,D
Turn/Look	R	R	Mouse
Toggle Sprint	L	L3	Left Shift
Toggle Iron Sights	R	R3	Middle Mouse Button
Navigation Aid	◎	✚	N
Jump / Attach to Sky-Line	A	X	Space
Crouch / Reverse (While on Sky-Line)	B	◎	Left Ctrl, C
Use / Reload Weapon	X	□	F to Use, R to Reload Weapon
Melee / Execute (Hold Button)	Y	△	V
Swap Vigors	LB	L1	Q
Open Vigor Menu	LB (Hold)	L1 (Hold)	Hold Q
Fire Vigor	LT	L2	Right Mouse Button
Fire Alternate Vigor	LT (Hold)	L2 (Hold)	Right Mouse Button (Hold)
Switch Weapon	RB	R1	E or Mouse Wheel
Fire Weapon	RT	R2	Left Mouse Button

CHALLENGES OF COLUMBIA
★ DIFFICULTY ★

There are four difficulty modes in *BioShock Infinite*, if you're looking for additional challenge.

The game systems that are affected by increased difficulty are:

Cost to Respawn—When Booker dies, you are penalized a certain amount of Silver Eagles. The cost increases as the difficulty level becomes higher.

Damage Taken—Enemy attacks deal more or less damage as you raise or lower the difficulty level.

Damage Dealt—Your own weapons inflict less damage on higher difficulties.

Shield Regen Delay—After taking damage, your Shield waits the listed time before it starts recharging. The higher the difficulty level, the longer the delay in the recharge.

Shield Regen Time—On higher difficulty levels, your Shield takes longer to regenerate. The time listed is how long your Shield takes to regenerate when completely broken.

Difficulty	Cost to Respawn	Damage Taken	Damage Dealt	Shield Regen Delay	Shield Regen Time
Easy	$5	50%	125%	3 seconds	1 second
Medium	$25	100%	100%	4 seconds	2 seconds
Hard	$50	170%	60%	5 seconds	3 seconds
1999 Mode	$100	200%	50%	6 seconds	4 seconds

1999 MODE

1999 Mode unlocks after you've beaten the game on any difficulty or input a secret code that any true gamer should be familiar with on the main menu (Up, Up, Down, Down, Left, Right, Left, Right, **B/◎**, **A/✕**) and offers an even greater challenge than Hard difficulty, with an added twist: if you can't afford your respawn, it's game over!

If Booker dies in 1999 Mode with less than $100, you return to the Main Menu without the ability to respawn. To succeed in 1999 Mode, you'll need to save as much money as you can and make sure Booker is in peak condition before you get into battles.

Aim Assist and the Navigation Aid are completely turned off in 1999 Mode, so you'll need to work for each kill and know your way around Columbia. Also, once you've started 1999 Mode, you can't change difficulty, so once you're in, you're in for the long haul!

To triumph in 1999 Mode, be sure to save your money—don't buy upgrades for Vigors or weapons that you don't use very often, and try to keep your health and Salts up by using items in the environment.

★ FIGHTING ★

In order to complete your mission and bring Elizabeth to New York, you'll need to fight your way through Comstock's army of Founders and Vigor-enhanced minions, all while civil unrest is reaching its peak on the floating islands of Columbia.

Booker has a variety of methods to meet these challenges and vanquish his foes, including firearms, fantastical Vigors, and the wonderous Sky-Hook.

You'll do most of your fighting using the guns that can be found around Columbia that defeated enemies drop. Each gun has its own strengths and weaknesses, so be ready to switch your sidearm often to be prepared for any combat situation.

To pick up a weapon, hold **✕/◻** when close to it. If you already have the same weapon equipped as the one you're trying to grab, you won't be able to collect it, but you can walk over it to replenish the ammo for that weapon.

Booker can only carry two weapons at a time. If you want to change the equipped weapon, you'll need to have Booker drop one first. Picking up a weapon while he has two equipped causes Booker to drop the weapon he's currently using. It is very important that you don't lose the weapon that you want to keep in the game. You certainly do not want to run into a group of Founders and find out you have been carrying two weapons without ammo!

When using a weapon, you can fire normally by pressing  🔘/🔘, or aim down the barrel of your gun by pressing 🔘/🔘. Using Iron Sights increases Booker's accuracy but slows down his walking speed and narrows the field of vision. If Aim Assist is turned on, Iron Sights will also quick-snap the reticule to an enemy's head, allowing for quick and easy headshots. Try not to use the Iron Sights when enemies are close to keep from being taken by surprise.

You can knock back extremely close enemies by using Booker's Sky-Hook and pressing 🔘/🔘. The Sky-Hook does not require ammo, but after swinging it, you cannot fire or attack again for a brief period, so avoid using it if you are surrounded.

SKY-HOOK DATA

Minimum Damage	Maximum Damage
191	259

When enemies are low on health, a skull icon appears and you can perform a special melee execution by holding down 🔘/🔘 for a brief period. These graphic executions can only be employed on normal enemies, Zealots of the Lady, and Beasts, so don't waste your time trying these attacks on a Motorized Patriot or a Fireman.

Booker can also fight enemies using the fantastic Vigors found around Columbia, each of which has unique effects. Every Vigor is tied to an element or effect, and the effect of each has varying degrees of success against the different types of enemies. Check out the Enemies of the People chapter of this guide for more detail concerning the best attacks against each enemy type.

Vigors can only be used as long as you have the Salts to use them. To cycle between your Vigors, tap 🔘/🔘 to quickly switch between your most recently used Vigor or hold down 🔘/🔘 to open up the radial menu where you can freely select from all your collected Vigors. The game will pause while this menu is open, so use this command to take a breather and assess the situation while equipping the Vigors you'll need.

Each Vigor has two modes of fire—a standard attack that is performed by pressing 🔘/🔘 and a secondary attack that is performed by holding down 🔘/🔘. For several Vigors, this will allow you to place a trap for foes on the ground—Possession, Devil's Kiss, Murder of Crows, Shock Jockey, Return to Sender, and Bucking Bronco.

These traps trigger whenever an enemy comes close and can potentially hit multiple targets with one explosion or effect. It is advantageous to set up traps whenever you are fighting enemies in an enclosed space where they can't avoid them. Foes will often blissfully run right over them, allowing you to stun your targets and take them out!

The other Vigors all have their own unique actions when you hold the Vigor fire button down. For more information on these miracles of science, check out the in-depth section of this guide that discusses the Vigors in detail.

SHIELDED FROM THE TRUTH

Shortly after beginning the game, Booker receives a Shield Infusion from the mysterious duo that has been following him around. Once it is equipped, any damage that is taken will drain the Shield instead of Booker's health as long as the Shield is charged.

When the Shield is drained, there is a short delay before it recharges again. This delay resets if you suffer any damage while the Shield is down. While the Shield is depleted, it is important to find cover and get to safety so it can completely recharge.

You can increase the potency of the Shield by finding Infusions that are located around the world, but you should choose these Infusions wisely, since this choice comes at the expense of increasing the capacity of the Salts or Health Meters!

DYING IN COLUMBIA

In most difficulty levels, death is only a temporary setback. When Booker's health is depleted, he'll be resuscitated and moved into a safe place, only suffering a slight monetary penalty of Silver Eagles. When you revive, your health won't be fully restored and some of your enemies' health will be, but you will be granted additional ammo and Salts.

Unless you are playing the game in 1999 Mode, Booker can still revive even if you don't have the amount of Silver Eagles that the death penalty would drain. If you are having trouble in a particular encounter, don't worry about it. It may be frustrating at first, but you can keep trying to complete the battle until you are able to overcome it.

★ SKY-HOOK TRAVEL ★

Booker can travel quickly across the landscape of Columbia by using the Sky-Lines that are located around the floating city. To hop onto a Sky-Line, simply look at it until you see a green arrow indicating the direction that you would like to travel, then press Ⓐ/Ⓧ.

While Booker is on the Sky-Line, the controls for the game change slightly.

SKY-LINE CONTROLS

Function	Xbox 360	PlayStation 3	PC
Speed Up	🕹 Up	🕹 Up	W
Slow Down	🕹 Down	🕹 Down	S
Reverse Direction	Ⓑ	◎	Left Ctrl
Exit Sky-Line/Sky-Line Strike	Ⓐ	Ⓧ	Space

It's important to constantly adjust Booker's speed while on a Sky-Line—speed up when trying to get away from enemies, and slow down to fire on an opponent below. While he is on a Sky-Line, Booker won't be able to use the power of Vigors, so make sure you're not fighting an adversary that requires their use while Booker is riding a Sky-Line.

If you need to have Booker change directions while riding on a Sky-Line, press Ⓑ/◎, and he'll quickly jump to a Sky-Line going in the other direction. You can use this kind of movement to keep an enemy targeted while also moving fast enough to avoid their attacks!

While on a Sky-Line, Booker has access to a powerful attack called the Sky-Line Strike, which allows him to quickly travel from a Sky-Line directly onto an enemy! The Sky-Line Strike deals massive damage, easily enough to instantly kill any normal foe.

You'll also find many freight hooks located in the environment that you can jump to by pressing Ⓐ/Ⓧ. These hooks won't let you travel, but you can most certainly use them to perform a highly-damaging Sky-Line Strike.

CATALOGUE FOR 1912

During your travels in the floating metropolis, you'll find many useful items to help navigate its perils. Items can be found everywhere—on the bodies of defeated enemies, in barrels and boxes, and often, just lying around in the open! You should constantly search every nook and cranny for items to keep the Salts and Health Meters topped off, to fill Booker's pockets with Silver Eagles for purchases, and to provide new upgrades.

Additionally, it is a good idea to search every corpse you find. You should do this to keep ammo stocks at capacity and maintain a healthy condition with any food that is scrounged up. Occasionally after defeating an enemy, you might find a lock box on the ground. Check these special drops for items, as well!

SILVER EAGLES

Silver Eagles are the currency of Columbia and they can be found just about everywhere. Silver Eagles are a very useful commodity, since you can use them to restore health and Salts, to buy ammo, and to purchase new upgrades to make your weapons and Vigors stronger.

However, there is a finite amount of Silver Eagles in the world, and even if you collect them all, you won't be able to afford everything you want. Shop smart and only buy health, Salts, and ammo if you absolutely need them, so you can save the balance of currency to buy precious Vigor and weapon upgrades as they become available.

EAT, DRINK, AND BE MERRY

You'll find a wide array of consumables around Columbia, each with their own benefits. These fit into one of four categories:

Alcohol (Whiskey, Beer, etc.)—These items restore a lot of health but also decrease Salts a significant amount. These beverages should only be used in an emergency because the trade-off of health for Salts usually isn't worth it. These beverages can also make Booker drunk, which is required to unlock the Lost Weekend achievement.

Drinks (Soda, etc.)—Non-alcoholic beverages restore the Salts Meter a small amount. When it comes to Salts, every little bit helps, so pick up these supplies whenever they are avaliable.

Cigarettes—Smoking restores Salts, but at the cost of a large portion of health. These are almost never worth using because Salts are fairly plentiful. You probably want to leave these alone, unless you are in a situation where you really need the Salts.

Food (Hot Dogs, Cotton Candy, etc.)—These items restore the Health Meter a small amount. You'll find plenty of them all around, but it might take a few of these items to fully restore Booker's health if he is really hurting.

WEAPONS AND AMMO

You can collect weapons either from defeated enemies or from random locations around Columbia. Watch especially for weapons that are simply placed in the world, as these can provide a hint about what's coming up soon—if you see a Sniper Rifle on the ground, beware of enemy snipers!

You can find ammo for weapons separately. There are boxes of ammunition hidden all over the game world. These generally restock a large portion of your ammo supplies. It can also be scrounged from the corpses of your enemies, though this typically only replenishes your ammo a few shots at a time.

MEDICAL KITS AND SALTS PHIALS

Food isn't the only way you can restore your health and Salts, since you can also find Medical Kits and Salts Phials of various sizes located throughout Columbia. Small Medical Kits restore 25% of a meter, medium sizes restore 50%, and large sizes can fully restore a single meter. Salt Phials can range anywhere from 10-100%, but will generally restore more than finding drinks.

There are also many Vigor bottles in various places that can be picked up and used. If you haven't received a particular Vigor before, it will grant a new power for you to use permanently! If you have already found it, it will completely restore the Salts Meter, so you should pick up any Vigor bottle that you see in Columbia—you never know, it might power Booker up permanently!

GEAR

Booker can equip up to four pieces of ability-enhancing Gear to boost his powers and give him access to an array of new combat options and tactics.

Each piece of Gear attaches to one of four specific slots—Hats, Shirts, Boots, and Pants. Only one piece of Gear can be affixed to a slot at a time, so even if you have two different Hats, you can only equip one. Of course, you can just store any extra Gear in your inventory and swap it out when the need arises.

Whenever Gear is collected, the piece that is actually received is completely random—each time you play through the game, you may find a completely different set of Gear! Most Gear is carefully hidden, so you should always keep an eye out for more pieces. Also, you receive a piece every time you kill a Handyman, so pay close attention whenever you take one of these hearty foes down!

INFUSIONS

These rare items give you the ability to permanently boost one of your meters, allowing you to increase your Health, Salts, or Shield Meter each time you pick one up. Each Infusion bottle only allows you to boost one stat, so keep this in mind before you decide on the choice of upgrade.

Infusions are very well-hidden and incredibly rare. They also fully restore whatever meter you're upgrading. Consult the walkthrough of this guide to make sure that you find them all!

LOCKPICKS

Elizabeth has the unique ability to pick various locks located in the world. Many of these she can unlock with just her trusty hairpin, but often the most valuable items are hidden behind doors and safes that require lockpicks to open. These lockpicks are one-use only.

You typically find lockpicks one at a time but, occasionally, you'll find bags containing three. Keep an eye out for lockpicks at all times to open the locked doors of Columbia and collect hidden items!

KEYS AND CIPHERS

Occasionally, you might run into a chest that even Elizabeth can't open with a lockpick. These chests require special keys that you'll find elsewhere. If you see one of these boxes, you should search the area close to these chests and look for a key. These keys are also detailed throughout the walkthrough chapters of this guide.

There are also encrypted messages that Elizabeth can figure out as long as you have the code book for the message. If you see one of these messages, look around for a clue: it will point you to where the key to the puzzle is located. When you have both, you'll be handsomely rewarded!

BUYING A BETTER YOU

If you're looking for a place to spend those hard-earned Silver Eagles, simply locate one of Columbia's many vending machines!

There are three types of vending machines found in Columbia, each with its own set of items:

Dollar Bill—This store replenishes your consumable items and meters, since it sells healing items, Salts, and ammo for any weapon you've run into.

Minuteman's Armory—The armory sells upgrades for your weapons, allowing you to deal more damage, carry more ammo, and more! These upgrades are extremely important, and you'll definitely need them the further you get in the game.

Veni! Vidi! Vigor!—This fanciful vending machine sells permanent upgrades to your Vigors, giving them enhanced efficiency and (at times) completely new functionality!

In general, you will want to avoid replenishing your supplies using the Dollar Bill if at all possible: there is only so much money you can find, but you can scrounge up plenty of ammo everywhere. Instead, you should save your money for new upgrades for your favorite Vigors and weapons.

Whenever you reach a new area, check out any new Veni! Vidi! Vigor and Minuteman's Armory machines you find because they receive new stock all the time!

ELIZABETH

Through most of the game, you'll be escorting the mysterious Elizabeth around the perils of Columbia, as you attempt to escape the city in the sky.

While you are her escort, you never need to worry about Elizabeth in combat. She knows how to stay out of trouble, so you can fight your enemies without stressing about her safety.

Throughout the game, Elizabeth can assist you in a number of ways and allow you to reach areas that Booker wouldn't normally be able to traverse.

ASSISTS

When you're in trouble and running out of health, Salts, or ammo—or perhaps you even need some extra cash—Elizabeth will help you out by giving you items.

When you see a prompt, press ✗/■, and she'll throw the item in question to you. After Elizabeth throws you an item, she won't be able to help you out for a while, so you should try to make her gift count.

Also, whenever you find a lot of money lying around or visit a vending machine, keep an eye on Elizabeth—she tends to throw some additional cash your way! Visit every vending machine you see, if only to have Elizabeth offer extra cash for your cause!

LOCKPICKING

There are many doors in the world that only Elizabeth, the master of unlocking, can open. Look for doors with a large lock over them—Elizabeth can open these, granting you access to the rare items located behind them! However, Elizabeth will not pick open any locks while you are in combat.

To open many doors, you'll need to use consumable lockpicks, which are fairly scarce. Keep an eye out for them so you can get behind every locked door and collect every Infusion, Voxophone, and piece of Gear!

PIECES OF ANOTHER WORLD (TEARS)

During your journey, Elizabeth shows you her ability to peer into other worlds using her gift to "Tear" into them. This ability can be a very helpful asset, giving you access to new powerful tactics and weaponry!

Tear types include:

Allies—Elizabeth can summon mechanized allies, including Machine Gun and Rocket Automatons, Mosquitos, and even Motorized Patriots!

Recovery—You see glimpses of boxes full of Medical Kits and Salts to fill your Health and Salts Meters!

Weapons—Elizabeth can summon stacks of powerful weapons like RPGs, along with plenty of ammo.

Navigation—Elizabeth can create freight hooks out of nowhere, giving you the ability to maneuver around combat areas.

Traps—Elizabeth can summon pools of oil and water from other worlds, which you can use to create deadly flaming oil slicks using Devil's Kiss or electrocuted puddles using Shock Jockey!

Decoy—Create a decoy to divert enemy attention while you take them out.

Cover—Create cover from nothing to put something between Booker and his enemies and take a breather during combat.

Stores—In two places you'll find two Tears that give access to discounted Stores, one of which has discounted weapon upgrades!

There are other types of Tears, each of which compounds Elizabeth's secret past.

SIGHTS AND SOUNDS OF COLUMBIA

There are several objects located around Columbia that exist to inform the player about the history and culture of the city, as well as ways to simply see some beautiful scenic views. Each of these objects enriches the complicated story of *BioShock Infinite* and tells you more about its many characters.

You'll need to find all the Kinetoscopes and Telescopes to earn the Sightseer Achievement/Trophy, and find every Voxophone to earn the Eavesdropper Achievement/Trophy. The locations of all of these objects are described in detail throughout the walkthrough of this guide!

KINETOSCOPES

These inconspicuous boxes house miniature movie houses that tell you about the history of Columbia through primitive "films". To activate one, simply walk up to it, and press ✗/◼ to learn more about the world of *BioShock Infinite*.

TELESCOPES

These are usually located along railings and allow you to see some of the beautiful scenery located around each area. To activate a Telescope, move up to one and press ✗/◼ to check out an amazing view and earn progress toward the Sightseer achievement.

VOXOPHONES

Voxophones are short voice recordings that give you additional insight into the story or point you to a secret area you might not otherwise have found. Voxophones are very important for getting the whole story of Columbia and its secrets, so try to collect all of them!

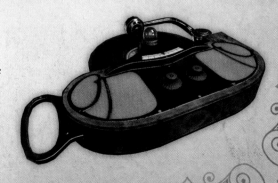

GUNS OF LIBERTY

During your stay in Columbia, you'll find a vast arsenal of weapons, each with its own unique strengths and abilities. Every gun Booker finds can also be upgraded up to four times, allowing a gun to be more efficient, deal more damage, or affect more enemies.

In this section, you'll find data for each weapon—including damage and rate of fire—along with tips on how to use every armament, as well as strategy for when and why you should upgrade.

Warning! There are spoilers in this section. You should not use this guide before you progress through the game if you do not want to discover any storyline-related details!

Weapon data contains the following stats:

Damage (Min): Damage dealt by a gunshot is random—this stat shows the minimum amount of damage a shot can inflict.

Damage (Max): As opposed to the minimum damage, this is the most damage a single shot deals. These two numbers are based on Normal difficulty; the numbers will be lower or higher on harder or easier difficulties, respectively.

Critical Multiplier: This is a measure of how much the damage will be multiplied on a critical hit. This is usually a headshot, but might be different on certain enemies like the Motorized Patriot.

Rounds per Minute: How many times you can fire the weapon if you press the button as quickly as possible—or hold down fire for a minute with an automatic weapon. Generally, the higher the number, the faster you can fire the weapon.

Magazine Capacity: How much ammo a single clip holds when you first pick up the weapon. You can increase this stat on several weapons through upgrades.

Reserve Capacity: How much ammo can be held for a weapon outside of the clip. You can likewise increase this stat through weapon upgrades.

Notes: If a weapon has any special feature or utility, it is listed in this field.

Lessons Learned from Wounded Knee

Here are some general tips to consider when picking your weapon load out:

★ **Use the weapon you want:** You can get through most of the game using only the weapons you prefer, as long as you keep upgrading them. Don't feel pressured to use a weapon just because it's new.

★ **Booker can only carry two weapons, so make sure the ones you have are fully loaded:** If you're running low on ammo, consider switching to a different weapon. You will often pick up ammo for weapons you aren't using, so switching to any available weapon should give you a fully loaded gun.

★ **Many weapons have increased accuracy when aiming down the Iron Sights:** You can control the random spray of gunfire by entering into Iron Sights, so use them especially when fighting enemies at a distance, even with the Pistol.

★ **Don't needlessly spend money on upgrades:** Don't buy every weapon upgrade available, especially if they're for weapons you don't use or prefer. Focus on a few weapons so you'll have enough money to afford the more expensive Vigor upgrades.

★ **Reload after every fight to stay prepared for anything:** After clearing out a wave of enemies, reload both your weapons before moving on. You don't want to run into a group of adversaries with an empty clip!

★ **Search everywhere:** You can not only find more ammo on enemy corpses and in boxes lying around, but you can also walk over defeated enemies' weapons to add their ammo to your own. If you've defeated an opponent using the same weapon as you, you won't receive a prompt to pick up their weapon, but you'll still get the ammo for your gun.

★ **Don't rely on Elizabeth too much:** Elizabeth does give you ammo, but not continually. After giving you ammo once, it'll be a while before she'll find enough to give you more for a particular weapon. If you run out of ammo after Elizabeth helps you out, consider switching to a different weapon.

BROADSIDER PISTOL

STATS

Damage (Min)	Damage (Max)	Critical Multiplier	Rounds per Minute	Magazine Capacity	Reserve Capacity	Notes
85	115	3.5x	400	12	108	—

UPGRADES

Upgrade	Cost	Function	First Available In
Damage Boost 1	$199	Increases damage by 25%	Inside Hall of Heroes
Damage Boost 2	$199	Increases damage by 25%	The Factory
Ammo Increase	$404	Increases reserve ammo to 162	Finkton Docks
Clip Increase	$275	Increases clip size to 18	Battleship Bay

STRATEGY

The Broadsider Pistol is the first weapon you'll find in Columbia. The Pistol doesn't deal much damage, but its speed and high ammo count make it a valuable weapon throughout most of the game.

Although it doesn't deal much damage per shot, the Pistol can fire very quickly—as fast as you can pull the trigger! The Pistol also reloads quickly, so when using the Broadsider, don't be afraid to spray ammo everywhere!

The Pistol deals huge damage on a critical hit, which is often enough to take out many soldiers in one to two shots. When using the Pistol, aim toward the heads of your enemies to take them out quickly.

TRIPLE R MACHINE GUN

STATS

Damage (Min)	Damage (Max)	Critical Multiplier	Rounds per Minute	Magazine Capacity	Reserve Capacity	Notes
72	88	1.5x	600	35	105	—

UPGRADES

Upgrade	Cost	Function	First Available In
Damage Boost 1	$236	Increases damage by 25%	Welcome Center
Damage Boost 2	$236	Increases damage by 25%	The Factory
Accuracy Boost	$512	Reduces spread by 75%	Inside Hall of Heroes
Clip Increase	$391	Increases clip size to 70	Finkton Docks

STRATEGY

Shortly after escaping Raffle Square, you'll find the Rolston Reciprocating Rifle or Triple R, an automatic rifle that can quickly unload into your enemies. The greatest asset of this Machine Gun is its availability—almost every group of enemies you'll fight has at least one soldier carrying one, giving you many opportunities to replenish your ammo.

Unfortunately, you'll need to replenish its ammo fairly often, as it chews through your supply almost immediately. Even though you can carry a reserve of 105 bullets, this is only enough to reload three times, so you might quickly find yourself low on ammo.

Damage dealt by the Machine Gun is very low, and the critical multiplier isn't very high, so don't waste your bullets aiming for headshots. Target the center of mass on enemies to compensate for the Machine Gun's spread and ensure that all shots fired hit your target.

CHINA BROOM SHOTGUN

STATS

Damage (Min)	Damage (Max)	Critical Multiplier	Rounds per Minute	Magazine Capacity	Reserve Capacity	Notes
765	1035	1.5x	45	4	20	Damage degrades with distance

UPGRADES

Upgrade	Cost	Function	First Available In
Damage Boost 1	$255	Increases damage by 25%	Finkton Docks
Damage Boost 2	$255	Increases damage by 25%	Emporia
Reload Increase	$456	Increases reload speed by 50%	Finkton Docks
Spread Boost	$360	Increases spread by 20%	Downtown Emporia

STRATEGY

The China Broom Shotgun, most likely named for the way it spreads buckshot in a fan-shaped pattern, is a very powerful weapon that deals pretty good damage from far away and huge damage up close! This Shotgun is one of the best secondary weapons you can carry, since it gives you a powerful weapon that you can save for heavy hitters and close-range encounters.

Save the China Broom mostly for close confrontations. From point-blank, the China Broom can deal enormous damage, easily enough to kill a soldier enemy in a single shot and occasionally two foes at once!

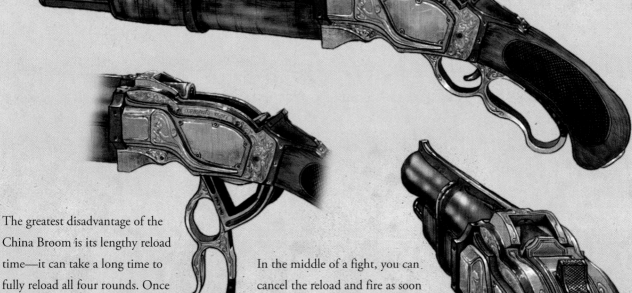

The greatest disadvantage of the China Broom is its lengthy reload time—it can take a long time to fully reload all four rounds. Once you can buy the Reload Increase upgrade, do it—it'll speed your reload significantly, nearly removing the gun's greatest drawback!

In the middle of a fight, you can cancel the reload and fire as soon as a single round has been loaded into the chamber. Don't waste time waiting to reload all four shots unless you are safely out of combat.

BIRD'S EYE SNIPER RIFLE

STATS

Damage (Min)	Damage (Max)	Critical Multiplier	Rounds per Minute	Magazine Capacity	Reserve Capacity	Notes
595	805	2.5x	50	4	20	Using Iron Sights activates scope

UPGRADES

Upgrade	Cost	Function	First Available In
Damage Boost 1	$349	Increases damage by 25%	Inside Hall of Heroes
Damage Boost 2	$349	Increases damage by 25%	The Factory
Fire Rate Boost	$654	Increases fire rate by 100%	Finkton Docks
Recoil Decrease	$288	Decreases recoil by 50%	Finkton Docks

STRATEGY

If you need to take out an enemy from a very long distance, the Bird's Eye Sniper Rifle is the perfect weapon. Activating Iron Sights allows you to use a scope that lets you target opponents from quite far away.

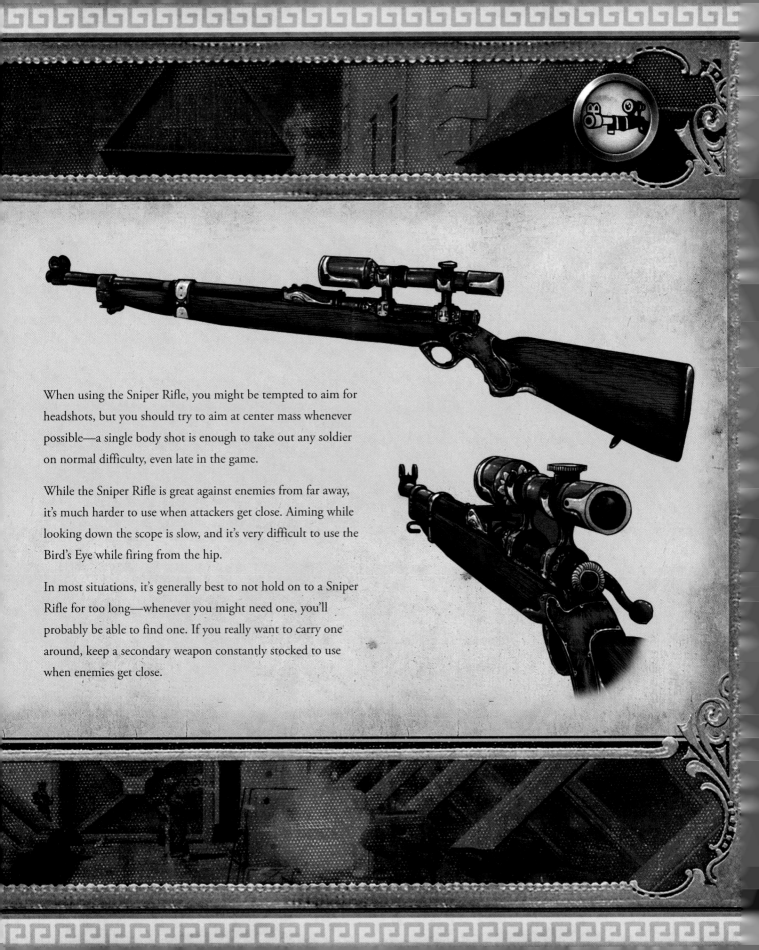

When using the Sniper Rifle, you might be tempted to aim for headshots, but you should try to aim at center mass whenever possible—a single body shot is enough to take out any soldier on normal difficulty, even late in the game.

While the Sniper Rifle is great against enemies from far away, it's much harder to use when attackers get close. Aiming while looking down the scope is slow, and it's very difficult to use the Bird's Eye while firing from the hip.

In most situations, it's generally best to not hold on to a Sniper Rifle for too long—whenever you might need one, you'll probably be able to find one. If you really want to carry one around, keep a secondary weapon constantly stocked to use when enemies get close.

BARNSTORMER RPG

STATS

Damage (Min)	Damage (Max)	Critical Multiplier	Rounds per Minute	Magazine Capacity	Reserve Capacity	Notes
1250	1750	—	40	2	8	—

UPGRADES

Upgrade	Cost	Function	First Available In
Damage Boost 1	$385	Increases damage by 25%	Inside Hall of Heroes
Damage Boost 2	$385	Increases damage by 25%	Emporia
Clip Increase	$816	Increases clip size to 3	Inside Hall of Heroes
RPG Speed Boost	$333	Increases projectile speed by 100%	Downtown Emporia

STRATEGY

The Barnstormer RPG is an incredibly powerful weapon that fires a slow-moving but deadly rocket-propelled grenade toward your enemies. These rockets inflict incredible damage and can take out several enemies in a single shot or destroy a heavy hitter very quickly.

It's best to employ the RPG against adversaries that are fairly far away, as using it too close can backfire, since Booker isn't immune to the explosion damage caused by RPG ammo. It's also generally not worth the ammo to use the RPG against single foes—save the RPG for heavy hitters or massive groups.

RPG explosions have the same fire effect as the Devil's Kiss Vigor, which allows you to use it instead of Devil's Kiss in certain combos. Also, it can set oil slicks on the ground ablaze, which allows you to create a devastating wall of flames!

Be careful when using the RPG against distant enemies because the grenade itself doesn't travel very quickly. You might fire a rocket at your opponents but find they've moved out of the way long before the rocket reaches them!

HUNTSMAN CARBINE

STATS

Damage (Min)	Damage (Max)	Critical Multiplier	Rounds per Minute	Magazine Capacity	Reserve Capacity	Notes
213	287	2.25x	240	8	72	—

UPGRADES

Upgrade	Cost	Function	First Available In
Damage Boost 1	$357	Increases damage by 25%	Inside Hall of Heroes
Damage Boost 2	$357	Increases damage by 25%	Emporia
Clip Increase	$484	Increases clip size to 12	Finkton Docks
Recoil Decrease	$333	Decreases recoil by 60%	The Factory

STRATEGY

The Huntsman Carbine Rifle is an incredibly powerful semi-automatic rifle that features a high rate of fire, a quick reload speed, and massive damage, especially on critical hits. From the first time you find one to the final battle, the Carbine can easily carry you through the end of the game as your go-to weapon.

The Carbine functions similarly to the Pistol, with longer range—though it fires rapidly, you should mostly attempt headshots. A critical hit with the Carbine does massive damage and can fell many soldiers throughout the game in one or two shots.

You can also use the Carbine with great accuracy even when firing from the hip. Simply aim toward an enemy's head, and watch them drop.

The Carbine is a very strong weapon and should be an integral part of your arsenal. If you've been using the Pistol or Machine Gun primarily, replace it with the Carbine as soon as you can.

THE PIG VOLLEY GUN

STATS

Damage (Min)	Damage (Max)	Critical Multiplier	Rounds per Minute	Magazine Capacity	Reserve Capacity	Notes
550+200	650+250	—	120	8	24	Damage degrades with distance from explosion

UPGRADES

Upgrade	Cost	Function	First Available In
Damage Boost 1	$522	Increases damage by 25%	Finkton Docks
Damage Boost 2	$522	Increases damage by 25%	Downtown Emporia
Radius Increase	$536	Increases explosion radius by 50%	Downtown Emporia
Clip Increase	$740	Increases clip size to 16	Downtown Emporia

STRATEGY

The Pig Volley Gun is a unique weapon that fires explosive shells in an arc, allowing you to lob projectiles behind cover, over obstacles, and into groups of enemies.

Volley Gun projectiles deal big damage, often taking out soldiers in a single shot. While Volley Gun projectiles do deal splash damage, it's not very much, and it'll take more than a few hits to inflict any significant damage on your opponents. You should focus on direct shots instead of relying on area-of-effect explosions.

You can use its low-damage explosions to your advantage, however, and employ the Volley Gun against enemies up close without hurting yourself too much. The Volley Gun also reloads very quickly, making it a decent close-range alternative to the Shotgun.

PADDYWHACKER HAND CANNON

STATS

Damage (Min)	Damage (Max)	Critical Multiplier	Rounds per Minute	Magazine Capacity	Reserve Capacity	Notes
510	690	3x	75	6	18	—

UPGRADES

Upgrade	Cost	Function	First Available In
Damage Boost 1	$448	Increases damage by 25%	The Factory
Damage Boost 2	$448	Increases damage by 25%	Emporia
Reload Increase	$656	Increases reload speed by 50%	The Factory
Recoil Decrease	$350	Decreases recoil by 20%	Downtown Emporia

STRATEGY

The Paddywhacker Hand Cannon is an immensely powerful pistol that has a slow rate of fire and low accuracy but deals enormous damage with every shot.

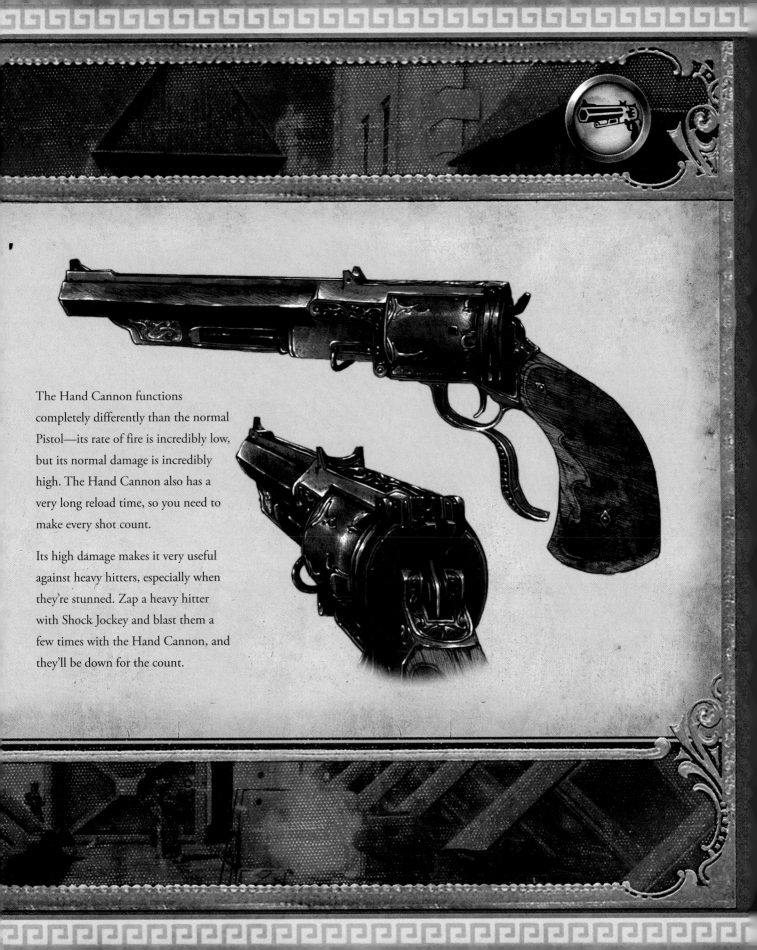

The Hand Cannon functions completely differently than the normal Pistol—its rate of fire is incredibly low, but its normal damage is incredibly high. The Hand Cannon also has a very long reload time, so you need to make every shot count.

Its high damage makes it very useful against heavy hitters, especially when they're stunned. Zap a heavy hitter with Shock Jockey and blast them a few times with the Hand Cannon, and they'll be down for the count.

PEPPERMILL CRANK GUN

STATS

Damage (Min)	Damage (Max)	Critical Multiplier	Rounds per Minute	Magazine Capacity	Reserve Capacity	Notes
70	130	1.5x	1500	100	100	—

UPGRADES

The Crank Gun has no upgrades.

STRATEGY

The Peppermill Crank Gun is the signature weapon of the Motorized Patriot and is a high-powered Gatling gun that chews through ammo and tears through enemies just as fast.

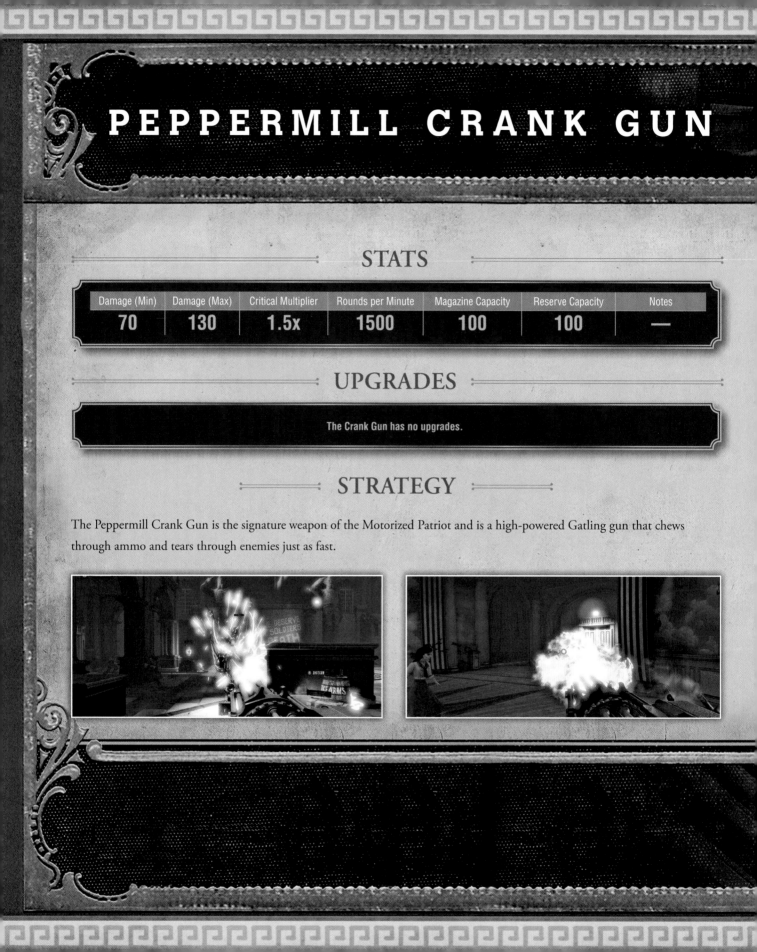

The Crank Gun is fairly uncommon, however, as it can only be found near defeated Motorized Patriots and in a few Tears located in the world. You can only replenish its ammo by finding another Crank Gun, so it's difficult to try to finish the game while Booker is equipped with it.

You should generally try to pick up the Crank Gun whenever possible. Though you probably shouldn't take it with you, use it to easily and quickly dispatch any soldiers or heavy hitters nearby.

VOX HUNTSMAN BURSTGUN

STATS

Damage (Min)	Damage (Max)	Critical Multiplier	Rounds per Minute	Magazine Capacity	Reserve Capacity	Notes
85	115	2.25x	265	30	120	Fires in three-shot bursts

UPGRADES

Upgrade	Cost	Function	First Available In
Damage Boost 1	$423	Increases damage by 25%	The Factory
Damage Boost 2	$423	Increases damage by 25%	Downtown Emporia
Recoil Decrease	$822	Decreases recoil by 50%	Downtown Emporia
Ammo Increase	$672	Increases reserve ammo to 180	Downtown Emporia

STRATEGY

The Burstgun is a modified version of the Huntsman that fires in a three-shot burst instead of a single, powerful shot. The Burstgun is the most common Vox weapon and is found everywhere in the latter half of the game.

Compared to the Huntsman, the Burstgun
is considerably weaker: its three shots—
even if they all hit—deal about as much
damage as one from the Carbine, but with
a chance that an individual round might
miss. When using the Burstgun, it's best
to aim for center mass to make sure all
three hits connect rather than risk losing
important critical damage.

However, since ammunition is plentiful,
it can be a very useful tool late in the
game. If you need a weapon, there's a good
chance there'll be a Burstgun lying around
that you can use while you collect more
ammo for your preferred weapons.

VOX TRIPLE R REPEATER

STATS

Damage (Min)	Damage (Max)	Critical Multiplier	Rounds per Minute	Magazine Capacity	Reserve Capacity	Notes
170	230	2x	350	20	60	—

UPGRADES

Upgrade	Cost	Function	First Available In
Damage Boost 1	—	Increases damage by 25%	—
Damage Boost 2	$416	Increases damage by 25%	Downtown Emporia
Recoil Decrease	$711	Decreases recoil by 50%	Emporia
Clip Increase	$449	Increases clip size to 40	Downtown Emporia

STRATEGY

This Vox-modified Triple R has a much slower rate of fire but deals significantly more damage per shot. The Repeater is a very useful late-game weapon, since it is very common throughout the latter stages, giving you many opportunities to refill your ammo.

Even though the Repeater is modified from the Machine Gun, it functions much more like the Carbine, but with a higher rate of fire. It doesn't deal quite as much damage on a critical hit, however, so enemies will require multiple headshots to take down.

The high rate of fire makes it very useful against heavy hitters, especially after they've been made vulnerable by a Vigor. Put the effect on an enemy, then lay into their weak spots to quickly take them down.

THE VOX PIG HAIL FIRE

STATS

Damage (Min)	Damage (Max)	Critical Multiplier	Rounds per Minute	Magazine Capacity	Reserve Capacity	Notes
580	820	—	545	5	25	Damage degrades with distance from explosion

UPGRADES

Upgrade	Cost	Function	First Available In
Damage Boost 1	—	Increases damage by 25%	—
Damage Boost 2	$688	Increases damage by 25%	Downtown Emporia
Radius Increase	$415	Increases explosion radius by 100%	Downtown Emporia
Clip Size	$399	Increases clip size to 8	Downtown Emporia

STRATEGY

This modified Pig fires projectiles that have the unique ability to bounce off walls and detonate in mid-air. While ammo for the Hail Fire is rare, its unique functionality makes it a powerful weapon.

The projectile fired by the Hail Fire differs based on how long you hold the trigger—if you tap it, the projectile bounces off walls until it hits an enemy. If you hold the trigger down, the projectile still bounces off walls until it hits a target, but will also explode when you release the trigger.

In general, you should use the normal fire version in most situations. However, if you're attacking enemies in a group or behind cover, lob a shot over cover, then release the trigger when the shot is near an adversary to detonate it, ignoring their cover!

Unfortunately, very few enemies carry the Hail Fire, so ammo for it is generally scarce. If you want to use this unique weapon, you'll often find yourself buying more ammo from Dollar Bill, so make sure you've purchased all the upgrades you can before committing to it.

THE HEATER

STATS

Damage (Min)	Damage (Max)	Critical Multiplier	Rounds per Minute	Magazine Capacity	Reserve Capacity	Notes
1360	1840	1.5x	35	1	8	Damage degrades with distance, sets enemies ablaze

UPGRADES

Upgrade	Cost	Function	First Available In
Damage Boost 1	—	Increases damage by 25%	—
Damage Boost 2	$554	Increases damage by 25%	Downtown Emporia
Spread Boost	$467	Increases spread by 20%	Downtown Emporia
Reload Increase	$752	Increases reload speed by 50%	Emporia

STRATEGY

The Heater is a modified China Broom that only holds a single bullet, but fires an extremely powerful shot that sets enemies ablaze and deals massive damage.

Any adversary caught up close is annihilated instantly by the Heater, and if the shot doesn't dispatch them immediately, they'll probably be finished off by the fire damage!

Unlike the Shotgun, the Heater is only useful at very close ranges. Even though it deals huge damage, be careful using it against heavy hitters that can seriously injure Booker whenever he gets too close.

Ammo for the Heater is very scarce, especially if you choose to steal it while you're in Soldier's Field. Much like the Hail Fire, you'll need to visit Dollar Bill for more Heater ammo, so try to use it sparingly.

VIGORS

Vigors are fantastical, wondrous tonics that grant a person who consumes one the ability to do otherworldly and amazing things. Booker will find a total of eight unique Vigors during his journey through Columbia, each with its own special abilities.

Each Vigor (save for Charge) has two separate attacks—a standard attack that is performed by pressing the Vigor fire button and an alternate attack when the Vigor fire button is held down. A meter appears in the crosshair while you're charging a Vigor, and when it is full, the alternate fire mode of the Vigor is available.

The first time you collect a Vigor, Booker experiences a short hallucination, giving you a preview of the Vigor's effect and its abilities—as well as its influence on Booker's mind!

When an enemy is hit by a Vigor, they have a chance of becoming vulnerable for a few seconds. While an enemy is reeling from the effects of the Vigor, you deal twice as much damage with your normal weapons! Each adversary is vulnerable to different Vigors, as illustrated by the following table.

The table describes how vulnerable an enemy is to each Vigor. If an opponent is 100% or more susceptible to a Vigor, then they become vulnerable after being hit. Careful use of Vigors is especially important against heavy hitting enemies like The Beast, Zealot of the Lady, and Fireman!

ENEMY WEAKNESS TO VIGORS

Enemy	Possession (Duration)	Devil's Kiss (Damage)	Murder of Crows (Duration)	Bucking Bronco (Duration)	Shock Jockey (Stun)	Charge (Impact)	Undertow (Pushback)
Soldier	100%	100%	100%	100%	100%	100%	100%
Gun Automaton	200%	100%	Immune	Immune	100%	Stun	Stun
RPG Automaton	200%	100%	Immune	Immune	100%	Stun	Stun
Barrage Automaton	Immune	100%	Immune	Immune	100%	Immune	Immune
Fireman	50%	Immune	100%	100%	100%	100%	100%
Zealot	50%	100%	Immune	100%	100%	100%	100%
Mosquito	200%	100%	Immune	Immune	100%	Immune	100%
Beast	100%	100%	100%	100%	100%	50%	50%
Patriot	50%	100%	Immune	Weakened	75%	100%	100%
Handyman	Immune	100%	75%	Immune	10%	Immune	Adds Weakness
Siren	Weakness	150%	Weakness	Weakness	Weakness	Weakness	Weakness

By using certain Vigors in succession, you can create a combo, granting an extra damage boost and enhanced vulnerability. Using Vigor combinations also contributes toward the Combination Shock achievement. Be sure to use them all to maximize your Vigor potential!

To hit with a combo, score a hit with the first Vigor listed, then use the second. You'll see "COMBO" appear on your target, and then you can watch the damage pile up!

POSSESSION

STATS

Cost per Use (Press)	Cost per Use (Hold)	Damage (Press)	Damage (Hold)	Effect Duration (Press)	Effect Duration (Hold)
50	100	—	—	10 seconds	20 seconds

COMBOS

This combo causes the enemy to become a walking Tesla coil, spreading electricity to anyone near them. It has a fairly low Salts cost for a Possession combo, making it a valuable option whenever you have used Possession on an enemy.

Using this combo causes a foe under the influence of Possession to become a walking firestorm, spreading fire to anyone they approach. While this costs more than using Shock Jockey, it deals more damage by setting enemies on fire. Use this combination whenever you want to deal more damage with Vigors instead of weapons.

UPGRADES

Upgrade	Cost	Function	First Available In
Possession Mod	$50	Adds ability to Possess humans who commit suicide when the effect expires	Raffle Square
Possession for Less	$1653	Decreases the Salts necessary to use Possession	Hall of Heroes Gift Shop

STRATEGY

The first Vigor you'll find in Columbia is the powerful Possession Vigor, which you can use to turn enemies into allies for a short period of time. Possession is an extremely powerful Vigor that has a multitude of uses throughout the game, both in and out of combat.

Possession, at the beginning of the game, is only usable on mechanical enemies like Automatons and Motorized Patriots. Once possessed, mechanical enemies like these become your ally for a few seconds, shooting any other opponents for you! Possessing turrets is a great way to get rid of them—let them thin out your attackers while they destroy the turret for you!

If you've been exploring Columbia, you'll soon be able to purchase an upgrade that lets you possess humans, as well, allowing you to make most enemies into allies. If you use Posession a normal soldier, they'll commit suicide after the Possession effect expires, causing an instant kill!

Only one enemy can be possessed at a time. If you possess a foe while one is already under the influence of Possession, the Possession effect immediately ends on the first enemy you possessed. While this is bad with mechanical turrets, a human you've possessed will instantly commit suicide!

Against heavy hitters like the Fireman, Zealot, and Motorized Patriots, Possession only lasts half as long, and they won't kill themselves when the effect is over. Possession doesn't work at all against the Siren or the Handyman, so don't waste your Salts trying it.

Possession's alternate fire is a mine that can possess multiple foes at the same time—which really means that one or two enemies might instantly commit suicide when they walk over it.

Even though it will quickly dispatch enemies, this method of attack isn't really worth the Salts, however, since it costs nearly an entire bar of the Salts Meter just to place one. However, once you get the Possess for Less upgrade, you may consider using mines more often.

Outside of combat, if you need some extra cash, you can cast Possession on one of the many vending machines around Columbia to cause them to spit out free money! This only works once per vending machine, but it is a free and easy way to get more money, especially if you have a full Salts Meter or you know that more Salts are nearby.

DEVIL'S KISS

STATS

Cost per Use (Press)	Cost per Use (Hold)	Damage (Press)	Damage (Hold)	Effect Duration (Press)	Effect Duration (Hold)
23	46	500	2100	3 seconds	5 seconds

COMBOS

After setting someone on fire, use Charge on them to create a series of molten projectiles that spew from the target's body. With the right timing and positioning, you can use this combination to create a series of additional firey grenades, spreading the damage throughout an entire encounter!

See Murder of Crows.   *See Bucking Bronco.*   *See Possession.*

UPGRADES

Upgrade	Cost	Function	First Available In:
Devil's Kiss Mod	$1241	Adds mini clusters for greater area-of-effect range and damage	Monument Island Gateway
Devil's Kiss Boost	$666	Increases damage	Finkton Docks

STRATEGY

The Devil's Kiss Vigor causes Booker to conjure a ball of magma and fire into his hands, which he can throw at his enemies. This Vigor essentially functions as a grenade, albeit one conjured out of the sky using fantastic power.

Devil's Kiss is a great way to use your Salts Meter just to deal damage to your opposition. A normal Devil's Kiss grenade inflicts a good amount of damage and is a great way to attack your enemies if you need to reload your main weapon.

The alternate fire of Devil's Kiss causes Booker to throw a projectile that sits on the ground like a trap, creating a high-damage landmine. This trap deals massive damage but doesn't cost many Salts, making it a very powerful and deadly tool. You can't detonate your own mine, but you can backpedal toward a mine to draw any ambitious enemies into it!

You can also place the Devil's Kiss trap on walls, giving you additional ways to attack adversaries on the ground or in the skies. Place a trap near a wall that a Sky-Line slides by, and any enemy chasing Booker down will trigger it and explode in a plume of fire!

MURDER OF CROWS

STATS

Cost per Use (Press)	Cost per Use (Hold)	Damage (Press)	Damage (Hold)	Effect Duration (Press)	Effect Duration (Hold)
28	56	60	300	4-5 seconds	9-10 seconds

COMBOS

By throwing Devil's Kiss at an enemy surrounded by crows, you can create a murder of flaming crows, which sets all your enemies ablaze while keeping them stunned! While this Vigor combo is expensive, it's especially useful against enemies vulnerable to the effects of fire and Murder of Crows, like the Handyman.

Much like the combo above, using Shock Jockey against an enemy surrounded by crows creates a legion of electric crows, capable of stunning any enemy nearby. This combo is fairly inexpensive and can instantly incapacitate an entire group of foes.

UPGRADES

Upgrade	Cost	Function	First Available In:
Unlock Murder of Crows	$150	Unlocks Murder of Crows if not found	Monument Island Gateway
Crows Trap Mod	$1485	Causes the corpses of Murder of Crows victims to become crow traps	Monument Island Gateway
Crows Boost	$545	Increases stun duration	The Factory

STRATEGY

Even for a Vigor, Murder of Crows is extremely unique, since using it causes Booker to send a, murder of damaging and annoying crows toward his enemies. Any adversary hit—as well as any opponent near him—is surrounded by a legion of crows that holds them in place and leaves them vulnerable, allowing you to deal additional damage with any weapons Booker has equipped.

Against many normal enemies, Murder of Crows is quickly outpaced by Shock Jockey, which performs the same function but costs significantly fewer Salts. However, the hardest-hitting enemy, the Handyman, is only briefly stunned by Shock Jockey but is totally distracted by Murder of Crows, giving you several valuable seconds to lay into him with gunfire!

Using the secondary fire version of Murder of Crows allows you to place a trap that, when approached, unleashes an onslaught of crows. This allows you to quickly dispatch any enemy foolish enough to trigger the trap with your equipped weapons. Be careful when setting a Murder of Crows mine, however, since it has an extremely high cost in Salts per use.

BUCKING BRONCO

STATS

Cost per Use (Press)	Cost per Use (Hold)	Damage (Press)	Damage (Hold)	Effect Duration (Press)	Effect Duration (Hold)
15	30	0	0	3-3.5 per second	6-7 seconds

COMBOS

By using Devil's Kiss on an enemy that has been levitated with Bucking Bronco, you can create a cluster of explosions! This combo is particularly useful before you buy any Bucking Bronco upgrades. As soon as you get it, you can make Bucking Bronco effective against every single enemy in an encounter.

Using Charge against an enemy that has been levitated by Bucking Bronco causes them to fly extreme distances—which, in Columbia, usually means flying off the city to their doom! Use this combo against the Zealot, Fireman, and Beast to save ammo and instantly defeat them.

UPGRADES

Upgrade	Cost	Function	First Available In:
Unlock Bucking Bronco	$175	Unlocks Bucking Bronco if not found	Finkton Docks
Bronco Mod	$777	Adds ability to chain floating effect from one enemy to others	Finkton Docks
Bronco Boost	$421	Increases duration of enemy's float time by 2x	The Factory

STRATEGY

Bucking Bronco is an incredibly powerful Vigor that allows you to turn the tides against any group of enemies attacking you. Simply pressing the Vigor fire button levitates any enemies in front of you, allowing you to punish them for extra damage while they float defenselessly in the air! If an enemy reaches less than 25% health while under the effect of Bucking Bronco, they will be slammed into the ground and instantly defeated!

This Vigor is especially useful against heavy hitters like the Beast, Fireman, and Zealot. Stop the Zealot from teleporting around you by holding him in the air, then attack him with your equipped weapon to immediately end him!

Since foes that have been levitated by Bucking Bronco are also impaired defensively, you can make short work of any Beast, who generally ignores many of your attacks. Also, if you're anywhere near a ledge, simply attack a levitated adversary with your Sky-Hook to push them off of Columbia, ending their threat immediately!

The alternate fire version of Bucking Bronco creates a trap that levitates anything near it. While this isn't as useful as the normal version, it costs little Salts, allowing you to create the perfect blend of offense and defense, especially near any of Columbia's many railings!

SHOCK JOCKEY

STATS

Cost per Use (Press)	Cost per Use (Hold)	Damage (Press)	Damage (Hold)	Effect Duration (Press)	Effect Duration (Hold)
16	32	45-55	45-55	2.8-3.2 seconds	4-5 seconds

COMBOS

See Murder of Crows.   *See Possession.*   *See Undertow.*

UPGRADES

Upgrade	Cost	Function	First Available In:
Shock Jockey Mod	$1265	Add ability to chain lightning strikes from one enemy to others	The Factory
Shock Jockey Boost	$575	Increases effective range (2x)	Downtown Emporia

"Who Needs The POWER Company?"

STRATEGY

Shock Jockey gives Booker the power to throw electricity, which is just as powerful as you might imagine!

The normal fire version of Shock Jockey is both incredibly powerful and incredibly cheap in terms of Salts, making it a useful tool throughout the game. Simply press the Vigor fire button, and voila: a stunned enemy that can't fight back and that takes double damage for a short period of time!

The normal fire version of Shock Jockey is incredibly useful against mechanical adversaries like the Motorized Patriot and any Automaton emplacement. Shoot Shock Jockey at them to keep them from firing at you, then lay into them for double damage while they're stunned!

The alternate fire version of Shock Jockey allows you to lay a series of traps that create a chained lightning effect. These traps zap any foe that walks in between them. Employ multiple alternate fire versions of this Vigor to create a defensive wall that severely punishes any enemy trying to move toward your position!

CHARGE

STATS

Cost per Use (Press)	Cost per Use (Hold)	Damage (Press)	Damage (Hold)	Effect Duration (Press)	Effect Duration (Hold)
25	25	350	700 + 200	1-2 seconds stun	1-2 seconds stun

COMBOS

See Devil's Kiss.   *See Bucking Bronco.*

UPGRADES

Upgrade	Cost	Function	First Available In:
Unlock Charge	$250	Unlocks Charge if not found	Emporia
Charge Mod	$1614	Adds brief invulnerability on attack and recharges Shield	The Factory
Charge Boost	$555	Adds explosive damage to Charge attack	Downtown Emporia

STRATEGY

Unlike most attacks, Charge does not have a normal method of fire; it only has an alternate. When you use it, you'll see why—Booker charges up his Sky-Hook, then flies toward his enemies with a single powerful blow!

Any enemy hit by Charge is left vulnerable, so you can continue dealing extra damage after you hit them. You can also use Charge against opponents on different levels of elevation—reach areas you didn't think you could by using Charge to attack an adversary standing on one!

Be careful when using Charge against heavy hitter enemies—often, they won't be stunned by the effects, and Booker will end up on the business end of an RPG. Check the vulnerability table to see which foes you should and shouldn't charge.

UNDERTOW

STATS

Cost per Use (Press)	Cost per Use (Hold)	Damage (Press)	Damage (Hold)	Effect Duration (Press)	Effect Duration (Hold)
31	31	0	40-150 on impact	3 seconds stun	3 seconds stun

COMBOS

By using Shock Jockey on an enemy affected by Undertow, you can cause extreme damage—the same damage caused by using Shock Jockey on a water puddle! Use this combination if you've caught multiple opponents with a single Undertow shot and want to finish them off immediately.

UPGRADES

Upgrade	Cost	Function	First Available In:
Unlock Undertow	$150 ($125 from vending machine)	Unlocks Undertow if not found	Emporia
Undertow Mod	$306	Increase number of enemies you can pull at one time	Emporia

STRATEGY

Undertow, on its own, does not deal damage against most enemies and might be considered useless in many combat scenarios. However, any enemy hit by Undertow is either propelled forward or pulled toward you, making it an excellent utility tool, especially late in the game.

In any scenario where you are near a ledge, Undertow can instantly end a combat encounter in seconds—simply use it to fling your enemies off of the confines of Columbia! This is especially useful against heavy hitters like the Zealot, Fireman, and the Beast, since it can end an encounter with any of these foes in an instant!

Undertow will do damage to mechanical enemies such as the Handyman, Motorized Patriot, and Turret Automatons in addition to stunning them, making it a useful attack when squaring off against these mechanized foes.

The alternate attack of Undertow allows you to pull an enemy toward you from nearly infinite distance. If there's a sniper you can't defeat with your current weaponry, it's no problem—simply pull him toward you! Any adversary pulled in by Undertow is left vulnerable and held in position, allowing you to unload an arsenal against a defenseless opponent!

RETURN TO SENDER

STATS

Cost per Use (Press)	Cost per Use (Hold)	Damage (Press)	Damage (Hold)	Effect Duration (Press)	Effect Duration (Hold)
20	10 per second	0	900+	3 seconds	As long as Salts allow

COMBOS

None.

UPGRADES

Upgrade	Cost	Function	First Available In:
Unlock Return to Sender	$200	Unlocks Return to Sender if not found	Hand of the Prophet
Return for Less	$898	Increases Shield duration (when pressed) and decreases Salts cost (when held)	Downtown Emporia
Sender Aid	$1287	Adds ability to absorb and collect incoming ammunition.	Downtown Emporia

STRATEGY

Return to Sender gives you the unique ability to both shield Booker while preparing an attack and create a forcefield that replenishes your ammo, depending on which attack you use.

The normal fire version of Return to Sender creates a shield that lasts for four to five seconds that, while active, absorbs any ammo fired at you and puts it into your own reserve. This replenishes your ammo while protecting you from damage.

The alternate fire version of Return to Sender also creates a shield but drains your Salts as long as you hold the button. Releasing the button sends out an explosive projectile that deals a huge amount of damage, compounded by any bullets sent your way! This is extremely useful against enemies like the Motorized Patriot—absorb a hail of Crank Gun fire, then send it back toward your attacker!

THE HEIGHT OF COLUMBIA FASHION
★ GEAR ★

COLUMBIA CHRONICLES

As you journey through Columbia, you'll find many pieces of Gear located throughout the city, each of which provides a different boost or unique ability beyond Booker's normal capacity. In this chapter, you'll find a description of all the Gear in the game, as well as their different effects.

Gear is divided into four categories—Hats, Shirts, Boots, and Pants. Only one piece of Gear can be equipped in each slot at one time, so you can have a Hat and Shirt equipped, but not two Hats.

When choosing what Gear to equip, consider two things—the way you like to play, and Gear that complements that style. If you think melee first, guns later, you should equip Gear like the Burning Halo and Gear that makes you faster. If you like to use Vigors, consider Gear like Storm and Blood to Salt to make your Vigors more powerful and the Salts plentiful.

Also, consider not only what you're fighting, but where—having a full set of Sky-Line Gear equipped all the time might not make sense, but if you're in an area with Sky-Lines everywhere, then kit up to take advantage of them. Carefully managing your Gear is key to victory—change your Gear often to take advantage of every situation!

LUCK OF THE DRAW
★ RANDOMIZED GEAR ★

Most of the Gear you'll find around Columbia is completely randomized. Each time you play through the game, you'll generally have a completely different set of Gear by the end of the game.

As you progress through the game, you have a better chance of collecting the more powerful Gear, even though you do have a chance of receiving it the first time you find a Gear Box.

HATS

Icon	Name	Function
	Hill Runner's Hat	Shield breaking increases movement speed. 50% faster for for 5 seconds.
	Ammo Cap	When shooting, empty clips have a 40% chance of automatically filling without the need to reload.
	Sheltered Life	Grants brief invulnerability when gaining health from snacks and Medical Kits.
	Gear Head	Makes you harder to detect by automatons, zeppelins, and Motorized Patriots.
	Storm	Killing with Devil's Kiss, Shock Jockey, or Bucking Bronco causes effects to chain to nearby enemies.
	Throttle Control	Increased throttle and braking control on Sky-Lines.
	Quick Handed	Decrease weapon reload times by 30%.
	Electric Touch	50% chance that a melee target is stunned. Victim is vulnerable for 3 seconds.

SHIRTS

Icon	Name	Function
	Scavenger's Vest	Enemies provide ammo upon death 40% of the time.
	Blood to Salt	Enemies provide Salts upon death 40% of the time.
	Nitro Vest	Increases radius of explosive weapon splash damage.
	Drop Cloth	Landing off a Sky-Line increases movement speed. 50% faster for 5 seconds.
	Shock Jacket	When struck, 50% chance to shock nearby enemies. Victims take 50 damage, vulnerable for 2 seconds.
	Executioner	Melee strikes against staggered enemies adds 60% chance to critical hit, and victims take 25% more damage when struck.
	Pyromaniac	When struck, 50% chance to burn nearby foes, Victims take 400 damage over 3 seconds.
	Sky-Line Accuracy	Increase weapon accuracy on Sky-Lines.
	Coat of Harms	Enemies become easier to melee execute.
	Winter Shield	Jumping to or from a Sky-Line grants a brief period of invulnerability.
	Bullet Boon	Increases clip size for all weapons by 50%.

BOOTS

Icon	Name	Function
	Fit as a Fiddle	When revived, Booker returns to life at full health.
	Nor'easter	Killing an enemy from a Sky-Line gives a 50% chance of a brief period of invulnerability.
	Newton's Law	Landing off a Sky-Line knocks back nearby enemies.
	Overkill	Killing with excessive damage stuns nearby adversaries.
	Kill to Live	Melee executions have a 65% chance to give health.
	Vampire's Embrace	Melee kills give health.
	Tunnel Vision	Aiming down Iron Sights increases damage by 25%, while aiming from the hip decreases damage by 25%.

PANTS

Icon	Name	Function
	Sky-Line Reloader	Jumping on or off a Sky-Line reloads your weapon.
	Angry Stompers	When extremely low on health, damage is increased by 2x.
	Brittle-Skinned	Hitting an enemy with a melee attack causes them to suffer 2x more damage for five seconds.
	Deadly Lungers	Melee strike range is increased by 3x.
	Head Master	Critical hit damage is increased by 50%.
	Fire Bird	Jumping from a Sky-Line sets nearby foes ablaze, dealing 400 damage over three seconds.
	Urgent Care	Shield recharge delay is decreased by two seconds, but Shield recharge time is increased by 2x.
	Last Man Standing	When very low on health, killing an enemy restores health.

★ GUARANTEED GEAR ★

While most Gear is random, there are five pieces of Gear you'll always find in the same place and you are guaranteed to have these pieces every time you play, as long as you are thorough! Check the walkthrough for the locations of where to find this unique Gear.

Icon	Name	Body Part	Function
	Burning Halo	Head	70% chance that a melee target is set ablaze. Victim takes 300 damage over 4 seconds.
	Spare the Rod	Head	30% chance melee target becomes Possessed. Possessed victim is an ally for a few seconds.
	Rising Bloodlust	Head	After each successive kill (up to five), weapon damage is increased. Boost resets if no enemies are killed within 10 seconds.
	Health for Salts	Legs	When out of Salts, health is consumed when Vigors are used.
	Spectral Sidekick	Legs	Dropping a weapon creates a ghostly ally for a few seconds.

MATCHING OUTFIT
★ BUILD EXAMPLES ★

You might notice that a lot of the Gear in *Bioshock Infinite* may have limited uses or may not seem that great on its own. However, when you combine certain pieces of Gear with others, you can create powerful and deadly combinations. Here are a few examples of set-ups that you can create by combining Gear pieces together.

GUNSLINGER

This build is specially built to emphasize firearm combat, especially using weapons that cause critical hits like the Pistol, Carbine or Repeater.

Hat	Ammo Cap or Quick Handed	
Shirt	Scavenger's Vest	
Boots	Tunnel Vision	
Pants	Head Master	

With this build, you'll find more ammo, reload faster, and you're your headshots will connect with extreme power! The buffs on Tunnel Vision and Head Master stack, causing enormous damage with a critical hit from a gun that is used with Iron Sights!

Depending on your preference, you can switch out Ammo Cap with Quick Handed—both increase your ability to reload in different ways, so this choice mostly comes down to personal preference.

DEMOLITION MAN

This example build is completely based around explosive weapons like the RPG and Volley Gun and causing extreme mayhem with them.

Hat	Quick Handed	
Shirt	Nitro Vest	
Boots	Tunnel Vision	
Pants	Angry Stompers	

This build is mostly centered around the Nitro Vest, which increases any explosive damage you cause. When you combine that with Tunnel Vision, you'll deal even more explosive damage per shot!

Quick Handed is better in this build than Ammo Cap, since the reload time on the RPG and other explosive weapons can be pretty lengthy and you'll need to reload these weapons more often.

BERSERKER

In this build, Gear is chosen to maximize your efficiency as a melee powerhouse, bent on crushing enemies with the Sky-Hook!

Every piece of Gear in this set is designed to maximize your Sky-Hook attacks, allowing you to attack from farther away, deal fire damage while striking, steal health after killing an enemy, and deal more damage in general!

If you're fighting stronger enemies like the Siren or Handyman, you can equip Sheltered Life instead, which gives you invincibility after eating food or finding a Medical Kit. Be sure to search enemies while you're fighting to maintain invincibility!

Hat	Ammo Cap or Quick Handed	
Shirt	Scavenger's Vest	
Boots	Tunnel Vision	
Pants	Head Master	

WIZARD

The Wizard build is focused on efficiently and powerfully attacking with an array of Vigors. This Gear is meant to allow you to primarily attack using Shock Jockey, Devil's Kiss, and other elemental attacks.

Hat	Storm	
Shirt	Blood to Salt	
Boots	Overkill	
Pants	Head Master	

To see the full effects of this build, zap an enemy with Shock Jockey, then blow them away with a Devil's Kiss projectile. You'll spread the effect to all enemies using Storm and stun them all using Overkill!

Once your foes are stunned, take out your enemies with headshots to fill your Salts Meter back up and do it again! If you want to limit your gun usage completely, consider Brittle-Skinned to turn your melee attacks into defense draining, debuff strikes!

SKY-LINE NINJA

This build is focused on striking your enemy and quickly escaping, constantly moving and suffering as little damage as possible.

Hat	Sheltered Life	
Shirt	Winter Shield	
Boots	Newton's Law	
Pants	Brittle-Skinned	

Since two of the Gear items in this build require Sky-Lines to be effective, you might not want to use these builds in areas with little-to-no Sky-Line combat, like Finkton and the first part of Emporia.

With this build, you should fly in, use a melee attack on an enemy once or twice then jump back onto a Sky-Line—you'll be invincible after you jump off and again when you jump back on!

DEFENDER

Defender is a build focused on keeping the Health and Shield Meters from draining. This build is better on harder difficulties or when you're having trouble advancing through some of the more difficult points in the story.

Hat	Hill Runner's Hat		
Shirt	Shock Jacket\Pyromaniac		
Boots	Vampire's Embrace		
Pants	Urgent Care		

This build is mostly focused on Urgent Care and Hill Runner's Hat. When combined, you can use the effect of Hill Runner's Hat to get away from foes, making it easy to keep your Health Meter filled.

On the Torso slot, you can use either Shock Jacket or Pyromaniac interchangeably, since they both punish any enemy that tries to attack up close. Use the one that better suits your play style—Pyromaniac does more overall damage, but Shock Jacket keeps enemies in place, allowing you to escape or drain health with Sky-Hook strikes that are charged with Vampire's Embrace.

SKY-LINE SNIPER

This is another build focused on being more efficient while fighting on and around Sky-Lines, but with guns instead of fists.

Hat	Throttle Control	
Shirt	Sky-Line Accuracy	
Boots	Nor'easter	
Pants	Fire Bird	

When using this build, slow down to shoot a few rounds at grounded enemies from a Sky-Line, then speed up to avoid their counter strike. After killing an enemy, shoot at another while you're invincible!

If you're being overwhelmed from the ground, try and jump towards multiple enemies if possible—Fire Bird will ignite them all! Instead of trying to finish off the flaming enemies, jump back on the Sky-Line to keep taking your enemies out from up high!

IN THE NAME OF THE PROPHET

The details are hazy, but the debt must be paid. That much you do know. The year is 1912, and you, Booker DeWitt, find yourself being tossed about in rough seas aboard a rowboat hailing from an unknown port. The couple before you prattles on back and forth as if you aren't even there, leaving you to mull over the contents of the box you've been given: a pistol, a key, a couple of postcards, and a message to bring the girl, unharmed, to New York City. There's a question for every whitecap on the horizon, and not an answer in sight.

"Bring us the girl and wipe away the debt."

★ LIGHTHOUSE ★

Climb the ladder to the dock and search inside the shed for a few loose coins, known locally as Silver Eagles. These coins may not be worth much where you've been, but they're the currency of choice where you're going. You'll need as much of this currency as you can find. Ascend the stairs to the base of the lighthouse and search the barrel off to the left prior to knocking on the door. This search should yield additional Silver Eagles and get you started on unlocking the "Coins in the Cushion" Achievement.

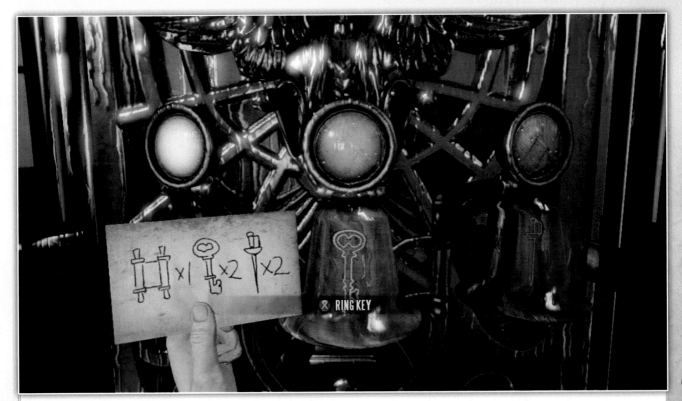

A curious assortment of items befitting this most unusual mission…

Enter the lighthouse and take a moment to have a look around. Get in the habit of scouring the areas you visit for Silver Eagles, consumables, various collectibles, and ammunition. The majority of the items you'll encounter, including ammo, are found in searchable barrels, crates, pieces of furniture, and yes, corpses. The wash basin near the entrance is just one of the many types of items you can interact with that doesn't yield items. You can also inspect radios, phonographs, telescopes, and many other devices. Take a moment to interact with each item whenever you see the button prompt. You never know what may happen.

Make your way up the spiraling staircase to the top of the lighthouse and approach the gate in front of the lamp. One of the postcards Booker was given reveals a pattern that matches that of the bells on the gate. Ring the bells the number of times shown on the card (Scroll x1, Key x2, and Sword x2, in that order), and watch the lighthouse transform before your very eyes. Take a seat in the chair whenever you're ready.

Ring each bell the number of times shown on the postcard, in sequence order from left to right.

The Lighthouse

The lighthouse for Infinite had to serve two purposes: The first being to set the religious nature of Columbia (much in the same way the original BioShock lighthouse gave a glimpse into Andrew Ryan's philosophical beliefs). The very first thing you see upon entering the lighthouse is the basin to wash away your sins, which is a very strong theme running throughout Infinite's story.

The Lighthouse's second purpose was to set the stakes for Booker's quest. Earlier versions of the Lighthouse didn't have things like the note on the door, or the dead man upstairs. By adding these, you immediately get a sense of urgency as well as what the stakes are if Booker should fail to retrieve Elizabeth from Columbia.

Drew Holmes
Lead Writer

WRITTEN IN THE CLOUDS

You might not have had any idea where you were going, but you have to admit the view sure is nice!
The rocket touches down softly, but you're not free to roam the city just yet.

ENTER THE CITY

The lighthouse-turned-rocket blasted you high into the stratosphere, to a place unlike any you ever dreamt possible. It's a city in the clouds, comprised of floating islands and bridges, where a man named Comstock is deemed a prophet. The rocket touches down atop a tower, then immediately lowers deep into a holy temple below.

THE WELCOME CENTER

Descend the stairs toward the sounds of the choral voices and inspect each of the two chapels flanking the large statue. The small chapel on the left contains a **Voxophone**. Voxophones (80 in total) are personal recordings made by the city's residents that often reveal interesting details concerning the history and politics of Columbia. Both chapels also contain a number of baskets, gifts, and other containers that you can search for Silver Eagles. Don't let the small denominations fool you, for even these small handfuls of coins can yield a tidy sum over time!

Descend the stairs past the robed man to the temple below, and wade through the water toward the preacher in the distance. Enter the circle at the end of the sermon to be baptized, for only those who have been cleansed of all sin can enter the wonder of Columbia.

	Voxophone
LOVE THE SINNER	
AUTHOR:	Lady Comstock
DATE:	April the 1st, 1893
LOCATION:	Welcome Center

Love the Prophet, because he loves the sinner. Love the sinner, because he is you. Without the sinner, what need is there for a redeemer? Without sin, what grace has forgiveness?

Walk along the watery path of forgiveness and accept the baptism.

Collectibles

Infusions

\-

Voxophones

1

Kinectoscopes

\-

Telescopes

\-

A DAY AT THE FAIR

★ TOWN CENTER ★

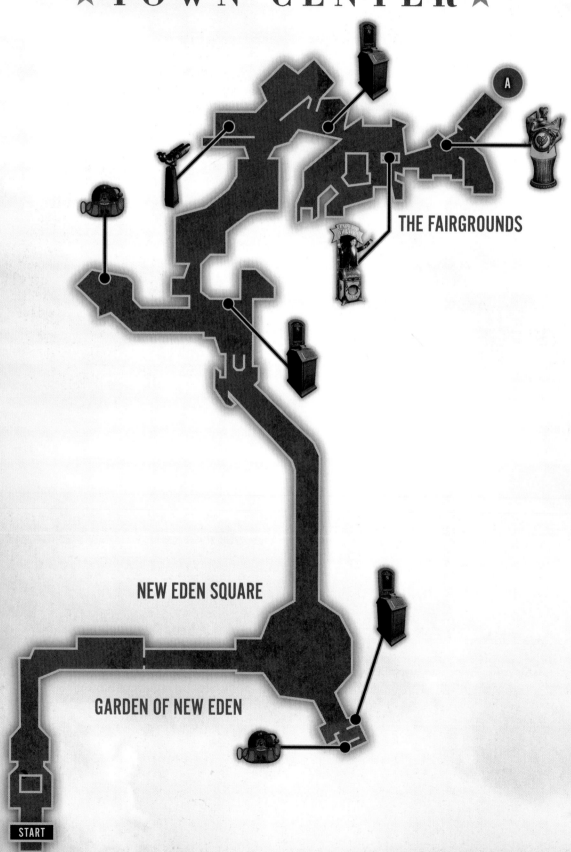

THE FAIRGROUNDS

NEW EDEN SQUARE

GARDEN OF NEW EDEN

START

RAFFLE PARK

SHADY LANE

EXIT

A

PATH OF THE SCROLL

First Encounters

POLICE (BATON)
POLICE (PISTOL)
GUN AUTOMATON
FIREMAN

New Vigors

Possession

Devil's Kiss

New Weaponry

Sky-Hook

Broadsider Pistol

Collectibles

Infusions

-

Kinectoscopes

3

Voxophones

4

Telescopes

1

FIND THE MONUMENT

THE GARDEN OF NEW EDEN

Booker comes to his feet in a sacred garden where Columbia's devout pay their respects to Fathers Washington, Franklin, and Jefferson. Ascend the stairs and continue beyond the other worshippers to the doors ahead. Throw the doors open to watch as the Garden of New Eden docks with New Eden Square. For a nonbeliever like Booker, it doesn't come a moment too soon.

You survived the baptismal dunking only to awake in a land where patriotism and religion have blended.

NEW EDEN SQUARE

New Eden Square is a lively area where folks come to shop, socialize, and enjoy a certain recreation in the leisurely manner befitting their standing. Enjoy the walk along the path leading to the square while making sure to collect any hotdogs or other food along the way. Booker still isn't feeling 100 percent after that dunking, but every bit of food he eats helps replenish his condition, which is represented by the Health Meter.

> **"Just 'cause a city flies don't mean it ain't got its fair share of fools."**

Voxophone

UNDESERVING

AUTHOR:	Zachary Hale Comstock
DATE:	September the 9th, 1893
LOCATION:	New Eden Square

And then, the archangel showed a vision: a city, lighter than air. I asked her, "Why do you show this to me, archangel? I'm not a strong man. I'm not a righteous man. I am not a holy man." And she told me the most remarkable thing: "You're right, Prophet. But if grace is within the grasp of one such as you, how can anyone else not see it in themselves?

The Garden of New Eden

As Booker awakes from his dream he finds himself staring at angelic statues of George Washington, Thomas Jefferson, and Benjamin Franklin. These American "Founding Fathers" are core to Columbia's religion. As Comstock tells it, the Angel Columbia gave the Founding Fathers three gifts to aid in the creation of America. They were the Sword, the Scroll, and the Key.

Drew Holmes
Lead Writer

Booker DeWitt

You take the role of Booker DeWitt, a former Pinkerton detective faced with mounting debts and forced to take one last job… You must travel to the city of Columbia to find a young woman and bring her safely to New York City. Unfortunately, that may not be as easy as it sounds…

Father Comstock's Gift of Prophecy

The first Kinetoscope is located inside Hudson's Fine Clothing shop, at the left end of the counter. The clothing shop is docked at the cul de sac, to the right of the statue where folks are having a picnic.

Continue up the path, past the horse and cart, to the drawbridge in time to see the parade floats and learn a little history about the founding of Columbia, a place where people can be free from "the Sodom below." Follow the others up the road to the on-your-honor Grocery and the sign announcing the fair and raffle today. Inspect the flower shop up the stairs to the left for additional coins, then proceed toward the sounds of the barbershop quartet, that dock on a floating stage. Soon, a distant chorus of bells and applause replaces the sound of their singing. Proceed along the path to spot the Angel Columbia monument. A young boy arrives to gives you a telegram from someone named Lutece: you're not to alert Comstock to your presence, nor should you pick #77.

The boy's telegram indicates someone knows you've arrived, but who?

Beware the False Shepherd!

This Kinetoscope is positioned near the large poster outside the grocery. Watch the short film to learn who the False Shepherd is and how the Lamb, the Miracle Child, can be protected from him.

	Voxophone
EVERYMAN, ALL AT ONCE	
AUTHOR:	Zachary Hale Comstock
DATE:	March the 29th, 1911
LOCATION:	Parade Crossing

One man goes into the waters of baptism. A different man comes out, born again. But who is that man who lies submerged? Perhaps that swimmer is both sinner and saint, until he is revealed unto the eyes of man.

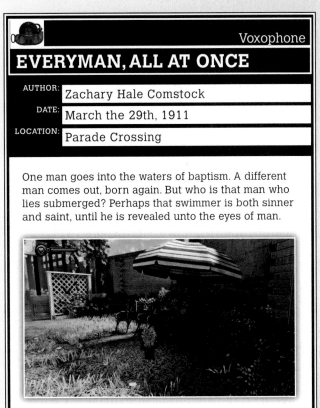

GO TO MONUMENT ISLAND

TELESCOPE

Find the first of 12 interactive Telescopes located on this road, off to the left. It's free to use and grants the viewer a tremendous close-up of Monument Tower.

Take a moment to look through the **Telescope** on the left after receiving the telegram, then proceed along the road to the gate up ahead. The policeman there explains that the road is closed for the night's fireworks show. It's for your safety, so you'll have to find another way around. That way is through the Fairgrounds. Ascend the stairs to the sounds of the carnival barkers.

THE FAIRGROUNDS

The Columbia Raffle & Fair is taking place today, July 6th, to celebrate Columbia's Independence Day. And nobody has pumped more money into this year's fair than Fink Manufacturing, creator of the drinkable, powerful Vigors. Stand in slack-jawed amazement as the Vigor barkers and their assistants demonstrate the power of Vigors, then step up to the "Cast Out the Devil" carnival game to give the Bucking Bronco Vigor a try! This game and several others in the fair give you a chance to try out some cutting-edge technology, win some money, and have a little fun for no cost at all. The Fairgrounds are roughly circular in shape, so take a moment to explore the area and try each of the three games, as well as the Voxophone recording demo. There's also a Veni! Vidi! Vigor! vending machine selling the Bucking Bronco Vigor for the lofty price of $375.

The Envy of All His Peers

Find this particular Kinetoscope opposite the Vigor demonstration at the top of the stairs, near the entrance to the festival. Don't be so distracted by those feats of wonderment that you miss the Kinetoscope on the right.

After you finish trying out the carnival games (covered on the next page), make your way to the ticket vending machine near the gate by the Handyman exhibit. The talking machine informs you that the raffle is all sold out, and entrance is reserved for dignitaries and VIPs only. Lucky for you, there's a free sample of the Possession Vigor just steps away! Take the bottle of **Possession** from the lady on the left to gain the ability to turn machines into allies! Put it to use on the ticket vendor machine, and watch as it mistakes you for the esteemed Assemblyman Buford and opens the gate on your behalf.

Use the free sample of Possession to trick the vending machine controlling the gate.

CARNIVAL GAMES

CAST OUT THE DEVIL

PRIZE: Silver Eagle Purse

It's up to you to use Bucking Bronco to knock the devil out of hiding without hitting the woman and child. Watch for movement behind the pieces of furniture, wait for the cardboard woman and child figure to slide out of the way, and press the Fire Vigor button to release Bucking Bronco. The devil changes his hiding place each time, but he's never hard to spot. Hit him three times to win the prize! Just don't think that you get to keep Bucking Bronco—this special formula was created specifically for the fair, and its effects wear off immediately. Sorry, pard'ner!

Wait for the woman and child to slide out of the way to avoid hitting them with the Vigor.

BRING DOWN THE SKY-LINE VOX

1ST PRIZE: Silver Eagle Purse
2ND PRIZE: Coins
3RD PRIZE: Cigarettes

Walk on up to the counter and grab the air shotgun to start playing. You have 40 seconds to shoot as many of the Vox Populi off the Sky-Lines as you can. The Vox rebels slide across the target area from either direction and on each of three different Sky-Lines. Use the air shotgun to blast them as quickly as you can to win the top prize! Booker automatically pumps the weapon to load it after each shot, so you needn't worry about reloading (in fact, pressing the Reload button causes you to exit the game prematurely). The air shotgun is accurate enough from this range to be used without sighting down the barrel, so just shoot from the hip and trust the weapon's spread to compensate for any error in your aim.

HUNT DOWN THE VOX

1ST PRIZE: Silver Eagle Purse
2ND PRIZE: Coins
3RD PRIZE: Cigarettes

This game uses an air rifle to shoot targets that pop up into view from three positions. Each target is worth one point, so it doesn't matter which one you hit. A fourth target, the infamous Daisy Fitzroy, appears once and slides across the rear of the target area. Shoot her to gain bonus points! The air rifle fires as fast as you can pull the trigger and is deadly accurate. It's certainly advantageous to aim down the sights by holding the Aim button before you pull the trigger, but this slows you down and narrows your field of view. Practice firing from the hip without aiming down the barrel when targeting enemies at this distance. Just aim the gun and wait for the reticle to turn red.

At this range, the air rifle is quite accurate before you even aim down the Iron Sights.

Fire as fast as you can to hit the Vox before they escape!

PATH OF THE SCROLL

Raid the provisions barrels for extra supplies, and continue along the path, past the policeman showing off his new Sky-Hook weapon, to the statue that is phased from male to female on the right. The plaque says that R. Lutece "Gave Columbia Her Wings," but more importantly, there's a **Voxophone** on the bench for you to pick up. Proceed toward the sounds of the singing crowd in the distance.

RAFFLE SQUARE

Follow the path around the lower level of Raffle Square, along the scenic walk to the police barricade. The road leading to Monument Island is closed, so Booker has no choice but to cut through the park. Head up the stairs near the fountain and continue down the other side toward the stage in the distance.

The raffle is about to begin, and whether you like it or not, the woman with the raffle numbers is waving you toward her. Talk to the woman to get your raffle number (#77) and watch as the announcer draws that very number out of the bowl. So much for heeding the advice of the telegram: you win!

As the winner, you're given the honor of making the first throw. The target: a shackled couple brought on stage to jeers and a mocking rendition of "Here Comes the Bride." Guilty of wanting to marry outside their race, they've been brought to the fair to serve as an example to the rest of Columbia. Their so-called crime is punishable by death, and death comes at an agonizing pace when the weapon is a barrage of thrown baseballs. And so it goes in 1912 Columbia, a city governed by a narrow-minded class of elites.

You're presented with a choice of throwing the ball at the couple or at the announcer, or doing nothing. This choice bears only slight significance that becomes clear in the next chapter. The immediate outcome is the same: one of the nearby policemen spots the brand on Booker's right hand. Booker uses some quick thinking to turn the tables on the cops who snag him. Once armed with the **Sky-Hook**, quickly press the Melee button to strike the cop as he approaches.

Voxophone

FOR I AM LONELY, TOO

AUTHOR: Constance Field

DATE: August the 1st, 1902

LOCATION: Path of the Scroll

Madame Lutece—I have read all of your books on the sciences. Mama says, "it's not a fit occupation for a lady," but I think she's jealous of our cleverness. Is it true that only you are allowed to visit the girl in the tower? If the Lamb is lonely too, I should like to meet her, as we would have much in common. —Warmest regards, Constance

Approach the lady with the basket of baseballs to get your raffle number.

Booker's quick thinking relieves this cop of his Sky-Hook, a multi-purpose weapon that then becomes permanently attached to Booker's left hand for the rest of the game.

Racism in Columbia

America's founding was the sign of a new order: Democracy triumphing over the will of a single ruler. But for all the enlightenment ideals it represented, there was the darker side most representative in its rampant slavery and ruthless oppression of minorities.

Comstock and his followers view themselves as the elite ruling class, and the minorities as nothing better than animals who can be "trained" to act civilized. It is through this oppression and demonization of minorities that the Vox Populi movement begins to take shape.

Drew Holmes
Lead Writer

DEFEND YOURSELF

The crowd vanishes at the first drop of blood, and the gate leading back the way you came is bolted shut. You're going to have to fight your way out of Raffle Square! Use the Sky-Hook to hit the two cops who come running at you, then search their bodies before heading up the stairs. The impressive bridge and island that you see dead ahead floats away as you approach. You'll have to loop around past the police blockade you saw earlier!

Hold the Melee button to perform an execution-style attack with the Sky-Hook once you've seen a skull icon appear over the enemy's head. This bloody assault isn't for the faint of heart, but it is effective! Although you can execute these coffee-and-donuts patrolmen when they're at full health, you'll need to soften up tougher enemies quite a bit before they'll be susceptible to a Sky-Hook execution.

Tap the Melee button for a quick strike, or hold it to perform an execution whenever a skull icon appears over the enemy's head.

Continue to assault the cops who approach near the fireworks display with melee attacks and take cover near the kiosk in the center, to stay close to the Health Kit if you need it. One of the cops who attacks in the area behind the stage drops a **Pistol**, making up for the one you lost during the rocket trip. Booker automatically equips the Pistol in his right hand once it is obtained.

Descend the steps to collect the **Voxophone** and the money from the Silver Eagle Bag near the vending machine. Purchase the **Possession Aid** upgrade from the vending machine for $50. This upgrade allows you to use the Possession ability to turn humans into allies who commit suicide when the effect expires. Shoot the fireworks barrel in the corner at the base of the ramp if any additional police approach.

Voxophone

SOLUTION TO YOUR PROBLEMS

AUTHOR: Jeremiah Fink

DATE: September the 16th, 1893

LOCATION: Raffle Square

I told you, Comstock—you sell 'em paradise, and the customers expect cherubs for every chore! No menials in God's kingdom! Well, I've a man in Georgia who'll lease us as many Negro convicts as you can board! Why, you can say they're simple souls, in penance for rising above their station. Whatever eases your conscience, I suppose.

Possession Aid makes it possible to use Possession on humans as well as automatons!

Ascend the ramp to the delivery barge and quickly Possess the Gun Automaton at the far end of the barge. Fire off a few rounds at the cops on the Sky-Lines above, then advance to the end of the barge to draw the cops into the turret's line of fire. Jump down (mind the gap!) and use advance and retreat tactics to pull the enemies back toward the Gun Automaton. Just be careful not to stay in this spot too long, because when the effects of Possession wear off on Automatons they do not suicide like human victims, instead they revert to attacking you!

Never hesitate to take possession of a Gun Automaton or other machine.

There's a second Gun Automaton located on a ledge near the flowering bushes on the right. Head up the stairs on the right to avoid detection, and use Possession on it as soon as you can. You can safely target it from the area near the fountain that is directly above the vending machine. Sometimes it's worth using Possession on a Gun Automaton not only for the help in defeating enemies, but as a way of saving you from having to spend ammo destroying it.

The green glow lets you know the Gun Automaton is still under the effects of Possession.

Vigors are powered by an electrochemical reaction that takes place in the body upon drinking. Once he's ingested a Vigor, that ability becomes part of Booker's DNA, and he'll never need to drink that Vigor again. Nevertheless, Vigors can only be employed if he has enough Salt in his system. Be on the lookout for Salt Phials or for bottles of Vigors you have already consumed to keep the Salt Meter full. Of course, you can always purchase additional Salt Phials from a vending machine, if necessary.

Booker can only use Possession on one human enemy at a time, but the length of the effect varies between enemy types. Human foes react to Possession differently. The effect wears off over time (its effect fades much faster on tougher enemies), but human enemies kill themselves as the effect fades. This makes it possible to eliminate a couple of foes by simply casting Possession at each one of them. As the effect shifts from one adversary to the other, the enemy no longer under the Vigor's trance will kill himself with his weapon. This is especially helpful when you're low on ammo, provided you have enough Salt to employ this expensive Vigor.

TAKE THE FIREMAN'S VIGOR

SHADY LANE

Gather up the ammo from the gun lockers in the park and continue past the police barricade to Shady Lane. Raid the grocery store on the left for food and do a thorough sweep of the area (and backtrack, if necessary) to replenish any lost health and Salt before approaching the gate at the end of the road.

★Fireman★

SHADY LANE FIREMAN'S VITALS

Health	Ranged Damage	Melee Damage	Special Damage	Special Attack
1430	240	300	360	Explosion

Beyond the Shady Lane gate stands an enemy of far greater threat than you've encountered thus far. The Fireman, clad in armor and rippling in flame, is capable of hurling small grenade-like firebombs at you from afar. These volatile firebombs explode with great force and shower everything nearby in flame. The Fireman is also quite capable at close-range combat and can strike with fire and fury should Booker dare to step within his range.

The very first thing to do upon spotting the Fireman is to cast Possession at him. There aren't any other enemies in the area, but this at least gets the Fireman to briefly stop attacking Booker. Unlike the feeble security force nearby, the Fireman does not commit suicide when Possession wears off.

Stick close to the entrance and pepper the Fireman in the head with gunfire. Continue to shoot as fast as you can while he's Possessed. He'll charge toward Booker in an effort to stand by his side; run from him as soon as he does. Cast Possession a second time if you have enough Salt (there's a Salt Phial on the left); otherwise, continue shooting while backpedaling away. Use the carts for cover and sprint away from any firebombs that he lobs your way. Continue to shoot at him while listening for the angry scream he unleashes right before initiating his self-destruct attack. The Fireman glows bright orange before charging toward Booker's position in an attempt to detonate against him. Give him a wide berth to avoid getting caught in the blast zone.

TAKE THE VIGOR FROM THE FIREMAN

PICK UP DEVIL'S KISS

Pick up the **Devil's Kiss** Vigor that the Fireman drops upon death, and watch as Booker gains the ability to hurl those very same fireballs that the Fireman was using. Tap the Switch Vigor button to alternate between Possession and Devil's Kiss, and note how the graduation on the Salt Meter changes. Devil's Kiss consumes less Salt than Possession and can be cast more times between refills!

Ascend the stairs engulfed in flames on the right to slip behind the white gazebo to get the drop on another Gun Automaton. Take Possession of it, then approach the edge to draw the cops out of hiding from behind the barricade. Switch to Devil's Kiss and lob a fireball at the fuel slicks on the ground. Target the red, white, and blue fireworks barrels with your Pistol if you run out of Salt and want to get the most bang out of your bullets!

Aim Devil's Kiss at the oil slicks on the ground to snare enemies in a pool of fire.

The path to Monument Island is out, it hasn't docked with Shady Lane and probably won't, given the flaming condition of the area. You'll have to continue through the restaurant instead. Push open the doors of The Blue Ribbon Restaurant and head inside.

First Encounters

FOUNDER (BATON)

FOUNDER (PISTOL)

FOUNDER (MACHINE GUN)

ZEALOT OF THE LADY

New Vigors

Murder of Crows

New Weaponry

Triple R Machine Gun

Collectibles

Infusions
3

Kinectoscopes
4

Voxophones
6

Telescopes
1

COMSTOCK ★ CENTER ★ ROOFTOPS

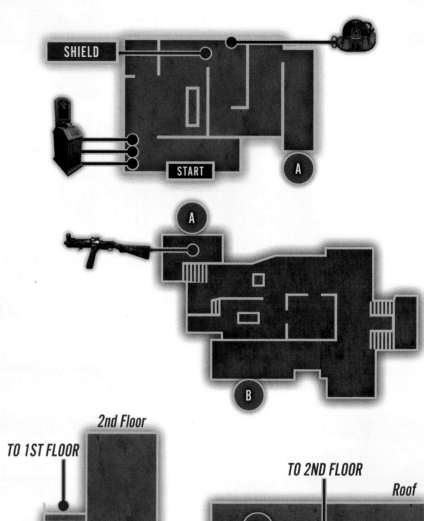

SHIELD

START

A

A

B

2nd Floor

TO 1ST FLOOR

C

LANSDOWNE RESIDENCE

TO 1ST FLOOR

QUEST CHEST

TO 2ND FLOOR

Roof

B

TO 2ND FLOOR

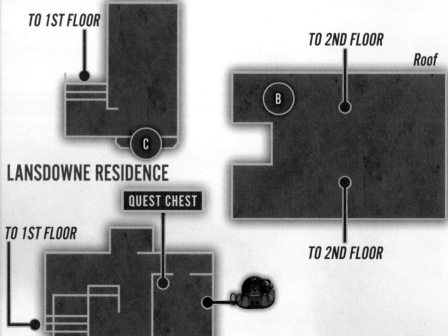

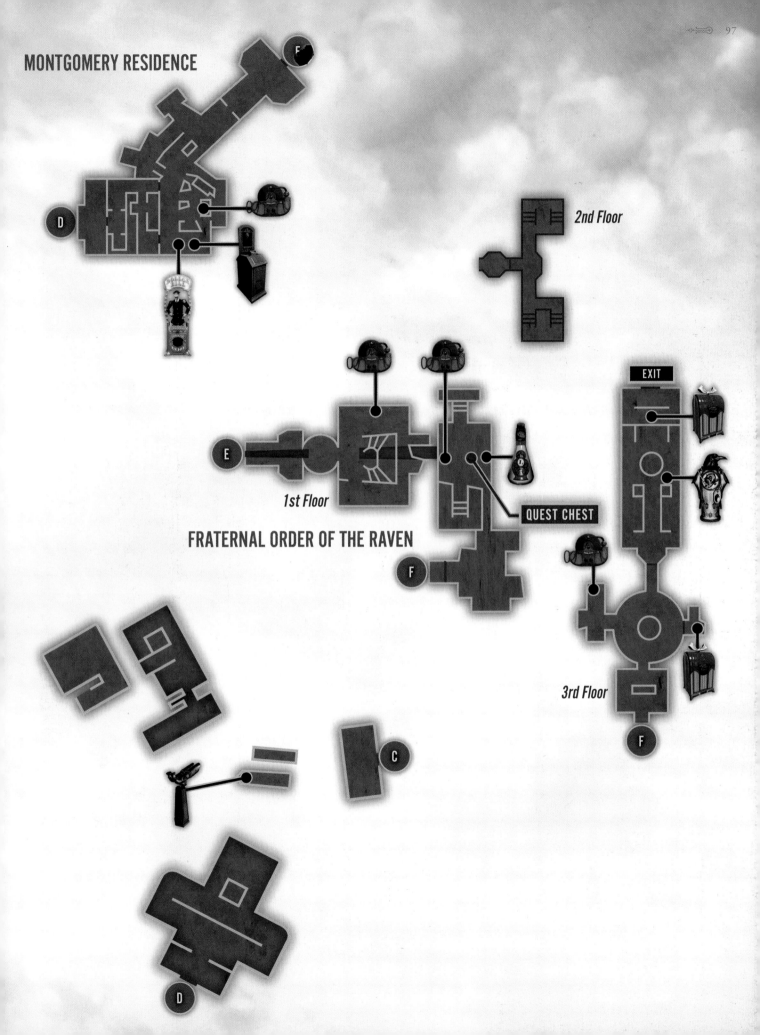

MONTGOMERY RESIDENCE

FRATERNAL ORDER OF THE RAVEN

2nd Floor

EXIT

1st Floor

QUEST CHEST

3rd Floor

GO TO MONUMENT ISLAND

THE BLUE RIBBON RESTAURANT

The restaurant isn't empty, but there aren't any hostiles in the immediate area, either: only the odd couple who asked you to flip the coin earlier. The man is busy scrubbing the bar, while the lady offers you an aperitif, a **Shield**. Take the bottle from her tray and bask in the comfort of knowing that you now have an electromagnetic force-field that can absorb incoming attacks and help to keep you safe from harm. Take cover and wait for the Shield to recharge whenever the yellow Shield Meter depletes and you see it "shatter" on the screen.

Approach the lady near the kitchen to obtain the Shield Upgrade.

A Look Back at Opening Day
The Prophet Stands up to Foes:
Within and Without!
We Secede from the So-Called "Union"

Enter The Blue Ribbon Restaurant and turn left to head down the hall. There, under a banner announcing "The Rise of Columbia," you see three Kinetoscopes. Take a moment to watch each of the three short films. This particular group of three Kinetoscopes is also found elsewhere in Columbia, so temper your excitement when you see other groups of three Kinetoscopes, as it will be these same three.

Collect the **Voxophone** on your way through the kitchen to the doors leading outside. There's a wealth of food and alcohol scattered about the kitchen, but take it easy on the latter. Though they do serve to replenish your health, alcoholic beverages drain your Salt and may leave you in the uncomfortable position of being unable to cast any Vigors when you need them most!

Voxophone

HALF A JEW

AUTHOR:	Ed Gaines
DATE:	March the 1st, 1912
LOCATION:	The Blue Ribbon Restaurant

Father Comstock called on me today to write his biography. Me! The man pays for exactly 100 pages, in advance. Now, I'm half a Jew when I smell silver, so I say, I say: "Father, your flock would pay for a thousand, you know. Why settle for less?" And then, the Prophet looks to me and says, "One hundred will suffice, as I know how it ends."

THE FREIGHT HOOKS

It's time to put the Sky-Hook to work in a less violent manner! Look toward the freight hook on the adjacent building and press the Jump button when it glows green, signaling that it's in range. The Sky-Hook's magnetic properties help propel Booker through the air from one freight hook to another. Make your way to the fourth freight hook, then target the enemy on the nearby rooftop. Line up the targeting reticle with your adversary and press the Jump button to perform a Sky-Line Strike. This type of attack is positively lethal against all but the strongest of foes and can successfully knock most opponents off buildings.

Pick up the **Machine Gun** near the crates and descend the stairs. A Founder with a Machine Gun patrols the area near the distant stairs and quickly spots Booker just as a police barge floats in from the left. Use Possession on the Founder just as the barge deploys its reinforcements. Head up the stairs on the right and slip into the small room where the generator is while the enthralled Founder deals with the Gun Automaton aboard the barge. Grab the Salt Phial near the door inside, and take Possession of the Gun Automaton on the barge. Open fire on it to destroy it before heading around the corner, else you could find yourself caught in crossfire between two Gun Automatons.

The green glow is your cue that Booker is within reach of the freight hook or enemy.

Use the maintenance building for cover when sneaking within range of possessing the Gun Automaton.

Round the corner and quickly head up the steps to the left as a fresh batch of Founders approaches from the right. Hit them with Devil's Kiss and open fire with your Machine Gun before continuing around the corner to the right, toward the roof overlooking the building with the large skylights. Search the multitude of lockboxes and gather the few Salt Phials you find. Quickly use Possession on the Gun Automaton that is on the barge near the skylights below, and let it aid you in clearing the roof. Shoot out the glass skylights and jump down to the bedroom below to enter the Lansdowne Residence.

Search the Lansdowne Residence for supplies and Silver Eagles. Descend the stairs inside the house to the lower bedroom and locate the **Voxophone** on the bookshelf, which reveals the history behind the strange chest on the floor to the right. You can't unlock this chest yet, but trying to yields an optional quest objective. The key to this chest is discussed later in this walkthrough.

Voxophone

OTIS' NIMBLE FINGERS

AUTHOR:	Byron Cotswold
DATE:	June the 23rd, 1912
LOCATION:	Lansdowne Residence

Otis works up at the lodge part-time. He took this box from one of their secret ceremonies, and I know for sure there is something dear inside. Problem is, Otis is more fool than not. He didn't bother to also secure a key from the feathered brothers to open the damn thing.

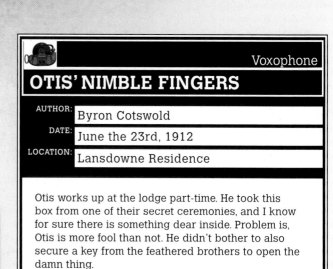

The chest is locked, but trying to open it nets you an optional quest objective.

Exit the house via the upstairs balcony and leap to the freight hook on the adjacent building. From there, target the patio outside the large building nearby and open the doors to enter the Montgomery Residence.

This building is home to the city's underground abolitionist movement, the Columbia Friends of the Negro Society, a group of people who no doubt did *not* participate in today's raffle. Make your way past the printing presses and down the hall on the right to the library. Exit through the doors on the left.

The replaying messages you've undoubtedly heard via the city's public address system have put the police on alert, and Constitution Square is

Not everyone is a foe; there's no reason to shoot this couple.

crawling with cops. You've got a fight brewing, but there's a vending machine straight outside Montgomery Residence, to the right of the stage, that sells Health Kits and Salt if you need it. Don't miss the **Voxophone** on the stage.

Voxophone

A NEW HUNT

AUTHOR:	Preston E. Downs
DATE:	June the 29th, 1912
LOCATION:	Comstock Center Rooftops

Comstock came by the wagon at dawn. Man was just… he just transfixed by my trophy scalps. Asked about the white ones, there. I said, "Well, sir—if your quarry dwells in the jungle, and beds down with the with the local color, why split hairs?" [Laughs] Not a chuckle out of him. Either he ain't seen a man go native, or maybe… maybe too many. Anyhow, now he's got me huntin' down this "Daisy Fitzroy." Hope he don't expect me to stuff and mount her.

Take cover behind the planter and cast Possession on the Gun Automaton far in the distance. It is located on the walkway, just beyond the grassy area. This helps draw a lot of the attention away from you, making it easier to pick off the Founders one by one. Hang back until you see the Fireman, and then move into cover near the pile of crates to finish him off. Look for a chance to detonate a barrel of explosives near the Fireman, but refrain from spending Salt on Devil's Kiss attacks aimed at the Fireman. Fire-based attacks aren't effective against him; you're better off opening fire with the Machine Gun. Another option is to cast Possession on him and shoot him while he's under the effects of the Vigor. Detonate the fireworks barrel to the right of the Gun Automaton to safely destroy it once the effects of Possession wear off.

Fight your way to the crates on the left, then turn and use Possession on the Gun Automaton that is stationed on the walkway beyond the tents.

Make sure you've completely destroyed the Gun Automaton, or your one-time ally may turn against you.

FRATERNAL ORDER OF THE RAVEN

The quiet halls of the Fraternal Order of the Raven provide a brief respite from the activity on the streets, but news of your arrival has spread here, as well. Enter the lounge to the left of the John Wilkes Booth statue, and open fire on the men inside as soon as they get to their feet. Watch out for one who may attack from the dining room on the other side of the hall. Take a moment to collect the **Voxophone** from atop the bar, then enter the dining hall on the opposite side of the foyer. There aren't many enemies here, but the squawking of the crows and "Order of the Raven" banner suggest the Founders' Lodge may attract a different clientele than expected.

Head up the stairs and through the double doors to the balcony overlooking the meeting hall. The leader of the Order of Black Raven has his audience in rapt attention, making them quite susceptible to a surprise Devil's Kiss attack. Hurl a pair of fireballs at the crowd downstairs, then fall back and wait for the survivors to charge up the stairs. Keep the action in front of you, and cut each of the attackers down with your Machine Gun as they charge forward. Some of the Black Raven Members attack with a Machine Gun or Pistol, but most simply charge Booker's position in hopes of landing a melee attack. On the left-hand side of the balcony, collect a small Salt Phial and Health Kit.

Hurl your fireballs down at the attendees,
then draw the Machine Gun and wait for them to run up the stairs.

Danger on All Sides

Exit the Montgomery Residence near the Wild West show and tend to the Founders and Gun Automatons in the area. Once done, head up the stairs near the Dollar Bill vending machine and around the corner to find this Kinetoscope.

	Voxophone
THE GIFT OF THE EMANCIPATOR	

AUTHOR:	Zachary Hale Comstock
DATE:	April the 14th, 1905
LOCATION:	The Fraternal Order of the Raven

And when the Angel Columbia gave unto the Founders the tools to build the new Eden, they did so without hesitation. For 85 years, they prepared the way of the Lord. But when the Great Apostate came, he brought war with him, and the fields of Eden were soaked with the blood of brothers. The only emancipation he had to offer was death.

Villains and Heroes

The statue of John Wilkes Booth is an image that represents Comstock's religious philosophy. In his view, America was an "Eden on Earth" ordained by God. The Constitution was a sacred religious document not to be altered. When President Lincoln issued the Emancipation Proclamation, Comstock argued it was an affront to God. Lincoln (whom the Founders refer to as "The Great Apostate") was therein viewed as a demon in the eyes of Comstock, and his assassin someone to be revered.

When creating complex and interesting villains, it's important to try to view them as human beings with real motivation and goals. Comstock isn't just the mustaches twirling bad guy—his actions are motivated by his background and his view on the world. Yes, they are warped and twisted (but in his mind his actions are justified. Few people view themselves as evil.

Drew Holmes
Lead Writer

Descend the stairs and raid the lockboxes left behind by your victims, and locate the **Voxophone** on the pew. The leader of the Order fled down the hall to the right, but there is an **Infusion** atop the altar that you shouldn't hesitate to grab. Infusions allow you to gain a small increase to your Maximum Health, Shield capacity, or Salts capacity. The key atop the table might also be of interest to you, because it unlocks the chest found in Lansdowne Residence.

Voxophone
THE LIE OF THE EMANCIPATOR

AUTHOR:	Zachary Hale Comstock
DATE:	April the 14th, 1905
LOCATION:	The Fraternal Order of the Raven

What exactly was the Great Emancipator emancipating the Negro from? From his daily bread. From the nobility of honest work. From wealthy patrons who sponsored them from cradle to grave. From clothing and shelter. And what have they done with their freedom? Why, go to Finkton, and you shall find out. No animal is born free, except the white man. And it is our burden to care for the rest of creation.

THE ORDER OF RAVEN'S CHEST

Descend the stairs in the Founder's Lodge and approach the altar to find a **key** next to the Infusion. This key opens a chest located in the downstairs bedroom of Lansdowne Residence. Exit the Fraternal Order of the Raven the way you came and cut back through the Montgomery House, where the poster printing was taking place. Use the Sky-Hook to leap back across to the house with the skylights on the roof. Make your way through the house to locate the chest in the bedroom downstairs, then open it to find another **Infusion**.

Exit the meeting hall through the doors at the end of the corridor on the right. This leads to the vacant library where several desks sit abandoned, their contents long since picked over. Enter the elevator in the library and push the button to ride it to the upper level, where a projector plays a a silent film to an invisible audience.

Locate the bookcase against the wall in the room with the projector and shove it aside (pushing only from the right) to uncover a hidden room. This secret storage room contains a new piece of **Gear** that grants Booker unique abilities when he wears it. The Gear that you find throughout Columbia is partially random. It is effectively divided up into various pools that become available as you progress through the story. The more powerful you are, the greater your odds of getting a more valuable piece of Gear. Booker can wear up to four pieces of Gear at any one time. However, only one piece from each of the following categories can be worn: Hats, Shirts, Boots, and Pants.

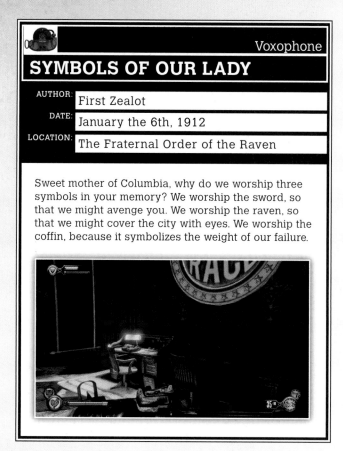

Voxophone

SYMBOLS OF OUR LADY

AUTHOR: First Zealot

DATE: January the 6th, 1912

LOCATION: The Fraternal Order of the Raven

Sweet mother of Columbia, why do we worship three symbols in your memory? We worship the sword, so that we might avenge you. We worship the raven, so that we might cover the city with eyes. We worship the coffin, because it symbolizes the weight of our failure.

There's a Voxophone in the room to the left, across from the hidden gear room.

Be sure to locate the Gear behind the bookshelf before you head up the stairs!

Go up the stairs and continue through the doors to the sounds, and sights, of torture. The man behind the vicious act you witness is the Zealot of the Lady, a commander of crows and leader of the Order of the Black Raven. He and his followers have transformed the roof into an aviary, and it is here where you will face him.

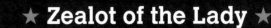

★ Zealot of the Lady ★

FRATERNAL ORDER OF THE RAVEN: ZEALOT'S VITALS

Health	Ranged Damage	Melee Damage	Special Damage	Special Attack
2356	N/A	532	N/A	N/A

Reload your Machine Gun and get ready for an attack, as the peaceful stroll through the aviary is about to be rudely interrupted. The crows you hear in the distance are drawing closer; they're on the upper walkway to the right and about to descend. Collect the Salts Phial on the left if you need it and switch to Devil's Kiss. Step out onto the grass in the center of the aviary while holding the Vigor button, and release it at the ground to set a trap. Walk away from it and set another where Booker stands.

The flock (a murder in zoological terms) bands together and creates the Zealot of the Lady, a dangerous entity capable of unleashing numerous flesh-eating crows on his target. With any luck, he materializes right near your trap. Open fire on the Zealot with the Machine Gun while he burns, and wait for the crows to appear and take off toward you. Back away from the second Devil's Kiss trap you set, and bait him into it. The crows gather into the Zealot, just in time to fall victim to the second trap.

The Zealot of the Lady has far more health than a standard Founder, but not enough to withstand multiple Devil's Kiss traps. There is an additional Salts Phial in the area, but if you are out of Salt and forced to confront the Zealot of the Lady without your Vigors, back away immediately and strafe behind cover. The key is to avoid his crows, so he can't emerge right on top of you. The crows home in on your position and gather up, and the Zealot of the Lady then descends on you in an instant, unleashing a painful melee attack.

Quickly pick up the **Murder of Crows** Vigor after defeating him—you can hold the Vigor Select button down to bring up the Vigor Radial—and lay a pair of Murder of Crows traps down. Place one on either side of the statue in the center of the aviary to catch the Founders about to descend the stairs. Murder of Crows does an excellent job of debilitating enemies, making them more vulnerable to weapon fire. Finish them off with the Machine Gun or Devil's Kiss, and head up the stairs to find another piece of **Gear**. This particular piece of Gear is one of five that isn't random. You will always acquire the Burning Halo hat, which adds a 70% chance to add a blast of fire to your melee attacks!

Murder of Crows traps are excellent for neutralizing and weakening multiple enemies at once.

GO TO THE GONDOLA STATION

Once outside, use the freight hooks to leap across to the second house, where the open doors are, and head inside. Several cops are interviewing the man and woman of the household here, so watch your aim. The crosshairs turn green to denote an innocent target: only shoot an innocent if you wish to draw additional law enforcement to the scene. There aren't any collectibles in this house, but you may find some Silver Eagles.

This house doesn't contain anything valuable, but you can search it all the same.

Continue across the rooftops via the freight hooks and leap to strike the enemy on the Gondola Station with a melee attack. Fight your way up the stairs, and head inside the Gondola Station entrance.

TELESCOPE

This easily overlooked Telescope is on the bow of the Founder barge to the left of the rooftops. Leap to it from the freight hook on the building before the one with the large patio.

MONUMENT ISLAND
★ GATEWAY ★

FIND A GONDOLA

Uncanny Mystery in Columbia...

This Kinetoscope is located on the right-hand side of the Gondola Station, directly across from the two vending machines. Inspect it before entering the lobby so you don't miss it.

Several police and Machine Gun units, as well as a Gun Automaton, heavily guard this station. Before you rush in to combat, use the vending machines on the left to replenish spent ammo, and to refill your Health and Salt Meters. The Veni! Vidi! Vigor! vending machine carries upgrades for Murder of Crows and Devil's Kiss, but it is highly unlikely that you'll have enough money to buy either of them.

Enter the main lobby on the right and use Possession on the Gun Automaton across the room. Switch to Murder of Crows, and cast it whenever two or more enemies approach simultaneously. Hang back behind the columns for cover so you can quickly retreat to the vending machines if you need more ammo or Salt.

The enemies here destroy the turret, but you shouldn't have much trouble fending them off with your newfound ability and Machine Gun. Gradually fight your way past the columns to the police barricade on the other side of the room; these provide excellent cover against any remaining foes. There are Salt Phials to find throughout the lobby, but you can make quick work of the Founders with your Sky-Hook melee strike, especially now that you have Burning Halo equipped!

Search the ticketing offices on the left and right and raid the many desks and cabinets for food, money, and ammo. Exit the station through the rear door and step out onto the balcony near the Sky-Lines.

Founder Police are no match for a Gun Automaton that has been possessed and Murder of Crows.

Don't hesitate to hit the baton-wielding Founders with melee attacks to save ammo and light them on fire.

★ MONUMENT ISLAND GATEWAY ★

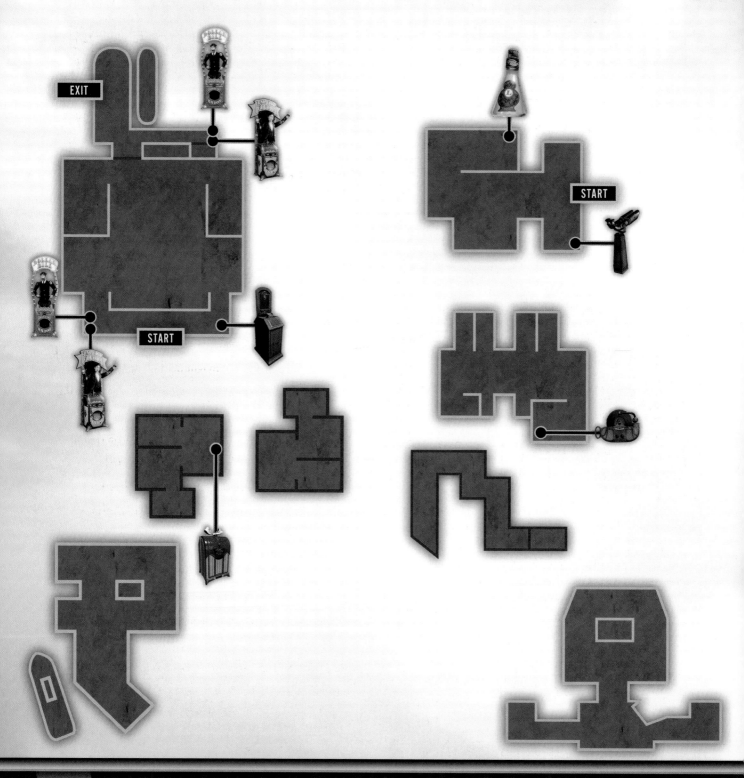

EXIT

START

START

Collectibles

THE TOLLING

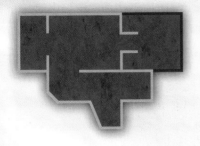

EXIT

USE THE SKY-LINES

Leaping on and off Sky-Lines soon becomes a valuable skill, so it is a good idea to start practicing now.

TELESCOPE

Sky-Line Strike the lone worker on the balcony, then inspect the Telescope in the corner before you grab the Infusion inside. Always leap off Sky-Lines to explore any platform you see for collectibles.

The gondola is out of service, so you're going to have to use the Sky-Lines to reach Monument Island. The Sky-Hook you've been using to attach to freight hooks is also capable of sliding along Sky-Lines, provided there isn't any cargo blocking the path. Human traffic on Sky-Lines stays to the left so that you can use the gun in Booker's right hand to fire on enemies as they pass by. Think of it as jousting, Columbia style! Press the Melee button to switch directions, and use the Movement Controls to control the speed of your slide: press up to increase your speed or down to go slower.

Leap onto the Sky-Line and pull down on the movement controls to keep from traveling too quickly. Watch for the lone Founder on the first tower you slide past, and leap to him for a Sky-Line Strike. Kill his companion to the left and enter the small tower to find an **Infusion** on the desk and a **Telescope** outside. Leap back to the Sky-Line, making sure to continue in a left-ward direction as viewed while exiting the tower.

Target the lone soldier outside this maintenance building, then go inside to find an Infusion.

Continue along the rails to the upper tower, leap off and kill the Founder, and grab the **Voxophone** from the control room on the right. Pull the lever on the Sky-Line control terminal to move the freight out of the way, then leap back onto the rail and continue to the police barge in the distance.

Sky-Line Strike the lone Founder on the barge, then take out the three Founders near the stairs. Booker needs to reach the upper Sky-Line if he's to get to Monument Island. Face the large hotel where the enemies were, and leap to the freight hook above the balcony. Find the **Gear** behind the nightstand as you cut through the hotel and exit via the rear patio. Continue along the Sky-Line to the next building in the distance.

	Voxophone

ANOTHER ARK FOR ANOTHER TIME

AUTHOR:	Zachary Hale Comstock
DATE:	September the 9th, 1893
LOCATION:	Gondola to Monument Island

"And the Lord saw the wickedness of man was great. And He repented He had made man on the Earth." Rain! Forty days and forty nights of the stuff. And He left not a thing that walked alive. You see, my friends, even God is entitled to a do-over. And what is Columbia if not another Ark, for another time?

You can't slide along Sky-Lines that have freight on them. Pull the lever to move the freight out of the way.

The easiest way to make a pinpoint dismount is often with a Sky-Line Strike!

ASCEND THE BUILDING

THE TOLLING

Leap down off the Sky-Line near the large squad of kneeling policemen. Their Prophet has ordered them to stand down. They're harmless, and you can choose to simply leave them alone. They also make for easy targets and can be annihilated with a single Devil's Kiss, even though they do not drop loot. The same goes for the group of kneeling men inside the tower. Ride the elevator up and follow the signs for rooftop access to the Sky-Lines.

You'll gain no loot for slaughtering these defenseless Founders, so hold your fire.

"For today, if I perish, what matter is that to me?"

BOARD THE ZEPPELIN

One of Comstock's zeppelins opens fire on the bell tower and destroys the upper Sky-Lines, leaving you no choice but to board his airship. Leap to the freight hook, then Sky-Line Strike the lone Founder on the wing. Raid the chests, then head inside, where several more enemies await your arrival. Open the door on the left to enter the cockpit. The room is empty save for a woman robed in white, praying to the painting of Father Comstock. Approach the control terminal and rig the steering.

Leap to the zeppelin, then fight your way inside to the controls!

Comstock appears before you on a small gondola, and instantly, your zeppelin is set ablaze. Run to the adjacent room, to the escape hatch in the floor, and leap to the Sky-Line below. This can take Booker where he needs to go.

WELCOME TO MONUMENT ISLAND

Your job was made a lot more difficult thanks to the raffle, but you've made it to Monument Island. The postcard says this is where you'll find the girl. You had better get searching.

★ Zachary Hale Comstock

Known as both Father Comstock and The Great Prophet, Zachary Hale Comstock is the leader of Columbia and the head of The Founders political faction. According to the city's religious doctrine, the Angel Columbia visited Comstock shortly after his victory at The Battle of Wounded Knee. There, she granted him a vision of the future mapping out the founding of the city and how to someday usher the world below into righteousness. Having repeatedly witnessed his gift of prophecy, Columbia's citizenry now trust him without question.

BRING US THE GIRL
★ MONUMENT TOWER ★
FIND THE GIRL

Leap to the freight hook high above the locked gates and jump down to the other side to bypass the deterrent and enter the monument, a structure whose interior truth belies its inspiring façade. Push open the doors to enter what amounts to the scientists' locker room and collect the **Voxophone** on the left.

Make your way through the series of laboratory rooms, past the growth charts and crackling cables of electricity, and onward into the area deemed to be quarantined. Pull the levers under the Siphon Passive sign to witness the remnants of the girl's past, three critical symbols of her childhood years, and then continue on deeper into the empty silence.

Push your way through the airlock door on the left to find another **Voxophone** before you continue down the hall. The darkroom on the left contains numerous photos of the girl. Similarly, the theater on the right contains a film reel showing various clips of the girl learning to pick locks, decipher codes, paint, and dance. Interact with the projector to view the film. Collect the **Voxophone** near the chalkboard and proceed past the room containing the siphon apparatus, then ride the elevator up into the observation portion of the tower.

Don't miss the Infusion located beneath the chalkboard tracking the siphon's power ratings.

 Voxophone

TIGER BY THE TAIL

AUTHOR: Ty Bradley
DATE: April the 8th, 1912
LOCATION: Monument Island

I guess even in a restricted area, these crackers need someone to clean the floors, hm? Hmph. Those politicians and scientists don't bother 'bout what they say 'round me, because I'm some half-lettered colored boy. But I can tell they scared out of their wits by that thing they got locked upstairs, yessir. They got a tiger by the tail, and they don't know whether to hang on… or run.

 Voxophone

TO: R. THOMPSON RE: FUSES

AUTHOR: Ty Bradley
DATE: July the 3rd, 1912
LOCATION: Monument Island

Uh, Mr. Thompson, sir, I replaced the entire fuse bank as asked, and the lights were all in working order last… last night … there they go again. We go through boxes of fuses every day as of late, just in the Siphon alone, I don't… Oh! Oh, Lord, something's happening! What— [Screams]

Collectibles

SPECIMEN OBSERVATION

Pull the lever near the shuttered window to reveal the girl's bedroom and study. She's not in either of these rooms right now, so you'll have to keep looking. Follow the green lights to the specimen tracker to learn that the girl is in the dressing room. Head through the door on the left and follow the wooden walkway to the next observation room. Pull the lever to get your first look at the girl through the one-way glass, then follow after her to the next observation room in time to see something truly special.

A flying city is one thing, but that's unbelievable!

Ascend the wooden ramp to the observation window overlooking the library and collect the **Voxophone** from the chair. Proceed through the airlock to the exterior walkway and reenter the tower via the door atop the stairs.

	Voxophone

A REWARD DEFERRED

AUTHOR:	Zachary Hale Comstock
DATE:	July the 5th, 1912
LOCATION:	Monument Island

It is one thing to imagine one's future. And another to see it. For I have seen the seeds of fire that will prepare the Sodom below for the coming of the Lord. But Elizabeth shall sow those seeds, not I. I will fall before the job is done… but she shall take up my mantle. The Lord is calling me home. I feel His love in every tumor, because they are the train which takes me to his station. And I go with joy, knowing that Elizabeth will take my earthly place. But the False Shepherd is coming to lead my Lamb astray. I will not board that train until she is safe from his deceptions.

	Voxophone

THE SOURCE OF HER POWER

AUTHOR:	Rosalind Lutece
DATE:	September the 5th, 1909
LOCATION:	Specimen Observation

What makes the girl different? I suspect it has less to do with what she is, and rather more with what she is not. A small part of her remains from where she came. It would seem the universe does not like its peas mixed with its porridge.

ESCAPE THE TOWER WITH ELIZABETH

Booker crashes through a weak platform and finds himself face to face with a wild-eyed and heavily frightened girl named Elizabeth. It's not until he shows her the key he was given on the rowboat that she realizes he might actually be helpful. Follow her through the heavy steel door and back through the observation corridor. Her guardian, a screeching beast whose goal is to ensure her captivity, is wreaking havoc on the monument. Continue running as best you can amidst the collapsing girders and ear-splitting noise, and follow Elizabeth to the elevator.

Elizabeth isn't used to guests dropping in unannounced.

The creature—Songbird—is nearly through the wall when the falling elevator blocks its advance. Drop down onto the wreckage, then head up the stairs to the top of the tower and exit through the door. Continue up the side of Monument Tower to the very top. Booker and Elizabeth are knocked from their perch, but Booker didn't come this far just to let her die. He catches her hand and manages to latch onto a Sky-Line below. He can't leap to the other Sky-Line because of the cargo and, with his right hand holding onto Elizabeth, he's unable to take control or fire any weapons. The two fall from the severed rails and crash-land in a faux ocean below.

Elizabeth

Imprisoned in Columbia since childhood, Elizabeth is a young woman whose only contact with the world has been the view from her tower and the books brought to her by her jailer, the massive creature known as Songbird. Finally freed by Booker DeWitt, she finds herself lost in the city and troubled by many questions. Who imprisoned her? Why? Where do her powers come from? And why is she at the center of the conflict that's tearing Columbia apart?

Elizabeth and the Songbird

Elizabeth is the heart and soul of Bioshock Infinite, and as such, her expressiveness is integral to the narrative. When designing her, we exaggerated her features so the player could clearly read her emotions at any given moment. We looked at some of the female leads from Disney animated movies and drew inspiration from their designs.

When it came to the Songbird, we wanted a creature that stood in stark contrast to Elizabeth, something obviously not entirely human, but at the same time capable of forming a believable and complicated relationship with Elizabeth. The end result is a creature that is physically imposing, but at the same time can appear gentle, especially in the presence of Elizabeth.

Shawn Robertson
Animation Director

The Songbird has but one purpose: to protect the girl at all costs!

Booker's hands are tied. He's at the mercy of the Sky-Line now.

Songbird

Songbird is the creature that serves as Elizabeth's jailer, protector, and only companion. Once Booker frees Elizabeth, Songbird will do anything and everything to return Elizabeth to her prison. His origins are known only to Father Comstock and his most trusted colleagues.

★ BATTLEFIELD BAY ★

GONDOLA STATION

B

A

THE ARCADE

A

EXIT

B

UPPER BOARDWALK

START

BATTLESHIP BAY

First Encounters

FOUNDER (SHOTGUN)

New Weaponry

China Broom Shotgun

Collectibles

Infusions
1

Voxophones
5

Kinectoscopes
2

Telescopes
1

FIND ELIZABETH

Booker escapes his flashback by once again opening the door he can't seem to keep from being knocked upon. This time, however, he awakes to find Elizabeth staring down at him. The two crash-landed in a beachside resort, one of Columbia's greater engineering feats. Music lures her away while Booker struggles to shake the cobwebs from his mind.

Make your way up the beach while stopping to ask the sunbathers if they have seen the girl. Search the baskets for money and food as you proceed past the maintenance structure on the right. Note the **Voxophone** on the ground beneath the cart.

With eyes that match the sky…

Battleship Bay

This Kinetoscope is on the small section of the Boardwalk separating the two beaches. It's around the corner to the right, against the other side of the wall where Booker spots the airship poster.

	Voxophone

BORN IN THE RIVER

AUTHOR:	Ed Gaines
DATE:	March the 6th, 1912
LOCATION:	Battleship Bay

The Prophet may know how his own biography's going to end—but I can scarcely fathom how I'm going to start it. Other than that the kid's stuff you get at the Hall of Heroes, anything prior to his baptism was, and here I quote, hang on, "left on the riverside." They'll call me a plagiarist, but I'm going to spend the first 30 pages regurgitating scripture.

Make your way across the sand and onto the pier to find Elizabeth dancing to the music. It's a shame you have to interrupt her pleasure, especially with it being her first time outside Monument Island, but you must keep moving. And the First Lady Aerodrome might just be the ticket out of here.

Follow the sounds of the music out onto the pier to find Elizabeth.

TAKE ELIZABETH TO THE AIRSHIP

Choose the cameo you want Elizabeth to wear for the rest of the game.

UPPER BOARDWALK

Make your way off the sand and through the turnstile to the Gift Shop. Head up the stairs to the upper level of the Boardwalk and make your way past the souvenir carts to the familiar couple you've encountered several times previously. They've snared Elizabeth's attention with a pair of cameos, and she wants your help choosing: bird or cage? This choice, unlike the one you made at the raffle, has only superficial significance: which pendant would you like dangling from Elizabeth's choker?

> **"Who knows what the Prophet foresees? He tells us what he deems wise."**

Elizabeth can open the most important doors with her hairpin, but you'll need lockpicks to access the optional areas that often contain collectibles.

Walk past the security checkpoint to the locked door at the end of the hall and watch as Elizabeth unveils her lock-picking skill. Elizabeth is a lock-picking expert, but she can't always work without the proper tools (though she can sometimes unlock doors with her hairpin). Keep your eyes peeled for lockpicks and try to keep at least five of them on hand at all times. Depending on the difficulty of the lock, she may require one, three, or five lockpicks in order to open it. Search the desks and filing cabinets in the office, and continue on through the small storage room beyond the door.

THE ARCADE

Elizabeth is just the type of proactive companion who can really come in handy. Not only can she pick locks, but she'll periodically toss you money, food, Salts, and ammunition. Listen for her audible cues, and press the Reload button to catch what she has ready to throw you. An icon appears on the lower portion of the screen to let you know what she has on hand.

The couple from the raffle gives you a piece of Gear if you opted to throw the ball at the announcer.

Continue to the far end of the hall and collect the **Gear** and the **Voxophone** from the washroom. Make a left past the segregated restrooms, and enter the main arcade area through the doors in the distance. Depending on how you handled winning first throw at the raffle—you did try to throw the ball, right?—you'll receive a piece of **Gear** either in the hallway or just inside the entrance to the main arcade area.

Flambeau, Mr. Fink's assistant, presents you with a piece of Gear inside the arcade if you wanted to throw the ball at the couple.

The arcade is abuzz with holidaymakers, and there are some interesting conversations to eavesdrop on if you seek them out. Have a look around, gather up the stray Silver Eagles, and search the restrooms on the far side of the room for a **Voxophone** and **Kinetoscope** (the three Kinetoscopes you first saw in The Blue Ribbon Restaurant are present here, as well). Once you're done looking around, head up the stairs flanking the Motorized Patriot photo exhibit and make your way to the turnstiles, where a peculiar lady mistakes Elizabeth for someone named Annabelle. Follow the ticketing signs up the stairs and down the hall. With any luck, you'll both be on the next gondola to the First Lady Aerodrome!

	Voxophone
HEAVEN	

AUTHOR:	Daisy Fitzroy
DATE:	February the 12th, 1912
LOCATION:	The Arcade

When I first see Columbia, that sky was the brightest, bluest sky that ever was. Seemed like... heaven. Then your eyes adjusted to the light and you saw that sea of white faces lookin' hard back at you...

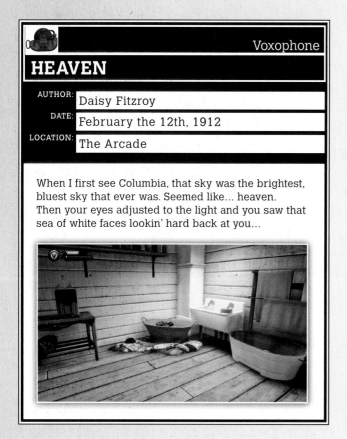

	Voxophone
A DOG'S LOYALTY	

AUTHOR:	Zachary Hale Comstock
DATE:	December the 18th, 1899
LOCATION:	The Arcade

As a boy, I had a dog named Bill. And like all dogs, Bill was a loyal friend. If we had not fed him, Bill would have been loyal. If we had struck him, Bill would have been loyal. Only when the colored man can make that claim will he take his place in society.

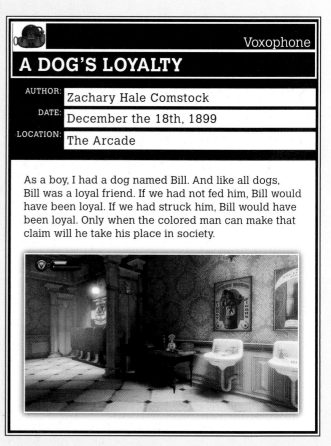

GONDOLA STATION

Cross the lobby to the ticket counter and ring the bell. The man behind the counter quickly reaches for the telephone as you draw near and seems to intentionally ignore you. Booker's instincts tell him something isn't right, and he's quickly given the choice of drawing his weapon—a risky move when trying to remain incognito—or demanding the tickets.

Solving the Irish Problem

Continue down the hall past the "whites" restrooms to the windows in the distance. The Kinetoscope is lined up in the center of the hall, facing Booker as he approaches.

Regardless of your choice, it's quickly made apparent that this was indeed a trap. The gates are immediately slammed shut, the windows shuttered, and the people in the room all draw their weapons.

Turn and cast Murder of Crows at the men near the violin cases, and open fire with the Machine Gun. Swap out the Pistol for the **China Broom Shotgun** near the violin case on the bench and set to blasting away at your would-be capturers. Use the counter off to the right for cover if necessary, and continue to stun and distract the assailants with Murder of Crows while using firearms to finish them off.

Failure to draw a weapon first allows the guy behind the counter to get the drop on Booker.

	Voxophone

TAKE HER ALIVE

AUTHOR:	Esther Mailer
DATE:	July the 6th, 1912
LOCATION:	Park Ticketing

This is the moment we trained for. The False Shepherd is here. The day was not exact, but… the Prophet's sight proves out again. The specimen must be taken alive. If she dies, I suspect they will give us to the bird. And whatever pieces it leaves behind will bear no names … That was cigarette number six. This waiting is insufferable.

Unleash Murder of Crows on the gang of attackers, then open fire at once!

Elizabeth, having never seen violence before, reacts as one might expect: she's horrified and quickly runs away. Set a Murder of Crows trap in the center of the room and remain in cover behind the columns. Hold your ground as a bright floodlight shines through the right-hand gate, and continue to defend yourself against the cops who charge in from the adjacent security office. Loot the bodies and desks for goodies and search the security office for a **Voxophone**.

PURSUE ELIZABETH

Elizabeth managed to slip through the gate and get a pretty good head start on Booker while he was busy trying to stay alive. Head down the hall after her, but first duck into the ticket office on the left to find the **Infusion** you most likely spotted behind the ticketing agent. The whitewashed stairwell beyond the door in the far corner leads down to a **Voxophone** and several bundles of Silver Eagles.

Elizabeth will bandage your stab wound if you choose the "Demand Tickets" option when dealing with the clerk.

Head out onto the platform to find Elizabeth near the gondola, atop the right-hand stairs. Board the gondola and pull the lever in the wheelhouse to reunite with her. This won't get you to the First Lady, but it does get you one step closer to it. Exit the gondola and scour the area for searchable gifts and the **Telescope**. Proceed through the turnstiles beneath the giant tank drawing to enter Soldier's Field.

TELESCOPE

Ascend the stairs from the gondola and take a moment to use the telescope near the railing. This set of high-powered optics grants you a great view across the sky, looking back at Battlefield Bay.

	Voxophone
THE GOLDEN PATH TO HEAVEN	

AUTHOR:	Zachary Hale Comstock
DATE:	September the 9th, 1893
LOCATION:	Park Ticketing

As the months and years turned to memories, so did the men of Congress turn to righteousness. And through the technology of men, the dollars of Washington, the Lord worked his will upon Columbia and raised her high above the Sodom below.

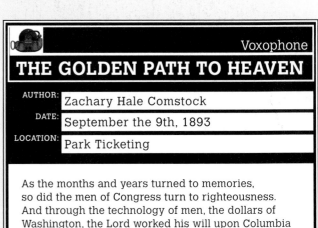

★ SOLDIER'S FIELD ★

TAKE ELIZABETH TO THE AIRSHIP

SOLDIER'S FIELD WELCOME CENTER

Soldier's Field is Columbia's twist on the amusement park. It's a place where kids can play games, ride a carousel, and spend all day awash in patriotic propaganda. Luckily for Booker, Soldier's Field has plenty of fun for big kids, too! Lead Elizabeth to the locked door (one lockpick) on the left, and instruct her to open it. You can find a lockpick on the floor near the locked door. Snag even more near the Minuteman's Armory vending machine. Gather up the **Infusion** and **Voxophone** inside the office, and spot the safe on the floor in the back room.

Return once you have five lockpicks to get the hundreds of Silver Eagles inside.

Locate the lockpick in the office to bring your total to three. You'll need to return here later, once you've collected the necessary five lockpicks it takes to unlock the safe.

Safes typically contain large sums of Silver Eagles, ammo, and Salts. Unlocking them all isn't paramount, but they're worth backtracking for once you have enough lockpicks. This is a great time to swap out the Shotgun or Machine Gun for the **Carbine,** as well. The Carbine is a powerful semi-automatic rifle with pinpoint accuracy—just watch for the targeting reticle to turn red, and fire.

MINUTEMAN'S ARMORY: NEW STOCK!

Item	Description	Price
Pistol: Clip Increase	Increases Pistol clip size by 50%.	$275
Machine Gun: Damage Boost 1	Increases Machine Gun damage by 25%.	$236

	Voxophone

A PLACE IN THE WORLD

AUTHOR:	Daisy Fitzroy
DATE:	February the 12th, 1912
LOCATION:	Soldier's Field Greeting Pavillion

Days at Comstock House was simple. Hard work, sure—but simple. Wringin' the linens, scrubbing the floors... Lady Comstock, she even had a kind word, now and then. Almost enough to make me think I had a place in their world. God made foolish girls so HE could have something to play with.

First Encounters

FOUNDER (CARBINE)

FOUNDER (SNIPER RIFLE)

BEAST (RPG)

New Vigors

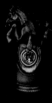

Bucking Bronco

New Weaponry

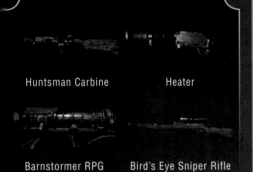

Huntsman Carbine   Heater

Barnstormer RPG   Bird's Eye Sniper Rifle

Collectibles

Infusions

3

Kinectoscopes

4

Voxophones

9

Telescopes

-

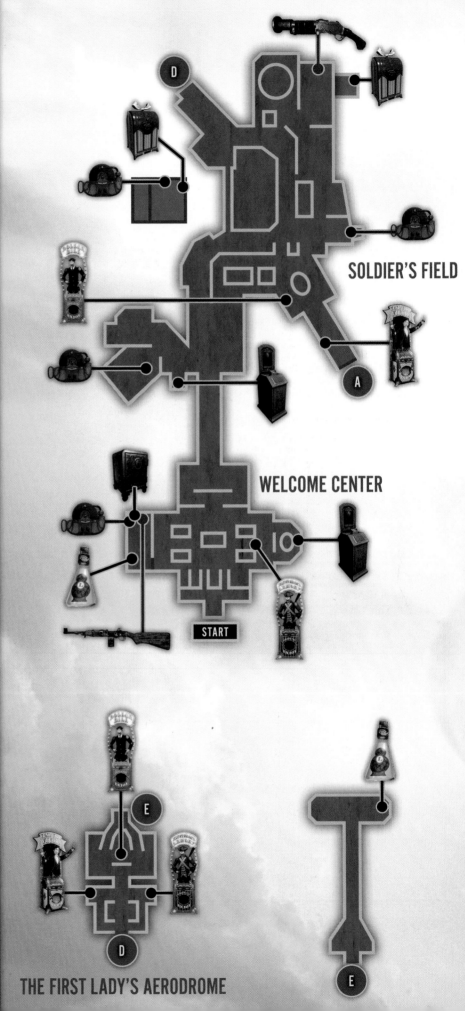

SOLDIER'S FIELD

D

A

WELCOME CENTER

START

THE FIRST LADY'S AERODROME

E

D

E

★ SOLDIER'S FIELD ★

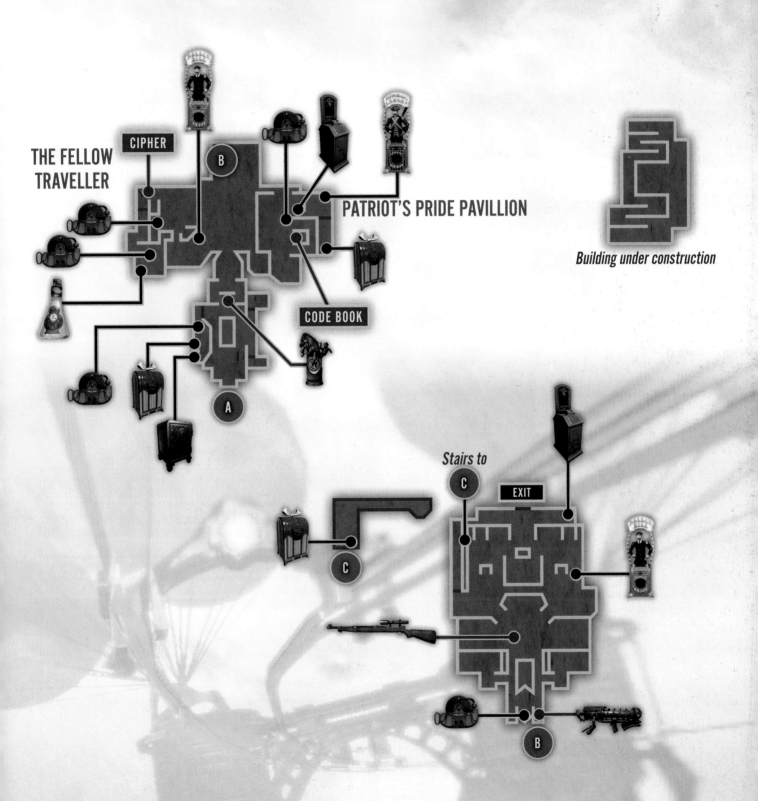

THE FELLOW TRAVELLER

CIPHER

B

PATRIOT'S PRIDE PAVILLION

CODE BOOK

A

Building under construction

Stairs to

C

EXIT

C

B

The gate closing the entrance to Soldier's Field Boardwalk is controlled by the power source on the left, but the darn thing goes on the fritz just as Booker approaches. Fortunately, he's strong enough to lift the gate by hand. Utilize the Salts machine around the corner—one whiff from the effervescent concoction is all it takes to replenish your Salt Meter—and head out onto the Boardwalk. Booker and Elizabeth arrive just in time to catch a glimpse of the First Lady airship as she heads to the dock. Booker and Elizabeth must ride a gondola from the pier to the airship if they're to board her.

The power's out, but Booker can open gates with openings in the bottom by hand.

SOLDIER'S FIELD

Despite the gate from the Welcome Center being sealed shut, the Soldier's Field amusement area is busy entertaining dozens of families when you arrive. Stealing is a big no-no in this family-friendly place, so keep your sticky fingers to yourself if you don't want to start a shootout! Pick up a snack from the shops on the left while you look for the **Voxophone** in the ice cream parlor before exploring the area to the right.

There are several vending machines near the dead-end leading to the currently closed Hall of Heroes exhibit. Be sure to locate the **Voxophone** inside Founders Books, and give the toy store near the carousel a look. The showcase weapon on the back wall, the **Heater,** is a devastatingly powerful shotgun you can steal, if desired.

A City in the Sky? Impossible!

Explore the Welcome Center fully and locate the Kinetoscope beyond the diorama off to the right-hand side. It's down the stairs, behind the Minuteman's Armory machine.

	Voxophone

I AM HIS MIRROR

AUTHOR:	Zachary Hale Comstock
DATE:	September the 9th, 1893
LOCATION:	Soldier's Field

And when I came to Washington, there were few in Congress who saw my vision for Columbia. But it is the burden of the Prophet to bring the wicked to righteousness. For what am I, if not a mirror to reflect the face of God?

Mighty Songbird Patrols the Skies!

This Kinetoscope is located between the Welcome Center gate and the ice cream parlor to the left of it. Behold the earliest footage of the Songbird, protector of the true patriots!

	Voxophone

VIEWING THE INFINITE

AUTHOR:	Rosalind Lutece
DATE:	August the 10th, 1890
LOCATION:	Soldier's Field

When I was a girl, I dreamt of standing in a room looking at a girl who was and was not myself, who stood looking at another girl, who also was and was not myself. My mother took this for a nightmare. I saw it as the beginning of a career in physics.

Just keep in mind that the security guard standing next to it will be quick to open fire if you take it. One shot from the Heater (a China Broom replica) is all it takes to drop him, but you're going to set the park on high alert if you take it. The owner and five additional police will attack, as well.

The Heater is extremely slow to reload, but it's incredibly powerful and capable of killing enemies with a single shell.

Continue on your way—peacefully—toward the "Gondola to Aerodrome" sign located to the left of the carousel. Pull the lever at the end of the dock to summon the gondola. Unfortunately, this leads to another blown power source. Elizabeth spots a nearby poster advertising a Shock Jockey display at the Hall of Heroes—it might not be all that stable, but it will have to do!

Where would we be without advertising?
Time to see the future of power at the Hall of the Heroes!

FIND SHOCK JOCKEY

Make your way back past the shops and the hotel toward the signs leading the way to the Hall of Heroes. Provided you found the lockpick near the carousel, the one on the ground to the left of the elevator should bring your total to five, just enough to open the safe back at the Welcome Center! A half-dozen Founders with Machine Guns and Shotguns attack as Booker gets closer to the elevator. Lob a Devil's Kiss fireball at them, then open fire on the survivors with the Carbine.

The crates that had earlier blocked off the elevator to the Hall of Heroes have since been removed. Ride the elevator until it comes to a halt, then access the fuse box on the left to get it working again.

Exit the elevator and have a look near the restrooms on the right. Grab the lockpick near the dolly in the center of the area and be ready for the Shotgun-wielding Founder in the toilet stall of the men's room—the one standing at the urinal isn't alone in there! Elizabeth alerts you to lockpicks that might escape your notice, such as the one in the stall in the ladies' restroom.

Have Elizabeth unlock the door to the Veteran's Affairs Office and quickly take Possession of the Gun Automaton in the back corner of the office. Don't waste any ammo trying to destroy it; just stay out of its line of fire while you collect the **Voxophone** and **Gear** on the right-hand side of the offices. You won't have enough lockpicks (five required) to unlock the floor safe in the back office, next to the Gun Automaton, but you'll be back through here soon enough.

SKY ROAD

Obtain the **Bucking Bronco** Vigor on your way out onto Sky Road. Bucking Bronco catapults enemies into the air, where they are briefly suspended for your shooting pleasure. Adversaries suspended in the air by Bucking Bronco take more damage when shot and cannot fire back.

Use the Carbine for distant enemies, then switch back to the Shotgun for lone Founders at close range.

Cast Possession on the Gun Automaton at the rear of the office, then step out of its line of sight.

	Voxophone

NEVER SEEN THE FACE

AUTHOR:	Captain Cornelius Slate
DATE:	May the 30th, 1912
LOCATION:	Soldier's Field

I served two-score years of soldiering. And every heathen land I've known is less peopled for my passing. I hated no special enemy. Until now. Comstock. He's made a vaudeville travesty of my battles, and cast himself as the white knight. I called him out over it, and he stripped me of my rank. That man has never seen the savage face of war. But he will.

Take cover behind the crates at the bottom of the stairs and listen to the rallying speech being given to the Founders up ahead. Cast your newfound Bucking Bronco ability at the group, and quickly lob a Devil's Kiss to engulf them in flame while they hover, helplessly, above the ground. Use the Sky-Hook to leap to the freight hook on the balcony to the right, kill the Founder stationed there, then switch to Possession and use it on the distant Gun Automaton. Maintain this upper position and use the Carbine to pick off those Founders that evade your deputized Gun Automaton. Cast Possession a second time if the Founders hadn't already destroyed the Gun Automaton.

Hit your foes with Bucking Bronco, then quickly lob a Devil's Kiss attack before they fall!

Possess the Gun Automaton, then set to sniping the remaining Founders with the Carbine.

Elizabeth alerts you to an incoming crow, otherwise known as a Zealot. Lead the Zealot into the large pavillion on the right-hand side of Sky Road, and blast it with the Heater (or China Broom Shotgun) and Bucking Bronco. Step back outside and finish off any remaining Founders from the relative safety of the balcony above the pavillion entrance.

DECODING THE VOX CIPHER

Enter the Vox Populi bar, The Fellow Traveller, and have a look around. There's a Voxophone in the kitchen and plenty of Silver Eagles and other supplies scattered about. Elizabeth draws your attention to a code scrawled on the wall in the first bathroom down the hall. She needs you to find the Code Book so she can decipher the code. The photo under the dead policeman's hand is your cue to its whereabouts. Now, where did you see that cannon?

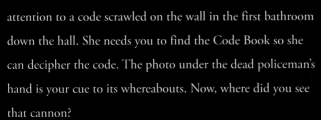

Exit the bar and cross Sky Road to the Patriot's Pride Pavillion nearby. You'll find the Code Book in the barrel of the cannon in the main lobby. Return to the cipher so she can translate it to read, "Tip the hat to the Vox." Enter the second bathroom and investigate the hat to uncover a secret Vox hideaway. Enter the hideaway to find a weapons cache, some locknicks, a Voxophone, and an **Infusion**. Among the weapons cache will be your first RPG Launcher

Enjoy the calm of a silenced Sky Road and have a look around The Fellow Traveller bar and Patriot's Pride Pavillion. The Minuteman's Armory vending machine, located in the candy store in the pavillion, has a number of new weapon upgrades for sale. There's also a number of **Voxophones** to find, as well as a **Kinetoscope** and piece of **Gear**, provided you have the three lockpicks necessary to pick the lock on the ticket office inside the pavillion.

MINUTEMAN'S ARMORY: NEW STOCK!

Item	Description	Price
Carbine: Damage Boost 1	Increases Carbine damage by 25%.	$357
RPG: Damage Boost 1	Increases RPG damage by 25%.	$385
Sniper Rifle: Damage Boost 1	Increases Sniper Rifle damage by 25%.	$349
Pistol: Damage Boost 1	Increases Pistol damage by 25%.	$199
Machine Gun: Accuracy Boost	Reduces Machine Gun weapon spread by 75%.	$512
RPG: Clip Increase	Increases RPG clip size by 50%.	$816

Voxophone

VOX CONTRABAND INVENTORY

AUTHOR:	Sergeant Leander Manley
DATE:	July the 6th, 1912
LOCATION:	Soldier's Field

Manley: "Got a tip there were contraband guns hidden in the Fellow Traveller. Didn't find 'em, but—funny thing—we found some old uniforms under the floorboards from the war. Took guesses as to why they were there but—[Door Opens] Who's there? You're Slate, right? Sir? Put the guns down! [Gunfire] [Screams]"

Slate: "Did you hear that, Comstock? That is the sound you have never heard—the sound of a soldier's end. Come to your 'Hall of Heroes.' Prove me a liar."

Voxophone

THEIR SUN IS SETTING

AUTHOR:	Daisy Fitzroy
DATE:	May the 1st, 1912
LOCATION:	Soldier's Field

The one thing people need to learn is that fear is the antidote to fear. I don't want to be a part of their world. I don't want to be a part of their culture, their politics, their people. The sun is setting on their world, and soon enough, all they gon' see… is the dark.

Voxophone

A TRUE SOLDIER

AUTHOR:	Lance Corporal Vivian Monroe
DATE:	April the 10th, 1911
LOCATION:	Patriot's Pavillion

God makes all kinds of soldiers, but he only made one Cornelius Slate. My father followed him up San Juan Hill, through the legations in Peking, and, as he put it," through hell, the order was given." At today's muster, Slate asked me if I was Sergeant Monroe's daughter. I said, "Yes, sir. I am." Slate said, "Your father always wanted a son. I hope the fool has wisdom enough to recognize his good fortune."

Who are the Vox Populi?

Learn who the Vox Populi are, in the eyes of Comstock, at the Kinetoscope on the ground floor of the Patriot's Pride Pavillion. It's located facing the couches near the candy store.

Booker likely encounters a pair of Shotgun-wielding Founders as he exits the Vox hideaway. Hit them with Bucking Bronco and a few rounds of the Carbine. Do the same to the two who approach from outside, and approach the Sky-Lines at the end of the Boardwalk.

A massive amount of cargo blocks the Sky-Lines. Pull the lever on the control terminal to get the freight moving. Once clear, Booker and Elizabeth can leap up onto the rail on the right-hand side of the control platform to get moving. Keep your eyes straight ahead and leap to the next Sky-Line as soon as you see the prompt signaling that it's okay to make the leap. Elizabeth found a Sky-Hook of her own and slides along behind Booker, enabling you to make use of his weapons while he's riding the Sky-Lines, if necessary.

Pull the lever to clear the Sky-Line of cargo while Elizabeth commandeers the Sky-Hook on the left.

Ride the Sky-Line up the slope, then leap across to the second track and ride it to the platform.

HALL OF HEROES PLAZA

Descend the stairs toward the gondola and consider swapping out your Shotgun or Machine Gun for the **RPG**. Don't miss the RPG ammo on the floor near the weapon. Collect the **Voxophone** in the pilot house of the gondola, then head up the stairs on the left toward the Hall of Heroes.

The sounds of sniper fire ring out as you make your way to the stairs. Listen for Elizabeth's shouts and take the **Bird's Eye Sniper Rifle** she throws you, making sure to hold onto the RPG you just acquired. Sprint up the stairs to the defaced statue—sacrilege!—and take cover behind it.

There's a Founder with a Sniper Rifle high on the roof to the left. Strafe in and out of cover behind the large statue and duel it out with your new Sniper Rifle. Zoom in for a precision shot—one bullet is all it takes to kill him. Unfortunately, his weapon is equally powerful. One shot from his rifle likely depletes your shield entirely, and depending on the difficulty level you're playing on, may even inflict some heavy damage, too. Take cover, pop out after he fires, then headshot him with your Sniper Rifle. Enemy snipers are easy to spot thanks to the sunlight reflecting off their scopes.

Switch to the Carbine before accepting the Sniper Rifle from Elizabeth so you don't drop the RPG.

Stay behind the large sign and statue for cover, and watch the gleam of the enemy's sniper scope.

Once you've killed the sniper, a large number of Founders attacks with Shotguns and Machine Guns. Quickly deploy Devil's Kiss traps at the base of the stairs and under the wooden bridge just beyond the statue. This prevents any enemies from getting the drop on Booker while he continues sniping those in the distance. Elizabeth likely lobs more Sniper Rifle ammo your way, but there's a Carbine to the far right should you need it. Stay behind the large statue while reloading the Sniper Rifle, then step out of cover, zoom in, and shoot any adversaries you see on the upper walkways.

	Voxophone
A FINAL STAND	

AUTHOR:	Captain Cornelius Slate
DATE:	July the 6th, 1912
LOCATION:	Hall of Heroes Plaza

Veterans! You shed your hearts' blood for Columbia, lost limb and viscera in the godless Orient! Comstock did nothing! And yet—look up! Whose image squats above you, even now? At every angle an insult! If the Prophet would make a painted whore of our past, what fresh rape does our future hold? Let us now make our stand, and fill yonder hall with true Heroes!

Who Needs the Power Company?

Once the fight is over, loot the enemy corpses and head up the stairs to the entrance to the Hall of Heroes. You find this Kinetoscope off to the right of the entrance.

★ HALL OF HEROES ★

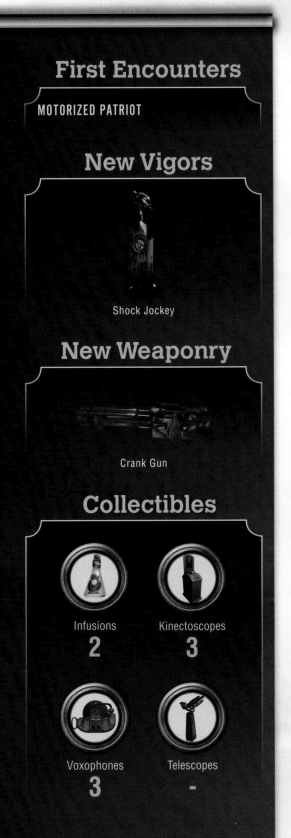

First Encounters

MOTORIZED PATRIOT

New Vigors

Shock Jockey

New Weaponry

Crank Gun

Collectibles

Infusions	Kinectoscopes
2	3

Voxophones	Telescopes
3	-

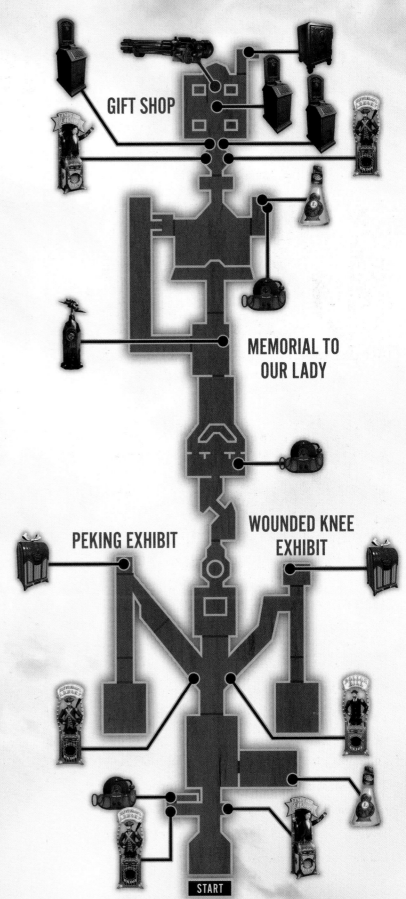

GIFT SHOP

MEMORIAL TO OUR LADY

PEKING EXHIBIT

WOUNDED KNEE EXHIBIT

START

FIND SHOCK JOCKEY

The Hall of Heroes appears empty, but you can bet the silence won't last for long. Head down the hall on the left and enter the office next to the Minuteman's Armory vending machine (no new items available). Find the **Voxophone** behind the door and lay low inside the office as two of Slate's men with Machine Guns patrol the area outside. Bounce them into the air with Bucking Bronco, and shoot them dead.

Approach the Father Comstock statue in the next room and listen in as one of Booker's former colleagues in the military addresses him from a remote location. His name is Slate, and he's waging a war against Comstock's revisionist history. Booker's sudden arrival on the scene is a wildcard Slate is all too happy to see revealed. Slate will give Booker the Shock Jockey Vigor, but he's going to have to fight his men for it first. Slate would much rather see his men die an honorable death at the hands of a real soldier than by those of a man like Comstock.

Place a Devil's Kiss trap on the floor in front of the door to your right along with a Bucking Bronco trap, in anticipation of the soldiers who emerge from behind the locked door. Help yourself to the **Infusion** at the rear of the storage room, and definitely pick up the two lockpicks also present. Return to the vending machines if necessary, then advance to the rotunda, where a large plinth reveals the timeline of the City of Columbia. Slate's men are stationed in the Boxer Rebellion and Battle of Wounded Knee wings of the Hall of Heroes.

You'll no doubt notice that there are plenty of Vigor bottles scattered around the Hall of Heroes, and nearly all of them are for Vigors you already have. Though you won't be able to gain a new ability, picking up a Vigor you already have is every bit as good as getting a full bottle of Salts. Vigors completely restore your Salt Meter and should not be overlooked!

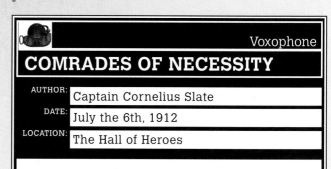

Voxophone

COMRADES OF NECESSITY

AUTHOR: Captain Cornelius Slate

DATE: July the 6th, 1912

LOCATION: The Hall of Heroes

The Fitzroy woman and her Vox are my comrades... but only of necessity. I doubt all the men who reddened Caesar's toga would still be seen breaking bread together in peacetime. With Comstock gone, my men's past deeds will be sacred — and they will claim the spoils due them. I need not live to see it.

"Tin soldiers don't fight wars... Men do!"

Placing traps from two different Vigors not only eliminates Slate's men but also counts toward the "Combination Shock" bonus.

DEFEAT SLATE'S MEN

As Booker enters, swap out the Carbine for the Sniper Rifle behind the rock on the left.

PEKING EXHIBIT

Enter the Boxer Rebellion wing and continue down the hall, through the display to where the path makes a hard turn to the left. Enter the storage room on the right to find a piece of **Gear**. Dispatch the soldier who attacks outside the room, and continue past the room with the George Washington display to the main Boxer Rebellion battle exhibit.

The doors lock behind Booker, and wooden cutouts block access to the pagoda on the right. Head up the rocky path on the left and swap out your Machine Gun or Carbine for the Sniper Rifle leaning against the rocks. Plant a Devil's Kiss trap on the floor at each side of the room, near the cutouts—they'll soon retract into the floor and allow Slate's men to charge forward.

A Fireman takes position in the pagoda just as several of Slate's men attack from the two sides. Your traps hold off the attackers, giving you time to focus on the Fireman with the Sniper Rifle. Stay behind the faux rocks for cover and pick off the remaining men with the Sniper Rifle. The Fireman is unlikely to cross the entire room during its self-destruct charge, but you can use Bucking Bronco on him if it happens. Be sure to loot the Fireman's corpse (or lockbox), as it contains a lockpick.

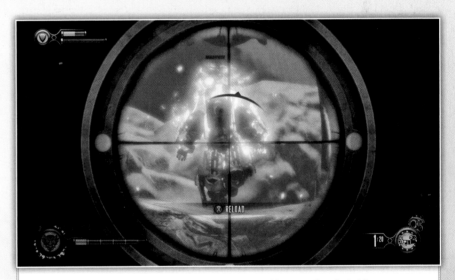

Fire the Sniper Rifle at the Fireman, then loot his corpse for a lockpick.

Recover your Carbine or Machine Gun and fight your way back to the rotunda. Restock your ammo and Salt supplies at the vending machines there before entering the second exhibit.

WOUNDED KNEE EXHIBIT

Make your way through Comstock's distorted rendition of the Battle of Wounded Knee, and enter the storage room on the left to find another piece of **Gear**. Continue on toward the flickering red lights and the main room beyond the doors.

Head to the right when you enter and lay multiple traps at the base of the stairs on either side of the rocks.

Once again, the doors lock behind Booker, and he's forced to fend off a number of Slate's men. Head up the steps on the right and lay Devil's Kiss or Bucking Bronco traps on the ground at the base of the stairs. Slate's men charge Booker's position from both directions, and these traps go a long way toward holding them off. Consider swapping the Carbine for one of the dropped Shotguns, and blast away any of the Founders who make it past your traps. Stay in cover to avoid incoming fire from the soldiers with Machine Guns on the catwalk high above the floor on the other side of the room. Pop out of cover, line up your shot, and take them down with one or two shots from the Carbine.

Once Booker has eliminated all these opponents, a Zealot of the Lady attacks. Use Bucking Bronco or Devil's Kiss to soften him up, then switch to the Shotgun and pump him full of lead. Another option, if you have it, is to use the RPG. Just watch for the crows to gather up, and fire a rocket at the floor to catch the Zealot in its blast as he takes shape.

This Zealot has considerably more health than the first one you fought, so don't let down your guard. Search the corpses and lockboxes for Salts and ammo should you need it. Return the way you came, but keep your Shotgun or Carbine on hand for any Founders patrolling the rotunda.

Quickly double-tap the Reload button to loot corpses during the battle to prevent you from running out of Salts.

FIND SLATE

FIRST LADY MEMORIAL

The doors between the two exhibits are now unlocked. Pass through them to enter the First Lady Memorial, a lovely garden display set to commemorate Lady Comstock. Walk with Elizabeth through the exhibit as Elizabeth reads the plaques adorning the displays. Have Elizabeth pick the lock on the door beyond the stone bridge— no lockpicks required—to learn about the murder. Search the adjacent rooms for money and a **Voxophone** before continuing to the room displaying Comstock's vengeance.

The memorial reveals more about Columbia's past than Elizabeth wanted to know.

	Voxophone
UNCONDITIONAL	
AUTHOR:	Lady Comstock
DATE:	April the 1st, 1893
LOCATION:	The Murder of Our Lady

To those who loved me, I was the most generous of souls. There was no pain I would deny them. No betrayal I would not gladly give. And when I had scorched the hearts of all who loved me, the Prophet said, "There is nothing you can do for which I will not forgive you, for God has granted me sight, and through His eyes, even you are loved."

The final area of the First Lady Memorial, the Courtyard, is still under construction, and a large gate blocks access. Elizabeth can slip between the bars, but Booker cannot. Fortunately, she manages to spot a Tear above the floor—it's a freight hook! Hold the Reload button to instruct Elizabeth to open the Tear, thus giving you a freight hook to have Booker leap to in order to scale the gate.

From your freight hook, Elizabeth spots additional Tears that can be opened: you must choose between three freight hooks high on the walls, or a large MG Turret in the center of the floor. A number of Slate's men has wandered into the room far below Booker's current position. Consider instructing Elizabeth to open the Tear for the MG Turret so you can gun down those enemies who are already present. Booker immediately falls to the balcony below, and though the MG Turret is destroyed in relative quickness, it sufficiently distracts enough attention to allow Booker to get into cover.

Instruct Elizabeth to open the MG Turret at the start of the battle.

The soldiers below cannot reach your position, provided you stay on the balcony with Elizabeth. Shoulder the Sniper Rifle, strafe past the scaffolding to the right, and take Possession of the Gun Automaton on the far side of the room. Remain crouched on the far right-hand side of the balcony to present a smaller target, and shoot each of Slate's men as they come into view. There's a Sniper Rifle on this balcony if you need it. Slate's men are all toting Machine Guns; dispatch them with a single bullet to the head.

Use Possession on the Gun Automaton, then use the Carbine or Sniper Rifle to pick off Slate's men.

Elizabeth's ability to open up Tears on Booker's command relies entirely on their presence in the area. Booker cannot request a Tear be opened for something that isn't there. That being said, there are often multiple Tears to choose from, and it's entirely up to you, as Booker, to decide which Tear to open. Once a Tear has been opened, you must wait 10 seconds before Elizabeth can open another one, at which time the first Tear disappears. Only one Tear can be open at a time. Not only can you reopen a previously opened Tear, but it even returns to its initial state. Watch to see if your MG Turret is destroyed, then quickly open another nearby Tear. Wait for the original MG Turret Tear to reappear, and reopen it to have it working again.

The Tear for the freight hooks makes it possible to Sky-Line Strike enemies throughout the Courtyard.

THE GIFT SHOP

The Veni! Vidi! Vigor! vending machine now contains the limited release Possession For Less Vigor upgrade, but the Minuteman's Armory machine contains no new products. The vending machines aren't the only devices of note in this area; there are also three **Kinetoscopes**.

Elizabeth can open any of three Tears in the Gift Shop: Salts, Medical Kits, or a Gun Automaton. If you need Salt or health, have her open either of the supplies Tears; otherwise, instruct her to open the Tear for the Gun Automaton on the right side of the room to prepare for the fight to come.

The Lamb is the Future of the City
Behold the Miracle Child!
A Prophecy is Fulfilled!

The small octagonal lobby in front of the Gift Shop contains two vending machines and a pair of Kinetoscopes. Watch the films and learn about the Miracle Child, the Lamb, the future!

A City Mourns...

This Kinetoscope is located in the center of the Gift Shop, near the Medical Kits. Whereas the two previous two told a story of hope, this is one of sadness.

GIFT SHOP MOTORIZED PATRIOT'S VITALS

Health	Ranged Damage	Melee Damage	Special Damage	Special Attack
5053	72	432	N/A	N/A

The Motorized Patriot subscribes to the motto that it's best to walk slowly and carry a big gun! An automaton in the form of seven-foot-tall George Washington wields a Crank Gun and is every bit as resilient to damage as his gun is lethal. Though he walks slowly, the Motorized Patriot has no fear and continues to march straight after its target, provided he can see it. Shooting his head off renders him unable to see, but he can still fire his weapon and wander around.

Being both heavy and made of wires and gears, the Motorized Patriot is invulnerable to attacks like Murder of Crows and Bucking Bronco. That said, he is highly susceptible to electric and water-based attacks, which you'll acquire eventually. For this fight, it's best to simply lead the Motorized Patriot out into the middle of the room, where the Gun Automaton that Elizabeth opened can shoot it.

The Motorized Patriot can be damaged from all sides, but his weakest point is in his back, right where his winding mechanism is located. Try to circle around a column or other obstacle to sneak up behind the Motorized Patriot for a clean shot. Similarly, see if he turns to fire on the Gun Automaton. If he does, run up behind him and unload on his backside with the Shotgun at close range! Lastly, though it isn't ideal, don't be afraid to hip-fire the Sniper Rifle at the enemy, as it packs a punch!

Motorized Patriot

The Motorized Patriot idea came about when we were looking at actual automatons and machinery of the time period represented in Bioshock Infinite. Most automatons were built specifically for one purpose. You had ones that could play chess, one that could write its name on a chalkboard, along with ones that could play an instrument. The great thing about these machines is that they were all created to look like a human, without ever getting it exactly right. What we are left with is the original uncanny valley: things that look almost, but not quite human. The end result is this amazingly creepy vibe that we wanted to capture in Columbia. Pairing the deification of the Founding Fathers with the automaton technology of the time seems like a perfect fit in creating the Motorized Patriot. The Gatling gun was the cherry on top!

Shawn Robertson
Animation Director

Swap out your Shotgun or Sniper Rifle for the **Crank Gun**, leave the Gun Automaton active (if it's still operational), and have Elizabeth pick the lock to the maintenance room in the rear right-hand corner. You'll find a safe in this room (five lockpicks), but the crates of Shock Jockey have been ransacked.

Plenty of Salt Phials, but no Shock Jockey…

Exit the maintenance room to the sound of the Gun Automaton acquiring a fresh target. Slate has laid several Shock Jockey traps in the gift shop —target them with the Crank Gun from afar to ensure that Booker doesn't get electrocuted. Follow the inky purple footsteps back toward the First Lady Memorial.

SUBDUE SLATE

THE COURTYARD

Cornelius Slate has taken the Shock Jockey Vigor back to the Courtyard and is on the far balcony where Booker first instructed Elizabeth in the use of Tears. Comstock's ships are circling above, but Slate isn't paying them any mind—he's going to lead his men into one final battle against Booker!

Slate glows pink from the effects of the Shock Jockey and periodically lobs electric traps throughout the area. These Shock Jockey traps take the form of electrified crystals; either avoid them, or better still, shoot them when Slate's soldiers are in range.

Open the Tear for the Medical Kits so that you can access them once necessary. Slate is going to conduct his assault in three waves, the first coming from the far balcony where Booker first entered the area. Use the cover near the two Tears and resist the

Mow down the early wave of attackers with the Crank Gun while also shooting the Shock Jockey crystals.

temptation to lay down a lot of Devil's Kiss traps, as many of Slate's men stick to the far side of the Courtyard for now. Strafe in and out of cover while popping off shots with the Carbine. Keep Bucking Bronco on hand in case any get too close; otherwise, try to shoot the Shock Jockey traps in the center of the room.

After a brief lull in the fight, Slate uses Shock Jockey to unlock the door on the lower left side of the room. Place both Devil's Kiss and Murder of Crows traps in front of the door to catch them as they emerge. A Fireman also attacks during this wave. Swap to the RPG or Crank Gun, and open fire. Listen for the whirr of its self-destruct charge, and try to snare it in a Shock Jockey trap or with Bucking Bronco to give Booker a means to escape.

The Devil's Kiss traps kill off the Founders, but the immunity warning lets you know a Fireman is also present.

The third and final wave comes from behind the door on the upper right-hand balcony. Place traps at the entrance to the room on the left, and head inside to force Slate's men to funnel through the chokepoint and right into your traps. Elizabeth alerts you to a Motorized Patriot—the one enemy most vulnerable to electrified attacks! Target any remaining Shock Jockey traps if you can; otherwise, consult your current Gear assortment and equip Electric Touch if possible. Electric Touch yields a 50% chance that a melee target is stunned and is perfect for use against Motorized Patriots.

The RPG is great for use against the Motorized Patriot when you don't have any way of electrocuting it.

Leap onto the table after picking up the Voxophone so you don't miss this Infusion.

Collect the **Voxophone** and **Infusion** from the storage room on the ground floor before chasing after Slate. The Infusion is inside the partially closed toolbox atop the workbench and can be hard to spot if Booker doesn't leap onto the table.

Voxophone

A SOLDIER'S DEATH

AUTHOR:	Captain Cornelius Slate
DATE:	July the 6th, 1912
LOCATION:	The Courtyard

My men and I are doomed, doomed as noble Custer was at Little Big Horn. But we shall not yield to Comstock and his tin soldiers. But my scout has seen him... Booker DeWitt is coming here, to the Hall! DeWitt... we called him the White Injun of Wounded Knee, for all the grisly trophies he claimed. A man such as he... might just grant us the peace we seek.

Slate retreats through the door opposite the Gift Shop, using it to head back towards the museum. Unable to access that ledge, you'll have to pursue him through the lengthy hallway to the right, taking down the enemies from an ambush attempt, and continue through the door to where he sits crumpled on the floor in a spotlight. Reach down to grab the Vigor, and watch as Slate musters the strength to give Booker one final order: he wants Booker to shoot him. The choice to spare or to kill Slate is yours, and, as with other choices that have been presented, the impact of this choice is relatively minor (largely just dialogue differences) and is revealed later in the walkthrough. Pick up the **Shock Jockey** Vigor after you make your decision.

You have to take the gun, but you don't have to use it in order to get the Vigor.

Cornelius Slate

A disenchanted, former military leader, Cornelius Slate has not only cut all association with The Founders and Father Comstock... he and his men have taken over The Hall of Heroes in an act of violent protest.

SHOCK TACTICS

Booker had no reason to suspect that Comstock wouldn't be the only man from his past running about in Columbia. Booker and Cornelius Slate shared a lot of tough moments on the battlefield, struggles that didn't exactly go as Comstock has since portrayed them to be. Slate knew the type of cold-blooded killer Booker had been (and is) and was eager to trade the Shock Jockey Vigor for an honorable death.

RETURN TO THE AERODROME GONDOLA

Fight your way back through the First Lady Memorial toward the entrance where the vending machines were located. Use your newly obtained Shock Jockey Vigor to immobilize any Slate's men you encounter along the way with a blast of electricity that renders them unable to fire their weapons as well as more susceptible to damage. Whenever possible, look to aim Shock Jockey at enemies standing in water, as the voltage gets amplified to lethal quantities!

Fire a dose of Shock Jockey at the glass power conductor across from the Salts machine to open the gate. It's time to head back across the sprawling Soldier's Field and power-up the gondola to the Aerodrome once and for all!

Fans of the *BioShock* series know exactly what to do when they see foes standing in water!

OUTSIDE THE MUSEUM

Booker exits the Hall of Heroes to find a full-scale battle taking place between Slate's devotees and Comstock's followers. Comstock's Founder Police are going to view Booker as being on the same side as Slate's men, so do your best to not shoot anyone with their back to you. Immediately open the Tear for the Mosquito in the far off distance so that it can start whittling down the number of Comstock's men. Watch for the gun balloon to be destroyed, then instruct Elizabeth to open the Tear for the Sniper Rifle on the left. This gives you plenty of ammo to pick off the numerous Founders approaching the steps outside the museum. Don't worry about any remaining units from Slate's makeshift army, as they're outnumbered and won't have the opportunity to turn against you. Reopen the Tear for the Mosquito as soon as it's ready.

Open the Tear for the Mosquito, then open fire on the enemies facing Booker's direction.

Descend the stairs on the right and use Shock Jockey to open the gated staircase on the far right side of the building (as viewed with Booker's back to the Hall of Heroes entrance). Ascend the stairs to find a wealth of crates to loot, as well as a piece of **Gear** and a Lockpicking Kit containing two lockpicks.

Don't hesitate to open the Tear for a Motorized Patriot when one is present!

Descend the stairs from the upper level and leap to the Sky-Line heading toward the Hall of Heroes maintenance platform off to the right. Open the Tear for the Motorized Patriot and leap to its side to fend off the other Founder Police (press the Crouch button to reverse direction if Booker happens to slide past the platform). A police barge rises up on the other side of the platform, so be ready for it. Stand guard with the Motorized Patriot and fire your preferred long-distance weapon at the enemies on the barge from the safety of the pile of wood.

Follow the Motorized Patriot up the stairs to deal with the Beast.

Sweep around the structure in a counter-clockwise direction to find a lockpick and to get the drop on an adversary with an RPG, known as the Beast. This helmeted foe is positioned atop the right-hand set of stairs, opposite the police barge, and he can fire RPGs in quick succession. Jolt him with Shock Jockey, then open fire or knock him into the air with Bucking Bronco. It's also possible to shoot his black metal helmet off. With his head exposed, you can go for the headshot! Clear the platform, then leap to the Sky-Line leading down and away toward Soldier's Field.

SKY ROAD

Hop off the Sky-Line and immediately take cover near the stack of crates. A large contingent of Founder Police has been assembled on Sky Road, and a Fireman accompanies the group. Pick off a couple of the ones nearest your position, then focus on the Fireman. Continue sniping him until he starts to rush Booker's position, then switch to Shock Jockey and the Shotgun or RPG to finish him off. Headshot the other enemies in the area, then round up the loot and continue up the stairs to the lobby. Be sure to loot the Fireman for the fifth lockpick you'll need to open the safe in the office up ahead.

Shock Jockey can briefly immobilize the Fireman, giving you time to open fire with your RPG.

A Motorized Patriot has escaped its display and is set to attack near the elevator. Though it's entirely possible to hit it with Possession and safely board the elevator without having defeated it, it's quite simple to kill it with Shock Jockey and a few rounds from the Carbine. The Motorized Patriot is highly susceptible to Shock Jockey. Stun it with the electric attack, then circle-strafe to its blindside and open fire on the sprockets and cogs. Snag the Crank Gun it drops, and board the elevator for the main Boardwalk at Soldier's Field.

Shock Jockey consumes very few Salts, so cast it repeatedly to keep the Motorized Patriot from firing its gun.

SOLDIER'S FIELD

Descend the stairs toward the Soldier's Field Hotel and leap to the freight hook on the balcony. Use Shock Jockey to unlock the gated door, and locate the **Voxophone** and **Gear** near the bed. There is a wealth of money and two lockpicks to be found in this room. Exit the hotel and make your way to the toy store, where you can use Shock Jockey to open yet another locked door. Lift the gate to enter the toy store after hours, then use Shock Jockey to gain access to the employees only closet to find another piece of **Gear**.

Voxophone

CALLING YOU OUT

AUTHOR:	Preston E. Downs
DATE:	July the 5th, 1912
LOCATION:	Soldier's Field

Ol' Preston is a sportin' man, Miss Fitzroy. I won't steal up on ya while you slumber like these Vox boys here, with their pigstickers...[Pleading] [Gunshot] That's... one scalp to me. [Screaming] [Gunshot] That's two. Now, when you hear this, I want you to square your affairs, and come die in the sight of the poets. You'll need a white man's weapon—give this a try.

The shops in Soldier's Field are closed at night, but you can still enter most of them by lifting the gates manually. With the shops empty, you don't have to fear alerting the local constabulary when you raid the cash registers or go behind the counter of the ice cream parlor.

There are several Tears available to you and Elizabeth when you return to Soldier's Field at night. There is a Motorized Patriot near the carousel, and Cover and a Gun Automaton on the roof of the ice cream parlor, as well as above the toy store. Open the Tear for the Motorized Patriot, and lead it toward the gondola lever.

Blast power conduits like these with Shock Jockey to open nearby locked doors.

CALL THE GONDOLA

Zap the power conductor near the lever with Shock Jockey to restore the power; now all you need to do is pull the lever. Before pulling the lever for the gondola, look out into the distance and note the two police barges flanking the tracks near the Aerodrome. Those barges will be headed straight for Booker once he pulls that lever, so make sure you're ready for battle! Now, pull the lever to call for the gondola.

Each of the two police barges contains a number of gun-wielding Founders and Beasts. The two barges slowly circle the Soldier's Field Hotel after affording the Founders a chance to either leap to the Boardwalk or onto the Sky-Lines that run around the area. Three Beasts are spread across the two barges and remain aboard and fire their RPGs continuously.

Hold your ground until the barges get close to keep the Motorized Patriot in position to help, then leap to the Sky-Line. Ride it past the hotel and leap to the upper Sky-Line to reach the roof of the ice cream parlor. Have Elizabeth open the Tear for the large Cover and grab the Sniper Rifle behind it. Lay traps down on the roof, near the Tear for the Gun Automaton, to catch any Founders that ride the Sky-Lines to this position. Use the Sniper Rifle to carefully snipe the Beasts that remain on the barges. Shoot their helmets off, then target their exposed heads.

Use the Cover Tear for protection while you snipe the Beasts on the police barges.

Open the Tear for the Gun Automaton if any of the barges get too close, and quickly leap to the Sky-Line to make a run for it. You can find Tears for Medical Kits on the roof of the shops, as well a Sniper Rifle Tear aboard one of the police barges. Equip any Gear you have that aids in Sky-Line Strikes, and consider leaping to one of the freight hooks on the police barges. Act quickly, and you can safely knock the Beast from its police barge with a Sky-Line Strike.

Shoot the Beast's helmet off to expose his head, then line up a headshot.

Leap to the Sky-Line when the Founders dismount, then fire an RPG rocket back at them!

Watch for the gondola's arrival, and soften up the Motorized Patriot with an RPG before it docks.

When the gondola arrives, have Elizabeth open the Tear to the Motorized Patriot near the carousel. The Motorized Patriot then takes care of the adversaries that exit the gondola you summoned, including an enemy Motorized Patriot. Leap to the lower of the two Sky-Lines, preferably with an RPG, and rain fire on the remaining Founders. You can use throttle controls and the ability to reverse direction to avoid return fire and position Booker in excellent position for a Sky-Line Strike.

BOARD THE FIRST LADY

Don't overlook this Infusion in your hurry to set a course.

Board the gondola and instruct Elizabeth to pick the lock to the cockpit. Grab the lockpick inside on the left and pull the lever to set the gondola in motion.

Ascend the stairs to enter the lobby and use the vending machines on either end to replenish your reserves. A half-dozen Founder Police are set to attack. Lay down some traps, and fall back toward the entrance to draw them into your traps. Switch to Murder of Crows to stun multiple foes at once if several are still standing. The Kinetoscope beneath the stairs is a duplicate of the one in the Gift Shop. Board the elevator across the room and ride it up to the First Lady Airship.

Collect the **Infusion** on the right and the Silver Bars across from the entrance (they're worth 100 Silver Eagles each). Be sure to gather these items before steering a course for your flight destination. Elizabeth knows her coordinates surprisingly well and detects your betrayal immediately. You'd have to be a tougher guy than Booker to stand hearing her cry; try talking to her.

FIRST LADY

Commandeering the First Lady was a stroke of genius! It wasn't easy, but you managed to get the girl and the Shock Jockey Vigor, and you made your way onto the airship. New York City… or bust.

GUNS FOR THE LADY

★ FINKTON DOCKS ★

FIND ELIZABETH

BEGGAR'S WHARF

There's no telling what happened after Elizabeth knocked Booker upside the head with that wrench, but she wasn't on the First Lady Airship, and now (thanks to Daisy's men) Booker isn't, either. Daisy says you can have the airship back if you get the gunsmith in Finkton to supply her Vox Populi with the arms they need, but first things first: you've got to find Elizabeth!

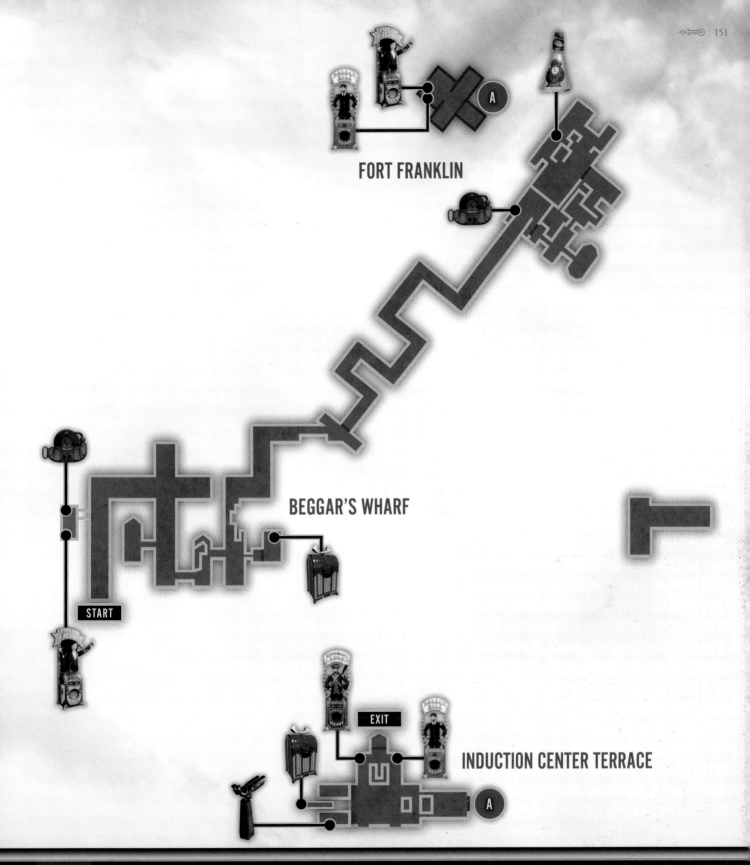

FORT FRANKLIN

BEGGAR'S WHARF

START

EXIT

INDUCTION CENTER TERRACE

First Encounters   Collectibles

Take a moment to scour the delivery center on the left and use the Veni! Vidi! Vigor! machine to purchase one of the new Vigor upgrades. Bronco Aid and Devil's Kiss Aid are now available. You should also locate the **Voxophone** nearby. Loot the desks for ammo and money, then continue around the corner, past the men scrubbing the dock, to find a pair of freight barges.

Keep your guard up at Beggar's Wharf, but don't fire unless fired upon. Those balloon-supported turrets mean business!

	Voxophone
GOD'S BLUEPRINT	
AUTHOR:	Hattie Gerst
DATE:	April the 19th, 1908
LOCATION:	Beggar's Wharf

Samuel always thought that the pew on Sunday went hand in hand with the desk on Monday. "Science is the slow revelation of God's blueprint." After two years in the Lamb's tower on the Monument Island, he took ill with cancer of the stomach. I prayed to the Prophet, and the Prophet delivered unto us a miracle through his servant, Fink. I do not know if I will ever get used to a husband bound in a skeleton of metal, but... better a Handyman than a dead one.

Daisy Fitzroy

The charismatic leader of Columbia's insurgent faction, the Vox Populi, Daisy Fitzroy yearns for the overthrow of Comstock and the Founders. She believes that the dramatic destruction of Columbia will undo all that they have worked for.

The Founder Policeman attacks with his baton the moment Booker inspects that piece of Gear or takes the silver from the safe.

The foreman watching over the barge on your right has a short temper and is quick to alert the authorities if you go trespassing. There's nothing of value on his boat, so just let it be and head up and over the barge to the left to avoid the fight. You'll get your chance to initiate a fight soon enough, and from a far more advantageous position.

Enter the small brick building on the other side of the second barge. This office contains a piece of **Gear** and

a jackpot of Silver Eagles and Silver Bars that a cop inside is closely guarding. The guard attacks with his baton if you so much as try to search or take anything in this room—and there's no way to keep him from putting all of Beggar's Wharf on alert (you can't even prematurely use Possession on him, so save your Salt).

Shoot the Mosquito out of the sky the moment the Possession wears off.

Go ahead and take the Gear, and take down the cop with melee attacks. Plant a Devil's Kiss trap near the door and hold your ground as four or more baton-wielding Founders come rushing in. With them out of the way, head to the door and use Possession on either of the two Mosquitoes hovering about. Mosquitoes are similar to Gun Automatons, except they are suspended by helium balloons. Take cover near the crates at the base of the ramp. Ready Shock Jockey and keep a potent weapon on hand for the Motorized Patriot that attacks last.

"They're selling dreams! And dreams, my friends, they don't come cheap!"

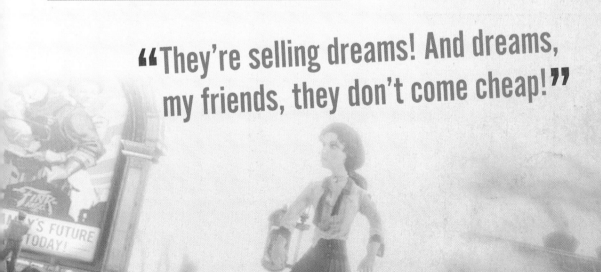

Elizabeth opens several Tears to slow you down. Just keep chasing her!

Make your way to the corner of the docks opposite where Booker was first dropped onto the wharf. Follow the path to where nearly a dozen Shock Jockey traps have been deployed as a result of some spilled cargo. Shoot a few of the crystals to safely reach the Salts, then continue through the angled container and pry open the door to spot Elizabeth.

Elizabeth was thrown off a barge just beyond this door, but she isn't about to let you catch her that easily. Chase after her through the loading area of the docks as she opens Tears to try to thwart you. Wait out each of the obstacles she opens in Booker's path and continue the chase to the police station ahead. There aren't any collectibles to find or crates to search in this area, so don't worry about combing the place.

Pursue her through the doors into the Fort Franklin area just in time to see her open a Tear to escape. Unbeknownst to Elizabeth, Booker wasn't the only one chasing after her. Locate the **Voxophone** in the office, then exit the station through the door on the right. Proceed along the path and up the stairs to the platform overlooking where the Founder Police have seized Elizabeth.

Elizabeth's captors have her behind bulletproof glass.
Hold your fire, and approach this strategically.

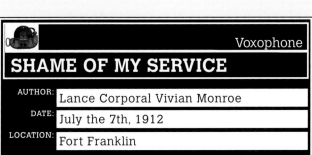

Voxophone
SHAME OF MY SERVICE

AUTHOR: Lance Corporal Vivian Monroe

DATE: July the 7th, 1912

LOCATION: Fort Franklin

They called Slate a monster and a traitor. I know the men who died in the Hall of Heroes with Captain Slate. There is no shame to be counted in their number. The shame lies to we who assembled outside the hall. Though we were not the ones who fell, I feel only envy for those who perished under his banner.

RESCUE ELIZABETH

FORT FRANKLIN PIER

Use Possession on one of the Founders, then use either the Sniper Rifle or RPG to shoot the others who attack your ally.

Elizabeth and her two captors are behind a sheet of bulletproof glass, so don't waste any bullets on them. Instead, use Possession on either of the Founders down low and shoot the others with the Sniper Rifle so that your ally will target the two holding Elizabeth. The enemies leave her locked away while they set out on patrol. Maintain this elevated position, and use Possession on one of the Founders to the right. Lob a Devil's Kiss bomb (or fire an RPG) at the group, then back away, grab the Salts on the right, and ready your weapon for the Founders who ride the Sky-Lines up to Booker's position. A police barge soon arrives on the right. Cast Possession on the Gun Automaton at the bow of the barge, then finish off any remaining enemies and gather up the loot from their corpses.

Drop down to the lower level and enter the jail area opposite where Booker arrived to find an **Infusion**, then ride the Sky-Line up to the platform where Elizabeth was. Open the door to the security office just in time to watch Elizabeth open a Tear for an entire Sky-Line. Leap onto the Sky-Line after her for a short ride to the cargo container that soon blocks the path. Jump down onto the platform and head left toward Elizabeth.

After some surprise drama involving a Handyman, Elizabeth has agreed to trust you once again. Now it's time to go meet that gunsmith! But first, instruct Elizabeth to pick the lock (five lockpicks) on the wheelhouse of the gondola near the **Telescope**. You'll find a piece of **Gear** and a Silver Bar inside. Search the workers' bags and visit the Minuteman's Armory and Dollar Bill machines atop the stairs before heading inside. The Dollar Bill machine on the right is one of the few vending machines that sells lockpicks ($48).

MINUTEMAN'S ARMORY: NEW STOCK!

Item	Description	Price
Shotgun: Damage Boost 1	Increases Shotgun damage by 25%.	$255
Volley Gun: Damage Boost 1	Increases Volley Gun damage by 25%.	$522
Shotgun: Reload Increase	Decreases Shotgun reload time by 50%.	$456
Sniper Rifle: Fire Rate Boost	Increases Sniper Rifle fire rate by 100%.	$654
Pistol: Ammo Increase	Increases Pistol reserve ammo by 50%.	$404
Machine Gun: Clip Increase	Increases Machine Gun clip size by 100%.	$391
Sniper Rifle: Recoil Decrease	Reduces Sniper Rifle recoil by 50%.	$288
Carbine: Clip Increase	Increases Carbine clip size by 50%.	$484

Save enough Salts so you can cast Possession on the Gun Automaton on the barge that shows up.

Leap off Elizabeth's temporary Sky-Line when you reach the yellow fuel tank, and continue after her on foot.

TELESCOPE

You've got Elizabeth back by your side and you need to find the gunsmith, but first, take a look through the **Telescope** near the gondola on the left. This gives those coming to work for Fink one last look at what they're leaving behind before they head into the factories.

★ FINKTON PROPER ★

FIND THE GUNSMITH

WORKER INDUCTION CENTER

Pay a visit to the vending machine on the left before circling around to the processing counter in the middle of the lobby. Locate the **Voxophone** in the center office, and search the desks for loose supplies. Provided you have enough lockpicks, instruct Elizabeth to pick the lock of the gate in the back corner of the lobby (five lockpicks). You'll find an **Infusion** inside the office, as well as a number of searchable desks and the **Pig Volley Gun**, an explosive launcher capable of lobbing projectiles at enemies.

No jobs means no elevator service.
Head down the stairs to the side, and pick the lock.

The main elevator in the Worker Induction Center is currently closed due to a lack of job openings. You'll have to descend either of the stairs flanking the elevator and have Elizabeth pick the lock at the base of the stairs. It doesn't require any lockpicks, so don't fret if you used your last one getting that Infusion.

The Path of the Vox Populi...

Elizabeth draws your attention to the Chen Lin poster on the right as soon as you enter the area, but don't let this distract you from the Kinetoscope on the left. It's located near the vending machine.

	Voxophone

A PRODUCT LIKE ANY OTHER

AUTHOR: Jeremiah Fink

DATE: March the 27th, 1893

LOCATION: Worker Induction Center

The truth is, I don't have a lot of time for all that prophecy nonsense. I tell you, belief is… is just a commodity. And old Comstock, well, he does produce. But, like any tradesman, he's obliged to barter his product for the earthly ores. You see, one does not raise a barn on song alone. No sir! Why, that's Fink timber, a Fink hammer, and Fink's hand to swing it. He needs me—lest he soil his own.

First Encounters

HANDYMAN

BEAST (VOLLEY GUN)

New Vigors

Charge

New Weaponry

The Pig Volley Gun   Hand Cannon

Vox Repeater

Collectibles

Infusions
3

Kinectoscopes
4

Voxophones
8

Telescopes
1

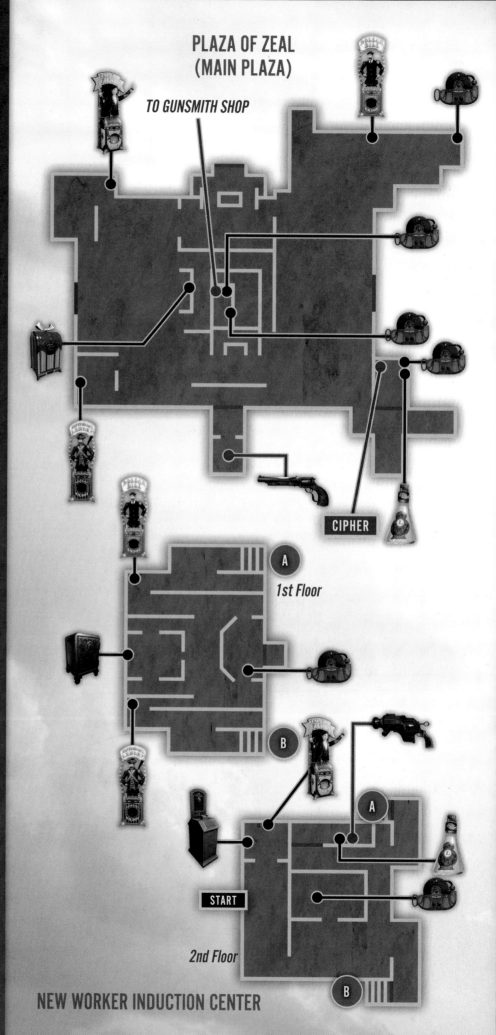

PLAZA OF ZEAL
(MAIN PLAZA)

TO GUNSMITH SHOP

CIPHER

A
1st Floor

B

A

START

B

2nd Floor

NEW WORKER INDUCTION CENTER

TO FACTORY

TO SHANTYTOWN

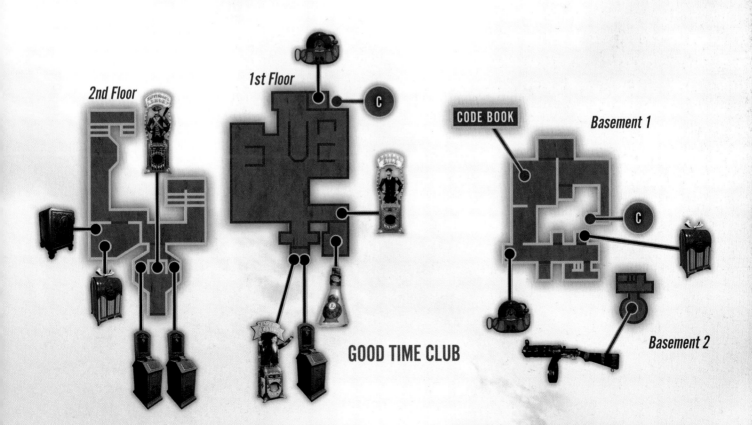

2nd Floor

1st Floor

C

CODE BOOK

Basement 1

C

Basement 2

GOOD TIME CLUB

Descend the stairs to the room below, where the Motorized Patriot and several Founders are standing guard. They'll spot you as you reach the ground level and immediately turn hostile. Cast Possession on the Motorized Patriot, then set to sniping the other guards as they try to fend off your new ally. You'll likely have to finish off the Motorized Patriot yourself, but you can make quick work of it with Shock Jockey and a Shotgun.

Use Possession on your enemies from the balcony, and open fire with the Carbine.

Elizabeth can't be harmed, so don't worry about firing an RPG into a crowd of Founders near her.

Pilfer the desks, cabinets, and mailboxes throughout the lobby, and have Elizabeth open the safe in the office (one lockpick). There may be a number of baton-wielding guards on alert in the lobby upstairs; head upstairs and kill them if Elizabeth is still "in combat." Enter the employees only area behind the sign for the service elevator. Call the elevator and grab the **Voxophone** from inside Slate's locker on the right before boarding it. The elevator ultimately comes to a halt, and then the phone starts to ring. Answer the phone to hear from Mr. Fink.

Voxophone

SEED OF A LIE

AUTHOR: Captain Cornelius Slate

DATE: June the 17th, 1912

LOCATION: Worker Induction Center

I hold in my hand the private journal of Comstock's wife. It puts the lie to this "Miracle Child" nonsense. She loved the child not. It seems the sainted lady would have preferred to let the "seed of the Prophet" just... dry out on the bedsheets...

Mr. Fink's assistant, Mr. Flambeau, greets you in the room at the base of the elevator. Fink has been watching you, and he's impressed. Collect the **Hand Cannon**, lockpicks, and coins from the Silver Purse on the table, and exit the room. The Hand Cannon is a deadly pistol that is arguably one of the finer close-range weapons in Columbia.

Flambeau

When one wants to make the best of impressions, one sends Flambeau. With impeccable manners and even finer style, Flambeau is the quintessential gentleman's gentleman. Industrialist Jeremiah Fink employs Flambeau as a personal assistant. Those who encounter him are struck by his generosity, discretion, and expertly folded pocket square.

PLAZA OF ZEAL

Finkton Proper is essentially a small town all to itself, with the Plaza of Zeal serving as the town square. The residential area lies off to the right, entertainment can be found on the far side of the plaza, and the factory extends off to the left. The Gunsmith Shop you seek isn't far—just enter the large center building via the door on the left— but Elizabeth suggests you scavenge supplies first. Just be warned that the Founder Police will attack, along with the Mosquito hovering overhead, the

You're free to roam around the Plaza of Zeal so long as you don't advance past these Fink Security barricades.

moment you employ a Vigor or fire a weapon. Additionally, be sure to mind the security checkpoint on the far side of the area, or else the Gun Automatons stationed there will commence firing.

Use the freight hooks high above the plaza to reach the awning on the left-hand side of the large building in the center. Grab the **Gear** there, then leap down and head through the doors to enter the Gunsmith Shop.

DECODING THE VOX CIPHER

Descend the stairs from the elevator entrance and loop around the corner to the docks on the right, and have Elizabeth unlock the gated door. Push inside to find a cipher on the rear wall of this clockmaker's shop. Now that you know there's another secret Vox hideaway around, you should keep your eyes peeled for the book containing the code to solve the cipher. You can't go and pick it up right away, but it is located in a room inside the basement of the Good Time Club. You'll have to walk right past it soon enough, once you make your way backstage at the theater.

Return with the Code Book later on so Elizabeth can read the clue: "the broken clock tolls at midnight." Approach the clock on the wall to the right of the poster with the cipher, and set the time ahead to midnight. Once set, the clock automatically slides away, revealing a secret cubby that holds a **Voxophone** and **Infusion**, as well as a Volley Gun and lockpick bag.

Voxophone
WE'VE NEED OF A SHEPHERD

AUTHOR:	Daisy Fitzroy
DATE:	July the 6th, 1912
LOCATION:	The Great Chen Lin, Gunsmith and Machinist

I have a pressing need to speak to this so-called "False Shepherd" stirring up so much trouble. We got enough problems without this damn fool shooting up the city and blamin' it all on the Vox. Though, if he's amiable... yeah... yeah, he might be just the fella we need for our... immediate concerns.

THE GUNSMITH SHOP

Head up the stairs inside the Gunsmith Shop to the small Buddhist shrine, then continue to the upper level. The machinery is running unattended, but there is nobody to be found. Search the crates and barrels for supplies, and grab the lockpick on the workbench. Elizabeth suddenly hears the sounds of someone downstairs. Descend the stairs to the shrine and speak with the visitor.

Mrs. Lin gives you the details about her husband's abduction.

Voxophone
A TRUER ALLEGIANCE

AUTHOR:	Lance Corporal Vivian Monroe
DATE:	July the 7th, 1912
LOCATION:	Plaza of Zeal

I came to Columbia because I believed in God and because I believed in honor. But Slate has shown me this: there is no God in shutting our brothers out from the family of man, and there is no honor in defending those who are strangers to its meaning. Perhaps in Finkton, there is one more deserving of my service...

GO TO THE GOOD TIME CLUB

Exit the Gunsmith Shop and turn to the right to spot the Good Time Club up ahead. You can't miss this massive building with the marquee bearing Booker's name, but there's something of far greater concern at the moment! A Handyman has tracked Elizabeth to the Plaza of Zeal and is ready for a fight. Immediately cast Possession on the Gun Automaton beyond the security barricades to the right (near the Good Time Club), and ready yourself for a fight!

★Handyman★

PLAZA OF ZEAL HANDYMAN'S VITALS

Health	Ranged Damage	Melee Damage	Special Damage	Special Attack
9952	1334	800	1382	Charged Slam

The Handyman is a massive, semi-robotic bruiser that has super-human strength, leaping ability, and speed. Although his primary attacks consist of a heavy pounding strike, a gorilla-like charge, and various melee assaults, the Handyman also possesses innate electric current that he can discharge at will. If Booker leaps to a freight hook or gains enough separation from the Handyman, he can summon a ball of electricity in his hands that he hurls at Booker. Similarly, if Booker leaps to a Sky-Line, the Handyman can jump up and electrocute the entire Sky-Line with his robotic hands. Lastly, the Handyman can perform an electrified ground pound that not only inflicts damage, but stuns as well, leaving Booker vulnerable to follow-up attacks.

It should come as little surprise then that using Shock Jockey against the Handyman is a bad idea, as it's just not very effective. He's also completely invulnerable to Possession and Bucking Bronco. As far as Vigors are concerned, it's best to unleash a Murder of Crows on him and then swap to Devil's Kiss (or Undertow once you get it), and engulf the Handyman in fire or water.

The single best way to defeat the Handyman is to focus your gunfire on his heart, which is visible through the large circular window in his suit. Aim for this red organ in the center of his torso, especially with the Hand Cannon, Sniper Rifle, or Machine Gun, and watch his health drain by the second. Fire, step or leap to the side, then fire again. It's tough to continue facing him without being hit, so don't hesitate to leap to a freight hook or momentarily flee the scene if you need to allow your Shield to replenish. The Handyman is vulnerable to damage anywhere on his body, but you'll inflict far more by targeting his heart. Of course, it doesn't hurt to employ Possession on any nearby Gun Automatons or Mosquitoes so that they can at least help to distract him and chip away at his overall health. The Handyman always drops a piece of Gear upon his demise, so be sure to look for it.

RESCUE CHEN LIN

THE GOOD TIME CLUB

Fink has been awaiting your arrival, and he's put together quite a show on your behalf. Top off your Salts and reload the Hand Cannon and one other weapon. This is also a good time to check your Gear to ensure you're taking advantage of those items that *do not* have anything to do with Sky-Lines, at least for the time being.

Fink wants to see you perform in the art of combat, and he's prepped the Good Time Club for a three-wave battle. Several Salts Phials and weapons have been scattered around the club, and there are three Tears available for your use: Medical Kits, an RPG, and a Volley Gun. Those lucky enough to have the Sheltered Life item equipped should immediately open the Tear for the Medical Kits. Sheltered Life gives Booker brief invulnerability whenever he consumes food or Medical Kits, making the Medical Kits Tear a particularly useful item to have handy.

Crime Comes to 'Shanty-Town'...

Enter the Good Time Club's lobby and head up the stairs on either side to find this Kinetoscope. It's just to the left of the Minuteman's Armory machine and does a good job of painting a bad picture of the folks in the area's housing district.

★ Jeremiah Fink

A wealthy industrialist and ruthless businessman, Jeremiah Fink is the head of Fink Manufacturing, which is responsible for many products found in Columbia, such as weapons, Vigors, and automatons.

Knock the Fireman into the air with Bucking Bronco,
then blast away with the Hand Cannon!

Lure the Zealot up to the balcony so you can fight him
before the other thugs get within range.

The Motorized Patriot's Crank Gun is a fine substitute
if you run out of Salts or Hand Cannon ammo.

The first wave of enemies consists of a Fireman and a number of Fink's thugs with guns. Cast Possession on the Fireman, and watch as he draws much of the gunmen's attention. Finish off the others with the Hand Cannon, then turn to the Fireman when the Possession wears off and take him down with Shock Jockey (or Bucking Bronco) and the Hand Cannon. Another option is to use Murder of Crows against the gunmen and simply avoid the Fireman until you are ready to face him. Either way, it's best to eliminate the fodder as fast as you can to avoid being shot at from all directions.

The second wave consists of a Zealot and several Machine Gun-wielding thugs. Buy yourself some time by heading to the balcony before Fink introduces the second wave. The Zealot can fly up to Booker's location, but the others have to make their way to the stairs. This gives you plenty of time to deal with the Zealot one-on-one. Hit him with Shock Jockey or Bucking Bronco, then fire away with the Shotgun or Hand Cannon. Sweep the area for the remaining enemies, then high-tail it back to the balcony and swap out one of your weapons for the RPG via the Tear.

The third wave doesn't contain any human enemies: rather, it consists of two Gun Automatons, a Motorized Patriot, and three Mosquitoes! (Fortunately, not all at once.) Stick close to the RPG Tear, and have Possession ready to cast. Aim it at the Gun Automaton nearest Booker's position on the stage. Switch to Shock Jockey and quickly electrocute the Motorized Patriot that appears at the end of the stage. Fire a couple of rockets at it, then finish off the Gun Automatons if they didn't destroy one another after your Possession. Switch back to Shock Jockey and the Hand Cannon, and use the column atop the stairs for cover. Three Mosquitoes fly in from behind the curtain. Shock them as they appear, then blast away with the Hand Cannon. It should only take two or three shots with the Hand Cannon to destroy each Mosquito. Work quickly, and you just might destroy all three before they so much as fire a single bullet at Booker!

Search the lower level of the club for an **Infusion** and a **Kinetoscope**, as well as some Silver Eagles and a lockpick. Enter the dressing rooms backstage to find a **Voxophone,** then continue down the stairs beyond the employees-only sign. Kill the two Founders in the storage room, and note the chalkboard in the adjacent room.

"Sometimes there's precious need for folks like Fitzroy... 'cause of folks like me."

The First Lady

This Kinetoscope is easy to overlook in your excitement to head backstage and continue the search for Chen Lin. Let the sound of the nearby Veni! Vidi! Vigor! machine lead you to it.

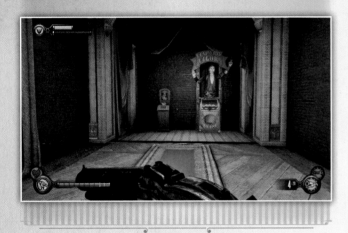

Voxophone

CHANGING MY TUNE

AUTHOR:	Jeremiah Fink
DATE:	August the 12th, 1894
LOCATION:	The Good Time Club

I had thought you a fool, dear brother. When you told me that you heard wonderful music trumpeting from holes in the thin air, I began to doubt your mental integrity. But not only have you made your fortune from these doodads, you have lit the path for me as well.

FIND CHEN LIN'S CELL

Instruct Elizabeth to pick the lock on the adjacent door, and locate the **Code Book** atop the crates nearest the furnace. Bring this back to the clock shop in the Plaza of Zeal after you find Chen Lin. Continue to the projector room, where Elizabeth turns on a film showing Chen Lin's interrogation. Kill any guards you spot, and push on to the cells up ahead. Grab the **Voxophone** from the right end of the hall, and pick the lock on cell #8 (five lockpicks) to find a piece of **Gear**.

Did you spare Slate? If so, he's in a wheelchair inside the first cell on the right. Go ahead and put him out of his misery if you'd like.

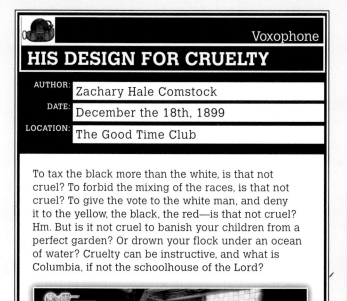

Voxophone

HIS DESIGN FOR CRUELTY

AUTHOR: Zachary Hale Comstock

DATE: December the 18th, 1899

LOCATION: The Good Time Club

To tax the black more than the white, is that not cruel? To forbid the mixing of the races, is that not cruel? To give the vote to the white man, and deny it to the yellow, the black, the red—is that not cruel? Hm. But is it not cruel to banish your children from a perfect garden? Or drown your flock under an ocean of water? Cruelty can be instructive, and what is Columbia, if not the schoolhouse of the Lord?

Ask Elizabeth to unlock cell #9, and descend the stairs to the basement. Cross the darkened cell to the dimly lit button to turn on the lights. Rouse Chen Lin to find that he is dead, butchered and bled out. The Lutece couple appears, and along with them, a Tear where Chen Lin's corpse was located. The Tear leads to another Columbia, another side of the same coin, as it were.

There's no going back once that Tear is opened.
And what you know to be true may no longer be right.

Give Elizabeth the command to open the Tear. The body and blood are gone, and the room is suddenly back to being a normal storage room. Grab the **Repeater,** a Vox-modified version of the basic Machine Gun.

RETURN TO THE GUNSMITH SHOP

Return the way you came, past the large group of imprisoned (but alive) Vox Populi and up the stairs to the projection room, where a very different interrogation video is playing. Chen Lin was cut free due to his wife's important friends at the Columbia Gazette.

Make your way back through the storage rooms to where the two guards you killed earlier are. Now they're flickering and suffering from steady nosebleeds. Something significant changed when Liz opened that Tear. They're back from the dead, but not quite alive. You can either let them be or shoot them dead again. The choice is yours.

Test out your first Vox weapon on the Founders
who attack with batons in the club.

Cut back through the dressing rooms to the theater, and watch as a large number of Founders suddenly starts to attack. This is no audition—these men mean business! The Tears you had access to are gone, and Booker is left to battle them with his newfound Repeater and Vigors. The addition of the Founders isn't the only change, however. The upper office is no longer gated, and you can now loot the **Gear** and safe (three lockpicks) from within it.

PLAZA OF ZEAL

The gate leading back up the road directly to Chen Lin's shop is sealed tight, forcing you to loop around the plaza in a clockwise direction. Equip Possession and Bucking Bronco, Devil's Kiss, or Murder of Crows, and head out the left-hand gate. Immediately cast Possession on the enemy that is on the stairs outside of the Shantytown entrance to the right, then head left toward the stacks of logs. Locate the **Voxophone** in the far corner, and use the Dollar Bill machine to stock up on ammo.

Booker won't be able to leap to any of the freight hooks above the road, but there is plenty of cover. The only problem is that there is a Beast firing a Volley Gun at Booker from the distance. Use Bucking Bronco or Murder of Crows along with the Hand Cannon to fight your way up the road. Stick to the cover on the far left, near the wooden boardwalk, and try to take Possession of the Beast when you get a chance.

There's a Tear for a Volley Gun on the left and another for Medical Kits in front of the clock store, should Booker need them. Use Possession on the Beast atop the stairs near the service elevator entrance, then run up those very same steps and take cover near the railing. Cast Devil's Kiss at the group of enemies down on the street below, then gather up some Salts and cast Possession on the Gun Automaton in the distance, near the entrance to the Gunsmith Shop.

Possess the Gun Automaton now positioned outside the Gunsmith Shop, then make a dash for the building.

Gunsmith Set Free!

This Kinetoscope sits to the right of the Minuteman's Armory machine in the lobby of the Good Time Club, but only after you've opened the Tear in Chen Lin's cell. Be on the lookout for Kinetoscopes and Voxophones in areas where they weren't in the *other* Columbia.

	Voxophone
THE INVISIBLE COLOR	

AUTHOR:	Daisy Fitzroy
DATE:	February the 12th, 1912
LOCATION:	Plaza of Zeal

One day, ain't nobody notice me. Then they I done for Lady Comstock, and, well—everybody noticed me. I head to Finkton, and I hide. I hide deep. The more they look, deeper I go. Only thing a colored child can count on is the fact they invisible.

GUNSMITH SHOP

Ascend the stairs inside the shop to find an empty workshop (no machinery at all) and a flickering vision of the machinist, Chen Lin. Speaking to him doesn't yield any information other than that you should talk to the lady downstairs. Descend the stairs to the shrine devoted to the Prophet and speak to the lady. It's Mrs. Lin, but she's no longer the short Chinese woman you met earlier. This alternate Mrs. Lin says that the police took Chen's tools and impounded them in Shantytown.

Chen Lin is alive and free, but his tools are locked up at the Bull House Impound.

FIND THE POLICE IMPOUND

Exit the Gunsmith Shop and loop back around to the other side of the Plaza of Zeal, then fight your way past the Founders to the building with the spray-painted Shantytown sign. Pull the lever opposite the vending machines to slide the freight out of the way. Doing so gains you access to Shantytown (the freight now blocks Booker's path back to the Plaza of Zeal and must be moved again when it's time to exit).

PATH TO SHANTYTOWN

The Gun Automaton distracts the Founders, leaving Booker free to snipe them with ease.

Open the Tear for the Gun Automaton on the upper ledge to the right, then use Possession on the Beast that patrols the overhead walkway with the RPG. He'll be able to rain fire down on the numerous enemies in the courtyard, including those making their way toward Booker. Watch your Gun Automaton closely, and immediately open the Tear for the Cover in the center of the road if it is destroyed.

One of the more rewarding ways of dispatching the Founders in this area is to use the leaking pipes to your advantage. Fire a blast of Shock Jockey at the water pouring from the pipes in the center of the area to trap and electrocute any foe that comes forward. Shock Jockey takes on lethal potency when combined with water. Open the Tear for the freight hook high on the left, and leap to the floating billboard platform to snag an RPG and some additional ammo if you want it. Note the location of the Vigor behind the locked steel gates inside the office near the elevator. You'll be able to access it on your way back through here in a few minutes.

Cast Shock Jockey at the leaking pipes to electrocute your enemies!

★ SHANTYTOWN ★

GRAVEYARD SHIFT BAR

START

SHANTYTOWN

QUEST KEY

A

A

THE BULL YARD

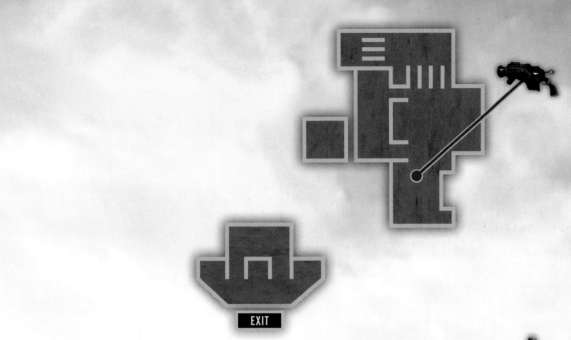

THE BULL HOUSE IMPOUND

TO 2ND FLOOR

START

1st Floor

TO BASEMENT 1

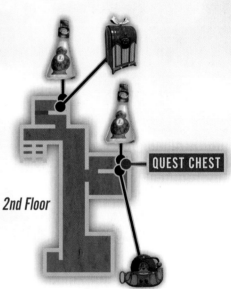

QUEST CHEST

2nd Floor

Basement 1

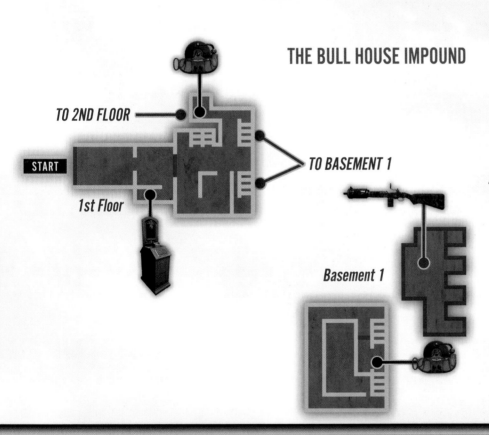

First Encounters

FOUNDER (HAND CANNON)

New Weaponry

Burstgun Carbine

Collectibles

Infusions

3

Voxophones

7

Kinectoscopes

1

Telescopes

1

FIND CHEN LIN'S TOOLS

SHANTYTOWN

Make your way down the road, past the poverty-stricken homeless of Shantytown, and turn left to find an **Infusion** behind the counter at a food rationing point. There's no way to get this Infusion without spilling blood during this initial trip through Shantytown (you can risk waiting until later if you'd like), so go ahead and unleash your Bucking Bronco attack to knock the crowd into the air, grab the vial, then open fire on the two men manning this black market shop.

Descend the stairs at the end of the road and enter the Graveyard Shift Bar. The upper level has all three types of vending machines, as well as a Shotgun-wielding barkeep who won't hesitate to open fire if you try to search any crates or grab a Salt Phial. Head on down to the basement, where there are no watchful eyes.

Pick up the guitar leaning against the chair to enjoy a brief reprieve from the gloom and sorrow of Shantytown. Locate the **Voxophone** in the basement, and pick up the **keys** from atop the barrel in the corner. These keys prove to be useful soon enough.

The two men with the suspenders attack once Booker takes the Infusion, but they pose no real threat.

Pick up the guitar in the corner of the basement to hear Elizabeth sing a song.

Voxophone

FANNING A FLAME

AUTHOR:	Daisy Fitzroy
DATE:	February the 12th, 1912
LOCATION:	The Graveyard Shift

When you forced deep underground, well—you see things from the bottom up. And down at the bottom of the city, I saw a fire burning. A fire's got heat aplenty, but it ain't got no mouth. Daisy... now, she got herself a mouth big enough for all the fires in Columbia.

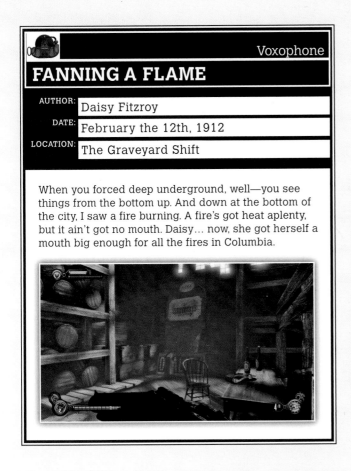

Exit the Graveyard Shift Bar and head back the other way, toward the steps leading down to where an angry crowd has gathered around a vending machine. Open the Tear for the Food Sacks to the right as a distraction; otherwise, you'll have to fight (i.e., kill) the bystanders to obtain the Silver Eagles scattered nearby the machine.

Open the Tear for the Food Sacks to distract the crowd from the Silver Eagles by the vending machine.

The people of Shantytown have scoured nearly every inch of their home in search of food and valuables. Don't expect to find much as you make your way through this depressing place. Descend the road toward the encampment up ahead, and locate the **Gear** at the entrance to the Bull Yard.

DESTROY THE DEFENSE TURRETS

THE BULL YARD

The Bull Yard is crawling with heavy-armored Founders, a Motorized Patriot, a Gun Automaton, and two massive defense cannons. Needless to say, if you're going to breech the security of the Police Impound facility, you had better have a plan!

Use the Sky-Hook to reach the Sniper Rifle by the Telescope, and snipe the enemies on the dock below.

Kick off the battle by using Possession on the Founder patrolling the area directly below the ledge where Booker first enters the Bull Yard. Shoot any remaining Founders down below with the Volley Gun, then leap to the balcony high on the left, via the freight hooks. Here, you can find a **Telescope** and a Sniper Rifle. Use the Sniper Rifle to take out the heavy Machine Gunners in the distance, especially any that have a Hand Cannon. Provided the defense turrets haven't been activated yet, try to cast Possession on the Motorized Patriot that appears so it can eventually destroy the Gun Automaton or vice-versa.

There are two Sky-Lines in the area that rise and dive as they loop around the area between the two buildings flanking the main path to the police station. They roughly parallel one another, but one track rises high to the building on the right and through the lower section of the left-hand building, whereas the other track does the opposite.

Explore the two Sky-Lines and the buildings nearby to find four Tears that you can utilize. The roof of the left-hand building (when facing the police station) leads to a Rocket Automaton, which unfortunately is instantly destroyed if the defense turrets are still active. To destroy them, you're going to have to get a hold of an RPG or make frequent use of a Hand Cannon or Sniper Rifle.

TELESCOPE

This Telescope peers out across the Bull Yard to the entrance to the Columbia Authority police station. You can access it right away if you want, but it's better to wait at least until after you've destroyed the defense turrets. Use the freight hooks above the balcony to reach it.

The balcony to the left of the one with the Telescope serves as a nice spot for targeting the defense turrets.

Open the Tear for the Mosquito flying around near the cannons and ride the Sky-Line to the roof on the right-hand building. Open the Tear for the RPG, and start shooting at the defense turrets. Consider riding the Sky-Line to the lower level of that same building so you can have Elizabeth open the Tear for the Medical Kits. Keep close to them, use the available cover, and continue firing Shock Jockey and the RPG at the defense turrets. Use Bucking Bronco and the Hand Cannon or Repeater to make quick work of any Founders that ride the Sky-Lines up to Booker's position.

Fire the RPG at any crowds you see, especially if there's a Motorized Patriot in their midst.

The Mosquito proves even more helpful once you've destroyed the defense turrets.

	Voxophone

TRAPPED

AUTHOR: Preston E. Downs
DATE: July the 5th, 1912
LOCATION: The Bull Yard

Well, Fitzroy—you... you got a low cunning in ya, if nothing else. Dropped a couple grizzly traps 'round the lines up here. Idea was to... to bleed one of your couriers till he gave you up. 'Cept, of course, you're using kids now. Now I got this... tiny Injun boy, eyeballing me. Had to take his leg off. Damn thing's just lying here between us. I sure wish he'd cry or something.

FIND THE CONFISCATED TOOLS

Fitzroy Spotted!

The lobby of the Bull House Impound is completely empty of foes. Use this opportunity to search the office on the right for the Kinetoscope between the desks.

THE BULL HOUSE IMPOUND

The interior is empty of enemies and completely silent at first. Take a moment to search the offices, then advance to the main lobby where numerous Founder Police are stationed.

Keep low and duck into the office on the right as soon as Booker passes through the doors. Have Elizabeth open the Tear for the Crank Gun, then turn and have her open the Tear for the Cover in the center of the hall. Use the Crank Gun together with Murder of Crows to mow down the Founder Police as they charge out of hiding. They'll come from the center office, up the stairs on the left, and from both sets of stairs leading to the basement. Head to the opposite side of the Cover Elizabeth opened, as a Motorized Patriot is going to enter through the doors behind Booker. Switch to Shock Jockey, and take it out!

The Founders are no match for Murder of Crows and the Crank Gun!

Open the Tear for the Cover, and switch to Shock Jockey when the Motorized Patriot enters from the lobby.

Voxophone

TERMINATED

AUTHOR:	Daisy Fitzroy
DATE:	February the 12th, 1912
LOCATION:	The Bull House

They argued somethin' fierce at night—Lady Comstock and the Prophet. Could never make out what it was about from my bunk, though. After the worst, I seen she ain't left for morning prayer... so I crept upstairs to check in on her. And like a fool... I lingered. "Scullery maid" was what they called me when I walked into Comstock House. "Murderer" was what they shouted when I ran out.

The confiscated tools are in the basement, but there's a lot of good stuff to find on the main floor and upstairs. Give the Bull House Impound's upper floors a thorough search to make sure you find the two **Voxophones**, **Gear**, and an **Infusion**. You'll need Elizabeth to unlock the door to the storage room on the second floor (five lockpicks), but it's worth it for what's inside. There are usually some additional Founder Police milling around in the locker room upstairs, so keep your guard up.

EVIDENCE LOCKER

The center office on the second floor contains a large blue storage chest—the evidence locker alluded to in Private Wilbur Sykes' Voxophone recording. Wilbur somehow left the key to the chest over at the Graveyard Shift Bar; perhaps you found it already? The keys are located in the basement of the bar, on a barrel in the corner opposite the guitar. Use the key to unlock this chest to gain another **Infusion.**

	Voxophone

THAT GODDAMN KEY

AUTHOR:	Private Wilbur Sykes
DATE:	July the 5th, 1912
LOCATION:	The Bull House

There's the job, and there's life. They pay me to hate the goddamn Vox, and I take their money, but... what's the harm of having a drink with Fitzroy's people? Face to face at the Graveyard Shift, why, they're... they're just folk. Hell, I guess I fell into the goddamn bottle, because I stumbled back without the evidence locker key. If Schmidt finds out... well, there'll be hell to pay.

THE IMPOUND

Descend the stairs in the lower level of the Police Impound until you reach the basement, where the gunsmith's tools have been locked up. There's no way to physically move them back to the shop, but Elizabeth spots another Tear, one in which the tools aren't there. Instruct her to open the Tear; the gunsmith's tools are instantly replaced by crates of confiscated Vox weaponry. Swap out one of your weapons for the **Burstgun**, the Vox's burst-fired take on the Carbine Rifle. Head back upstairs, but be sure to grab the **Voxophone** that now sits on the table.

Opening this Tear changes everything. Be on the lookout for new Voxophones in places where they weren't minutes ago—it's quantum.

ARMED REVOLT

When Booker first arrived in Finkton, the gunsmith Chen Lin was dead. Then you opened a Tear to a reality in which he was alive, but his tools were confiscated. This second Tear yielded a reality in which Chen Lin was free to carry out his trade—and the Vox were given the arsenal they so desired. Head back up the stairs and collect the **Voxophone** from the desk in the hallway before exiting the station.

RETURN TO THE GUNSMITH

SHANTYTOWN

Return the way you came to the Bull Yard, where a full-fledged war is taking place between the Vox Populi and the Founders. The Vox Populi are clad in red and will not fire on you—the reasons become clear soon enough. Use the Sky-Lines to cross the yard and use Possession on the Gun Automaton on the far side, below the Telescope you saw earlier. Finish off any remaining Founders, and lead Elizabeth back through Shantytown to the elevator leading back up to Finkton Proper. Be

Cast Possession on the Gun Automaton on the left, then assist it in defeating the armored Founders.

sure to inspect the area around the Graveyard Shift Bar for two **Voxophones** that weren't there during your earlier visit.

 Voxophone

THAT ETERNAL SHORE

AUTHOR: Hattie Gerst

DATE: July the 25th, 1908

LOCATION: Shantytown

Samuel, when the spells of anger come, I want you to play this recording and remember that I am the proudest woman in Columbia to have been your wife. They said your soul was choked by the fumes in that metal box, but this I do not believe. And we shall meet again, on that eternal shore—both of us whole and smiling. I love you. I love you. I love you.

The Vox Populi

The Vox Populi—Latin for "Voice of the People"—is the group opposing the Founders. Their leader is Daisy Fitzroy. The Vox Populi first began as a small underground group that worked to protect the rights of the working class. Following an inciting event in China, the Vox Populi staged protests against Founder oppression. The Founders retaliated with a violent lockdown in the lower-class parts of the city, such as Shantytown. Now, the Vox aim to destroy industry and government control in Columbia. They see these acts of destruction as revenge against the Founder regime and the delivery of their political message.

Exit the elevator and grab the **Charge** Vigor from the looted storage cabinet inside the office. Charge allows Booker to essentially harness the power of a tornado and fly through the air to melee attack an enemy from afar. It's exceptionally powerful for both attacking faraway adversaries and enabling Booker to move swiftly across the battlefield. Access to that Vigor wasn't the only thing that changed!

Charge allows Booker to instantly fly through the air like a tornado to melee a faraway foe.

Round the corner and immediately open the Tear for the Gun Automaton on the left. The same Tears available to you earlier, here on the Path to Shantytown, are back. This time, however, there's a police barge on the upper right, near the freight hook. Let the Gun Automaton do what it can, then open the Tear to the freight hook and use it to Sky-Line Strike any remaining Founders on the barge. From atop the barge, you should try out Booker's new Charge Vigor on any remaining enemies. Reopen the Tear for the Gun Automaton, and continue to the Plaza of Zeal.

You'll have to rev up the Charge Vigor longer to use it against heavy enemies like this Beast.

	Voxophone

DRAWING DEAD

AUTHOR:	Booker DeWitt
DATE:	July the 6th, 1912
LOCATION:	The Graveyard Shift

"Bring us the girl and wipe away the debt. As plans go, I'd seen worse—except this girl was already gone. Monument Island's a damn ghost town. Seems like they evacuated her when they heard I was here. An old friend told me Comstock spirited her off to that fortress of his. As a one-man job, this just went from bettin' on the river to… drawing dead.

The Vox Populi

The Vox Populi, recognizable by its trademark red colorings, is a workers' movement in Columbia. Led by Daisy Fitzroy, the Vox Populi has taken up arms against prophet Zachary Comstock and the Founders, the private citizens of Columbia. Where the Founders are upper class and predominantly white, the Vox are poor, and much more ethnically diverse. In developing the look of the Vox Populi, we used the color red to represent them and set them apart from the Founders. We also gave them a more working class feel; overalls, welding gloves, ripped clothes, all adorned with the color red somewhere on their body.

Shawn Robertson
Animation Director

The battle is every bit as intense in the Plaza of Zeal. Quickly leap to the freight hook directly in front of Booker, dismount onto the awning facing the Good Time Club, and drop off the other side to quickly reach the Gunsmith Shop. Once there, investigate the bodies on the floor of the entryway and collect the **Voxophone** on the shelf to the left—it's a new Voxophone that wasn't present in the previous realities.

Voxophone

ALL DEBTS PAID

AUTHOR: Booker DeWitt
DATE: July the 7th, 1912
LOCATION: The Great Chen-Lin, Gunsmith and Machinist

Looks like I got a friend in town after all… Slate. He's fell in with these "Vox Populi." And for irregulars, I will say—they are loaded for bear. Problem is, I got to help them with their damn revolution first… then we take Comstock House by storm. I do that, I get the girl.

RECLAIM THE FIRST LADY AIRSHIP

PATH TO THE FACTORY

The Vox Populi have just about cut through the locked entrance to the factory. Follow the mob through the gate to the flaming interior, and wait while the rebel with the blowtorch cuts through the interior door.

Follow them onto the lengthy exterior platform and immediately use Possession on the Gun Automaton nearest Booker. Open fire on any Founders close by, and push across the bridge alongside the Vox Populi forces. Make sure the Gun Automaton is destroyed before Booker runs past it so that it doesn't fire on his blindside. Open the Tear for the Rocket Automaton in the center of the area, and take cover to the left of it. Keep a safe distance, look for an RPG to pick up, and use Possession, Shock Jockey, and your heavy firepower to destroy the Gun Automaton and Motorized Patriot at the far end of the pathway.

Cast Possession on the Gun Automaton on the right, and use the available Sniper Rifle to pick off a few enemies before advancing.

Open the Tear for the Rocket Automaton, but be ready to open another Tear to start its cooldown the moment it gets destroyed.

The perfect dismount!

The Vox can't cut the gate leading to the factory entrance with the zeppelin circling overhead—it's up to you to take it out! You don't have enough firepower to destroy it outright, so you're going to have to sabotage it. Leap to the Sky-Line and ride it all the way up and around the back of the buildings to the wing on the other side of the zeppelin. It's a very lengthy ride on a Sky-Line, so be patient and wait to Sky-Line Strike an enemy on the wing.

Cast Possession on the Gun Automaton on the side of the zeppelin, and rush past it to enter the zeppelin. Cast Possession on the Motorized Patriot far to the right, then set about picking off the heavily armored Founders standing watch over the engine. Stay behind the cover near the control terminal, and dispatch them with Vigor combinations and your RPG or Burstgun.

Approach the engine at the rear of the zeppelin interior, and use the Sky-Hook to cut the cables. This sends the zeppelin into a tailspin. Head out onto the side of the ship opposite the one Booker entered, and wait for a freight hook or Sky-Line to come into view, then leap to it to get off the zeppelin before it crash-lands.

Be patient and wait for a Sky-Line to come within view. You may need to leap onto the rail of the zeppelin to get a better view.

Follow the Vox Populi up the stairs to the factory entrance, but don't let the crowd's excitement carry you past the **Telescope** perched atop the stairs. Give the rest of Finkton Proper one final look before heading inside.

TELESCOPE

Ascend the stairs from the gondola, and take a moment to use the Telescope near the railing. This set of high-powered optics grants you a great view across the sky, looking back at the spires of Finkton's buildings.

★ THE FACTORY ★

TAKE BACK THE FIRST LADY AIRSHIP

The Vox are launching a full-scale assault on the Finkton Factory and have every intention of taking it down. Follow them through the doors up ahead, and quickly cast Possession on the Rocket Automaton across the room. Sprint past it on the right, toward the next door, then turn and destroy it with Shock Jockey and the Burstgun once the Possession wears off. You won't have to worry about it turning and firing on Booker, as it is too busy targeting the Vox Populi.

Possess the Rocket Automaton, then attack its blind-side from around the corner. Otherwise, enter the next room.

First Encounters

VOX (BATON)   VOX (SHOTGUN)
VOX (PISTOL)   ROCKET AUTOMATON
VOX (MACHINE GUN)

New Vigors

Undertow

PLATFORM HANGING ATTACHED

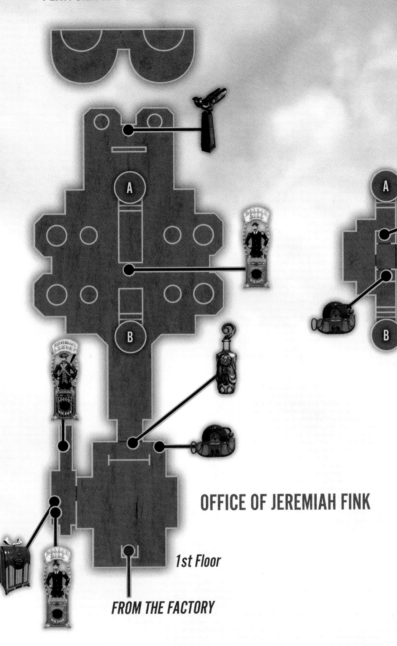

EXIT

A

B

A

B

2nd Floor

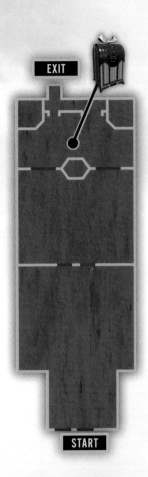

THE FACTORY

START

OFFICE OF JEREMIAH FINK

1st Floor

FROM THE FACTORY

Collectibles

Infusions	Voxophones	Kinectoscopes	Telescopes
1	2	-	1

Grab the **Gear** that had fallen off the dolly and ride the elevator up to Fink's office. The glass doors of the elevator provide you with an excellent view of floor after floor of manufacturing: Vigors, Salts, turrets, vending machines, and even teddy bears. Fink makes the stuff that Columbia wants. Answer the phone when the elevator stops—it's Daisy calling to tell you her Vox won't be taking it easy on you anymore.

OFFICE OF JEREMIAH FINK

Open fire on the Vox outside the elevator door, before they have a chance to get the drop on Booker. Kill the lot of them, then head behind Fink's desk to gather up nearly a thousand dollars in Silver Eagles, Gold Bars, Silver Bars, and purses. Use this newfound fortune to upgrade your Burstgun and Hand Cannon (or preferred weaponry) via the Minuteman's Armory machine in the room to the left. Also, grab the piece of **Gear** behind the Dollar Bill vending machine while you're there.

Collect the **Voxophone** and the **Undertow** Vigor near the exit before you leave. Undertow allows Booker to emit a blast of water that can knock enemies off ledges, Sky-Lines, and barges. It can also be used to yank enemies towards him. It's a perfect way to thwart lots of foes without spending any ammo! Have Elizabeth unlock the gate behind the desk and step out onto the distribution platform.

MINUTEMAN'S ARMORY: NEW STOCK!

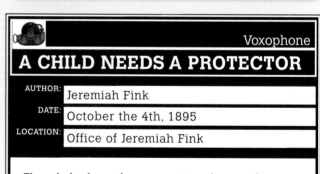

Item	Description	Price
Hand Cannon: Reload Increase	Increases Hand Cannon reload speed by 50%.	$656
Hand Cannon: Damage Boost 1	Increases Hand Cannon damage by 25%.	$448
Carbine: Recoil Decrease	Decreases Carbine recoil by 60%.	$333
Burstgun: Damage Boost 1	Increases Burstgun damage by 25%.	$423
Pistol: Damage Boost 2	Increases Pistol damage by 25%.	$199
Machine Gun: Damage Boost 2	Increases Machine Gun damage by 25%.	$236
Sniper Rifle: Damage Boost 2	Increases Sniper Rifle damage by 25%.	$349

Voxophone

A CHILD NEEDS A PROTECTOR

AUTHOR: Jeremiah Fink

DATE: October the 4th, 1895

LOCATION: Office of Jeremiah Fink

These holes have shown me yet another wonder, though I've yet to see the application for it. They illuminate a merger of machine and man that is somehow the lesser, yet the greater, of both parties. The process seems to be irreversible. Perhaps, though, Comstock will have some need of this kind of thing to keep watch in that tower he is building.

The incredibly rare Gold Bar is worth 500 Silver Eagles!

The Undertow Vigor emits a powerful blast of water that can knock multiple Vox to their death.

Step out onto the cargo distribution platform, and follow Elizabeth up the stairs to Daisy. Daisy may have gotten her guns, but she's not about to give you the First Lady Airship. In fact, her Vox Populi army is about to attack in great numbers. Leap to the freight hook off to the left, and wait for the first of several Vox Populi barges to pull within range. Jump to the barge and use Undertow to knock the Fireman and other Vox right off the edge!

Leap to the Sky-Lines and ride the oval-shaped track around the perimeter of the area until you see more Vox Populi. Vault into a Sky-Line Strike, then turn and blast them off the platform with Undertow. This is a good time to equip any Gear you have that boosts Booker's abilities while using Sky-Lines. Newton's Law, Death from Above, and Nor'easter are particularly useful!

Open the Tear for the Tesla Coil on the rear of the platform if within range, since it helps to stun any Vox Populi that approach (and helps contribute to the "Hazard Pay" bonus). Sweep the decks clear of Vox with Undertow and your Burstgun while trying to maintain a moderate supply of Salts.

Elizabeth does her best to stay close so she can continue to toss you supplies.

It won't be long before Elizabeth warns of a Handyman attack. The Handyman is susceptible to Undertow attacks, though he won't be knocked back. Stay on the move and pepper the Handyman in the heart with your Burstgun or RPG attacks.

The Handyman is capable of leaping onto the Sky-Line and electrocuting the entire track. Provided you manage to keep an eye on his position, it's possible to use this attack against him. Ride the Sky-Line until he finally leaps onto it, and listen for him to yell for Booker to get off. That's your cue that he's about to electrocute the rails. Dismount the Sky-Line, and open fire on him while he jolts the tracks with electricity. The Handyman can't cut this attack short, nor can he move once he starts the maneuver, thus leaving him a sitting duck for your attacks.

The Tesla Coil not only harms the Handyman, but it helps keep nearby Vox from attacking Booker.

Hit the Handyman with RPG rockets while baiting him to leap up and electrocute the Sky-Line.

Take out the Handyman, then head up the stairs to the upper level in time to assist Elizabeth. Follow her instructions to gain entry to the boarding platform for the First Lady Airship. But before you board the ship, make sure to find the **Telescope** on the front of this platform and the **Infusion** and **Voxophone** in the rooms on either side of the hall leading to the airship.

TELESCOPE

This Telescope is on the far end of the distribution platform. Don't worry about using it during the battle with the Vox, but make sure you pay it a visit before boarding the First Lady.

Voxophone

APOLOGY

AUTHOR:	Booker DeWitt
DATE:	July the 14th, 1912
LOCATION:	Office of Jeremiah Fink

[Coughs] Fitzroy... you win this fool war, you send this to New York. [Bloody Coughs] They ain't gettin' the girl. Whoever they are— [Winces] Maybe I did right by you and the Vox, but in the end... that don't square anything. Anna... Anna... I'm sorry...

BOARD THE FIRST LADY

Follow Elizabeth down the corridor into the First Lady Airship. Knock on the cabin door on the right, then head to the console and set a course. Elizabeth will meet you by the controls once she's slipped into some fresh clothes. Adjust the setting when prompted to bring this leg of the journey to an end.

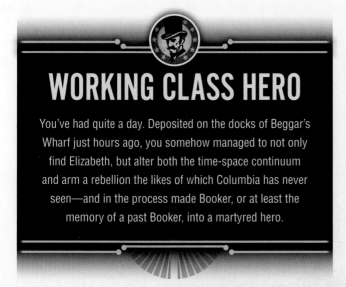

WORKING CLASS HERO

You've had quite a day. Deposited on the docks of Beggar's Wharf just hours ago, you somehow managed to not only find Elizabeth, but alter both the time-space continuum and arm a rebellion the likes of which Columbia has never seen—and in the process made Booker, or at least the memory of a past Booker, into a martyred hero.

Where will Booker steer the First Lady this time?

FAMILY REUNION

★ EMPORIA ★

Assist Elizabeth in opening the First Lady's hatch, and hurry toward the odd couple playing the piano. Elizabeth runs to them and tells them to stop, which they eventually do after realizing the piano isn't in tune. The male twin hands you a postcard detailing the Songbird Defense System. Take the card and push the piano out of the way to escape the crash site.

Help Elizabeth escape the crashed airship, and push the piano out of the way to continue.

GO TO COMSTOCK HOUSE

PROSPERITY PLAZA

Comstock House lies far off in the distance, on the other side of Emporia.

MINUTEMAN'S ARMORY: NEW STOCK!

Item	Description	Price
Repeater: Recoil Decrease	Decreases Repeater recoil by 50%.	$711
Heater: Reload Increase	Decreases Heater reload time by 50%.	$752
RPG: Damage Boost 2	Increases RPG damage by 25%.	$385
Hand Cannon: Damage Boost 2	Increases Hand Cannon damage by 25%.	$448
Shotgun: Damage Boost 2	Increases Shotgun damage by 25%.	$255
Carbine: Damage Boost 2	Increases Carbine damage by 25%.	$357

The tree-lined neighborhood of Emporia is evacuating as fear of the Vox Populi sweeps throughout Columbia. Citizens are lined up with their possessions, trying to clamber aboard barges that are already straining under the load. Some will survive to escape; others will be left behind to suffer their fate.

Scour the area's bags and garbage cans for usable items, and make your way along the terrace to the Minuteman's Armory vending machine in the tunnel on the right. Purchase the Sniper Rifle Damage Boost 2 upgrade if you're carrying a Sniper Rifle; otherwise, upgrade whatever Machine Gun you're carrying, or (better yet) the RPG.

Climb the stairs on the right, toward the sounds of a Vox mugging a civilian. Open fire on the Vox, then have Elizabeth open the Tear for the Mosquito in the distance. There are a number of Tears in this area, but the two you should focus on are the Mosquito and the Medical Kits directly ahead of you. A Vox Beast in heavy armor intensely guards the path ahead. This enemy is not only hard to kill, but it is also equipped with the Hail Fire weapon, which is the Vox equivalent of the Pig Volley Gun.

Maintain an elevated position, and try to shoot the Vox Beast that the Mosquito is targeting.

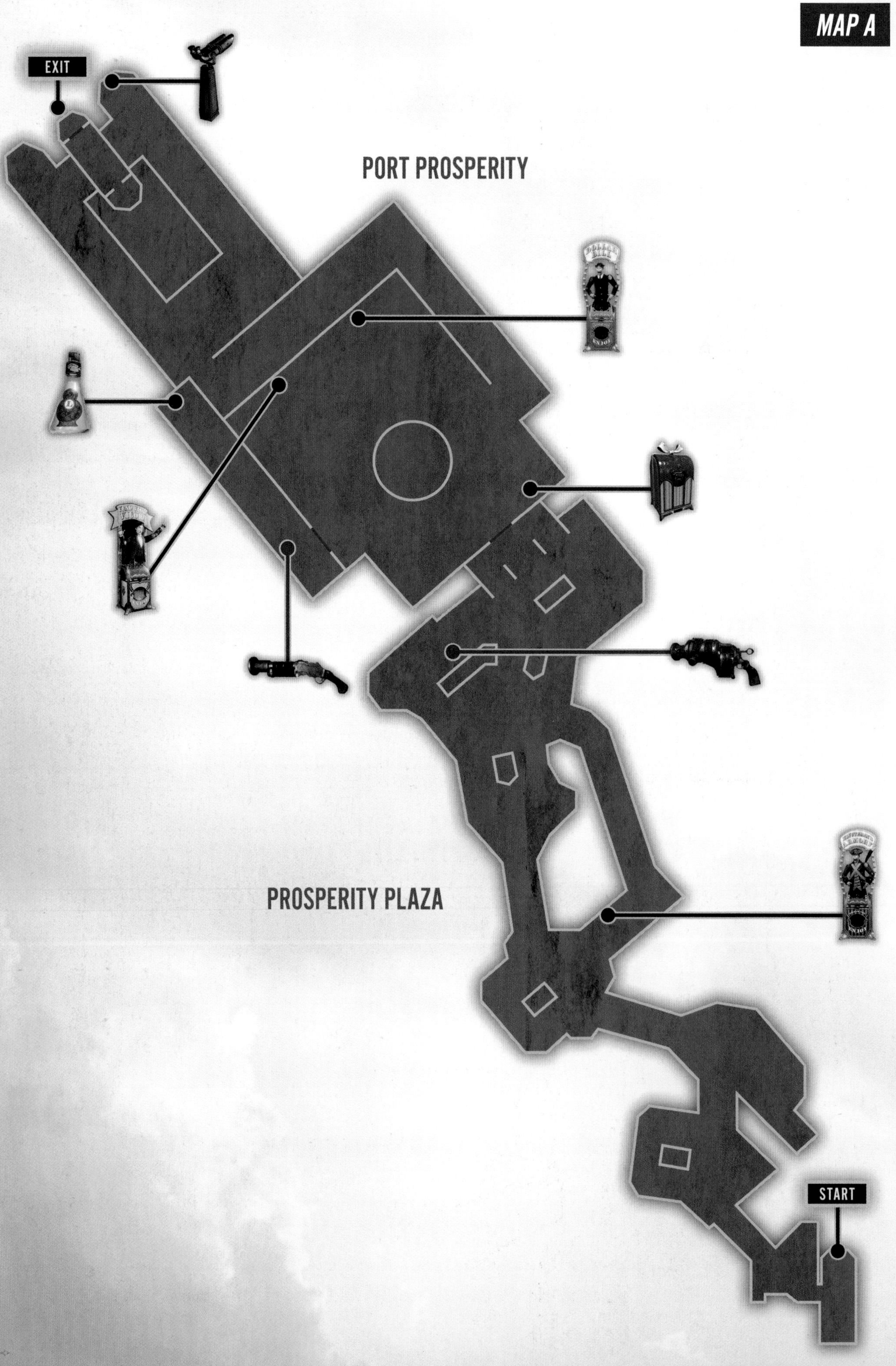
MAP A
EXIT
PORT PROSPERITY
PROSPERITY PLAZA
START

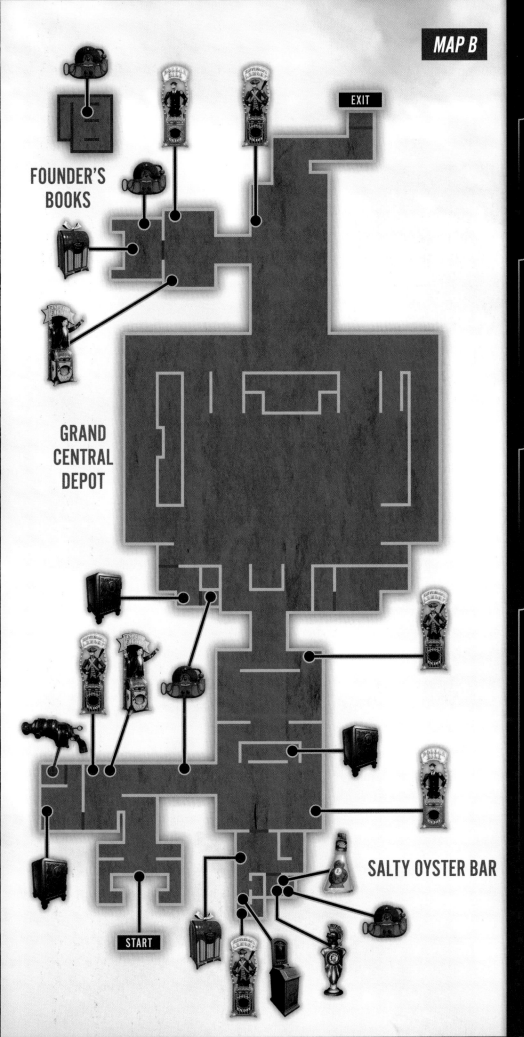

MAP B

FOUNDER'S
BOOKS

GRAND
CENTRAL
DEPOT

EXIT

SALTY OYSTER BAR

START

First Encounters

VOX (CARBINE)
VOX (HAND CANNON)
VOX BEAST (HAIL FIRE)

New Vigors

Return to Sender

New Weaponry

Hail Fire

Collectibles

Infusions
2

Kinectoscopes
1

Voxophones
5

Telescopes
1

Open the Tear for the Water Puddle, then use Shock Jockey to electrocute any nearby Vox.

The Vox destroy the Mosquito quickly, but don't worry. Open another Tear in the area and wait for the Mosquito's Tear to return, and then open it again. Maintain the elevated position on the right-hand walkway and use Undertow, Murder of Crows, and Devil's Kiss to hold back the attackers. This is a great place to snipe from if you have the proper weaponry; otherwise, be patient and let the Mosquito and your Vigors do the heavy lifting. Don't hesitate to double-back to the tunnel near the vending machine if you need to take cover while the Shield regenerates.

PORT PROSPERITY

Head up the steps and have Elizabeth pick the lock on the door. The main entry hall is empty, so take your time looking around. Open the Tear for the freight hook over the door Booker enters from to reach the piece of **Gear** atop the scaffolding. Be sure to have Elizabeth pick the lock on the gate to the left (three lockpicks) to access the Heater and the **Infusion** in the hall on the left.

Go fishing with Undertow and the Heater!

There are two heavily armored Vox in the hallway in the rear of this room. Put the Heater to work by using Undertow to reel in the enemies one by one, then blast them at point-blank range with the Heater. This one-two punch can kill all but the most dominant foes with a single squeeze of the trigger.

TELESCOPE

The Telescope is on the right-hand edge of the
Port Prosperity gondola platform. It's down the stairs
from the Motorized Patriot. Be sure to use it before
riding the gondola.

Head outside to the gondola platform, and open the Tear
for the Motorized Patriot on the right. Descend the far stairs
toward the **Telescope** and have Undertow and a Repeater or
Burstgun on hand. The gondola heading toward Booker is
loaded with enemies, including a Motorized Patriot.
Blast them with Undertow repeatedly while shooting the
Motorized Patriot. Your robotic ally may stay atop the
stairs, but it can fire its Crank Gun from above. Continue
blasting the enemies with Undertow, both to short-circuit the
Motorized Patriot and to knock the others off the platform.

Send Elizabeth to pick the lock on the gondola, and ride it
across to Grand Central Depot, one of Columbia's largest
gondola stations. Ascend the stairs and sneakily lob a Devil's
Kiss fireball at the two Vox standing near the oil slick. This
action guarantees a kill and also helps you earn the "Hazard
Pay" bonus. You can ignite the oil slick more than once; keep
that in mind for when the next two Vox come strolling in.

Undertow works just as well as Shock Jockey against
the Motorized Patriot and can impact multiple foes at once.

Oil slicks amplify the effects of Devil's Kiss
and instantly kill most anything caught in the area.

Enter the ticket office on the left to find a safe (three lockpicks to open it) and the **Hail Fire** weapon, the Vox equivalent of the Pig Volley Gun. The Veni! Vidi! Vigor! machine has new stock, although much of it may be a bit out of your price range at the moment.

Continue down the hall into the main gondola station and note the Gun Automaton on the landing above the ticket counter. Raid the safe inside the ticket office (three lockpicks required), as well as the nearby Salty Oyster Bar. The Salty Oyster Bar does contain a few Founders lying in wait, but it's worth dealing with them to access the **Gear** and **Kinetoscope**.

 Voxophone

COMING FOR COMSTOCK

AUTHOR:	Preston E. Downs
DATE:	July the 7th, 1912
LOCATION:	Port Prosperity

Mr. Comstock, when next we meet, it won't be to parley. See, I went out to that Hall a' Heroes to scalp your "False Shepherd" for you. Turns out, though—DeWitt speaks Sioux. He helped me swap words with this cripple child I've been uh… looking after. Now after hearing how the kid has fared in your city—I'm thinking, when we take your pelt, I'll let him hold the knife.

Rosalind and Robert Lutece

The Chief Scientist of Columbia, Rosalind Lutece devised the technologies responsible for launching the city into the sky. Her work is believed to involve the study of the mysterious dimensional Tears that have begun appearing, seemingly at random, throughout the city.

Little is known about the twin of Rosalind Lutece, the Chief Scientist of Columbia. The two seem utterly inseparable.

Lutece's Brother Arrives in Columbia!

This Kinetoscope is located inside the Salty Oyster Bar, between the two restrooms. You'll need three lockpicks to access this Kinetoscope inside the bar.

GRAND CENTRAL DEPOT

Open the Tear for the Gun Automaton atop the stairs to draw several Vox and a Fireman into combat. The Gun Automaton ends up destroyed, but not before it takes out a few of your foes. Use the ticket office for cover, and plant traps around the base of the stairs to finish your adversaries off.

> **"Once people get their blood up, it ain't easy to settle it down again."**

Ascend the stairs to the main lobby of the station and immediately cast Possession on the Motorized Patriot in the center of the room. Note the numerous Tears around the room (including the Medical Kits near the stairs), and open the Tear for the Tesla coil nearest the most enemies. The Tesla coil works much like Shock Jockey and automatically electrocutes any enemies that get too close. You can really take advantage of this by using Bucking Bronco just as an enemy starts to get zapped. This knocks your opponents into the air and effectively holds them in place for further shock damage. Enemies killed by the Tesla coil count toward the "Hazard Pay" bonus.

Stick close to the stairs that you came up and continue to use the Tesla coils, Bucking Bronco, and your weaponry to dispatch the numerous Vox Populi that attack. Elizabeth calls out a Fireman, the first of two. The same tactic works against the Fireman, but it's also worth hitting him with Undertow and your heavier firepower, such as the RPG from the Salty Oyster Bar.

A Tesla coil, a possessed Motorized Patriot, and the Hail Fire: what more could you ask for?

Stay close to the Tesla coil, and trap enemies in the air with Bucking Bronco for additional damage!

Enter the offices to the left of the Tickets sign and make your way to the back right-hand corner to find a small storage room containing another **Voxophone**. There's also a safe (three lockpicks required) to find in this office. A similar office on the other side of the room contains some valuables, as well.

Instruct Elizabeth to unlock the gate at the far end of the hall, and immediately open the Tear for the Cover directly ahead. There are two Vox Snipers in the area, one on the upper walkway and another on the scaffolding. Hit them with Undertow to knock them off their perch, then take them out at close range. Another option is to blast them with Undertow, then open the Tear for the freight hook near the ceiling above the turnstiles. Leap to the hook, then turn and Sky-Line Strike the snipers.

Use the freight hook Tear to get up above the snipers, then Sky-Line Strike them!

The turnstiles leading out of the area lock behind Booker, so heed Elizabeth's advice and check out the bookstore on the left first (one lockpick). Founders Books contains a piece of **Gear** and two **Voxophones**, one of which makes it possible to access the kitchen in the Salty Oyster Bar. Descend the stairs in the bookstore, and lay a Bucking Bronco or Devil's Kiss trap at the bottom of the stairs for the enemies that come down after you. Listen carefully to the recording on the Voxophone in the lower level of the bookstore.

Voxophone

WHISPERS THROUGH THE WALLS

AUTHOR:	Rosalind Lutece
DATE:	October the 15th, 1893
LOCATION:	Grand Central Depot

The Lutece Field entangled my quantum atom with waves of light, allowing for safe measurement. Sound familiar, brother? That's because you were measuring precisely the same atom from a neighboring world. We used the universe as a telegraph. Switching the field on or off became dots and dashes. Dreadfully slow— but now, you and I could whisper through the wall…

Voxophone

A WINDOW

AUTHOR:	Rosalind Lutece
DATE:	October the 15th, 1893
LOCATION:	Founders Books

Brother, what Comstock failed to understand is that our contraption is a window not into prophecy, but probability. But his money means the Lutece Field could become the Lutece Tear—a window between worlds. A window through which you and I might finally be together.

Fight your way back to the Salty Oyster Bar, and press the button beneath the cash register on the bar. This opens the kitchen door (though the button is only present if you found the "Sally" Voxophone at Founders Books). The kitchen contains another **Voxophone**, an **Infusion**, and the **Return to Sender** Vigor, which allows Booker to deflect and/or absorb and fire back incoming bullets.

Listen to the "Sally" Voxophone, then press the button beneath the register at the bar to access the kitchen.

 Voxophone

SALLY

AUTHOR:	Ronald Frank
DATE:	July the 16th, 1912
LOCATION:	Founders Books

Sally! The bastard snuck in while the Vox was shootin' up the place and took my girl! Got her locked up in the Salty Oyster—his hidden closet he keeps all his "treasures." Just need to hit the button under the register to open it, but…

Voxophone

ONE AND THE SAME

AUTHOR:	Rosalind Lutece
DATE:	October the 15th, 1893
LOCATION:	Financial District

You have been transfused, brother, into a new reality, but your body rejects the cognitive dissonance through confusion and hemorrhage. But we are together, and I will mend you. For what separates us now but a single chromosome?

Put your newfound Vigor to use as you exit the Salty Oyster Bar and fight your way back up the stairs. Head through the turnstile, and approach the locked elevator door on the right. This one can't be picked; it's a combination lock. Elizabeth says most fools keep the combination within 20 feet. Walk to the other end of the hall to the desk nearest the turnstiles to find the combination. Follow Elizabeth back to the elevator and talk to her as she enters the combination. Enter the elevator, and press the button.

Use Return to Sender to absorb enemy gunfire, then throw it back at them!

The combination for the door is located on the desk to the left, near the windows.

★ DOWNTOWN EMPORIA ★

GO TO COMSTOCK HOUSE

THOROUGHFARE

The elevator you're riding into Downtown Emporia is suddenly hit with stray artillery, where you're given a bird's-eye view of the war raging down below. Leap onto the Sky-Line and quickly dismount to the rooftop below, where the Tear for a crate of Salt Phials is located. Top off your Salt Meter here before riding the Sky-Lines up to the battle.

Those few Founders still trying to defend Emporia from the Vox Populi are fighting a gallant battle, but there are several Vox barges inbound, each containing at least one Beast. Things will get chaotic, and there will be a lot of firepower flying Booker's way, but this is a great battle to really put everything you've learned to work. There are two Sky-Lines, a number of upper balconies and rooftops Booker can leap to, and a variety of Tears that allow Booker and Elizabeth to effectively summon a Mosquito, Crank Gun, Medical Kits, and several other weapons.

Ride the Sky-Lines, then perform a Sky-Line Strike at the Vox stationed on the enemy barges.

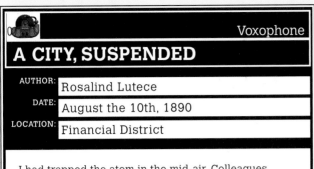

Voxophone

A CITY, SUSPENDED

AUTHOR:	Rosalind Lutece
DATE:	August the 10th, 1890
LOCATION:	Financial District

I had trapped the atom in the mid-air. Colleagues called my Lutece Field quantum levitation, but in fact, it was nothing of the sort. Magicians levitate—my atom simply failed to fall. If an atom could be suspended indefinitely, well—why not an apple? If an apple, why not a city?

Remember that one of the easiest ways to eliminate the Vox threat is to leap from a Sky-Line into a Sky-Line Strike on their barge, then quickly knock them off with a blast of Undertow. Vox can't fly, no matter how righteous Daisy thinks they are.

A Handyman eventually makes his appearance, but you can use the combating forces to your advantage. Use explosive weaponry to deal splash damage to the Handyman and other enemies while the larger brute is focused on other foes. The Handyman can leap far and wide and is also capable of grabbing the Sky-Lines, but you can stay one step ahead of him by moving along the upper Sky-Line between the rooftop and the upper ledge (above the vending machines). This helps you keep an eye on him, fire the RPG from the Sky-Line down at him, and also bait him into grabbing hold of the Sky-Line while Booker leaps off and fires at him.

Loot the corpses and lockboxes, then ride the Sky-Line up to the balcony above the vending machines. Unlock the doors to the hallway (three lockpicks required) to find a **Voxophone** a Handcannon, and a Heater. The vending machines in Downtown Emporia have new stock, so pay them a visit.

Wait for the Handyman to leap up to electrocute the Sky-Line, then open fire on his heart!

Open the Tear for the Decoy to attract any remaining Vox Populi away from Booker while he fights the Handyman.

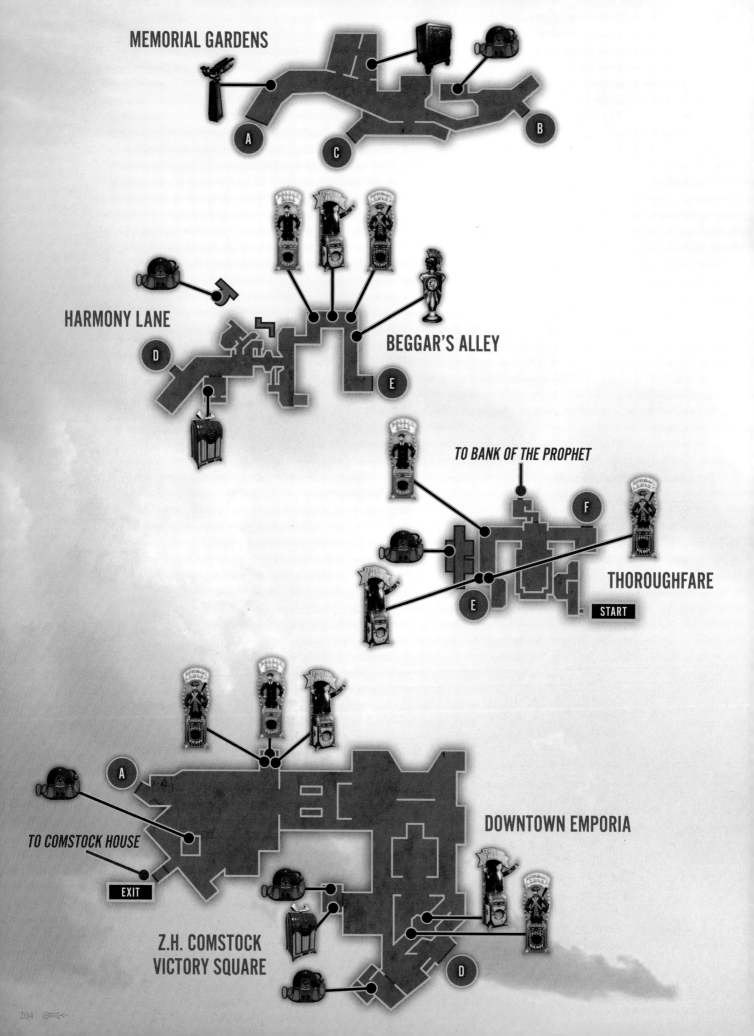

MEMORIAL GARDENS

A

C

B

HARMONY LANE

BEGGAR'S ALLEY

D

E

TO BANK OF THE PROPHET

F

THOROUGHFARE

E

START

A

TO COMSTOCK HOUSE

EXIT

DOWNTOWN EMPORIA

Z.H. COMSTOCK
VICTORY SQUARE

D

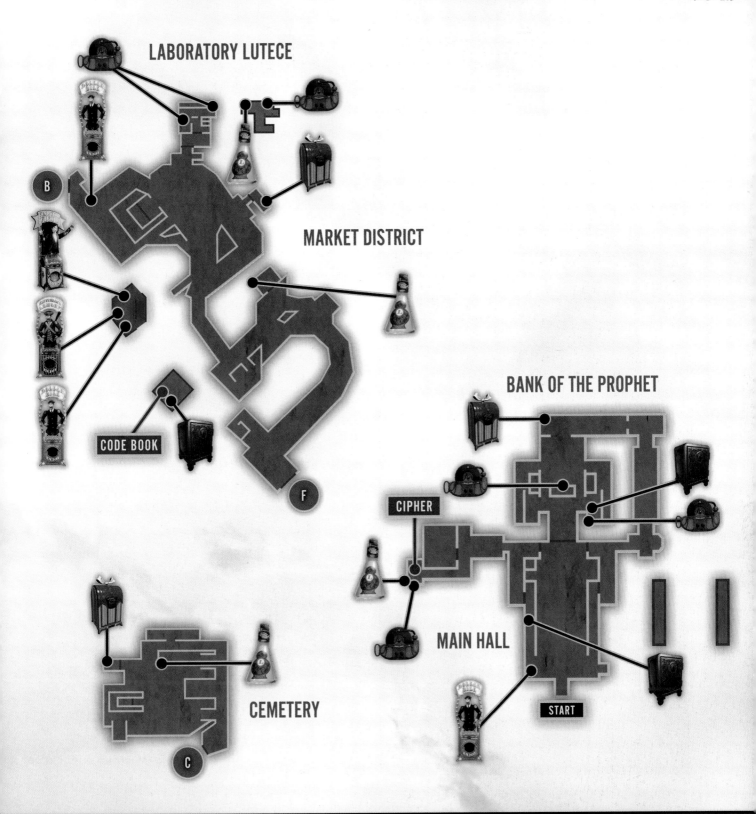

LABORATORY LUTECE

MARKET DISTRICT

CODE BOOK

BANK OF THE PROPHET

CIPHER

MAIN HALL

START

CEMETERY

B

F

C

First Encounters

SIREN

Collectibles

Infusions
3

Voxophones
12

Kinectoscopes
-

Telescopes
1

The Columbia Savings Bank is locked up tight for now (you can go inside the lobby, but that's it), thereby leaving you one of two directions to go: either through Beggar's Alley to Harmony Lane via the left-hand gate, or through the Market District to the right. There will be plenty of time to explore the Market District on your return (you'll essentially have to perform one and one half loops through Downtown Emporia), so take the path nearest the three vending machines first.

HARMONY LANE

Visit the vending machines in quiet Beggar's Alley leading past the shuttered shops, and continue up the stairs on the left. Elizabeth suddenly alerts you to a sniper on the rooftops in Harmony Lane, and he's not alone! There's a sniper high above the ground in the distance. The glimmer of his optical scope gives away his position. Open the Tear for the Sniper Rifle near the sign, and take cover. Use the Sniper Rifle and Return to Sender for protection, and take out the four Vox snipers manning the rooftops in the distance. Open the Tear for the Decoy in the center of the walkway, and stick close to the sign for protection. The snipers run around and take cover, so follow them with the scope and wait for a clean shot.

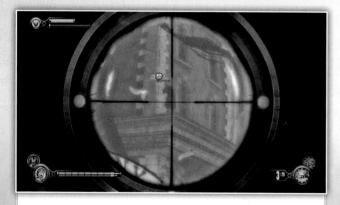

Elizabeth often identifies the enemy sniper with an on-screen icon.

MINUTEMAN'S ARMORY: NEW STOCK!

Item	Description	Price
Hail Fire: Radius Increase	Increases Hail Fire explosion radius by 100%.	$415
Burstgun: Recoil Decrease	Decreases Burstgun recoil by 60%.	$822
RPG: Speed Boost	Increases RPG projectile speed by 100%.	$333
Volley Gun: Radius Increase	Increases Volley Gun explosion radius by 50%.	$536
Volley Gun: Damage Boost 2	Increases Volley Gun damage by 25%.	$522
Burstgun: Damage Boost 2	Increases Burstgun damage by 25%.	$423
Repeater: Damage Boost 2	Increases Repeater damage by 25%.	$416
Hail Fire: Damage Boost 2	Increases Hail Fire damage by 25%.	$688
Heater: Damage Boost 2	Increases Heater damage by 25%.	$554
Shotgun: Spread Boost	Increases Shotgun cone width by 20%.	$360
Hand Cannon: Recoil Decrease	Decreases Hand Cannon recoil by 20%	$350
Volley Gun: Clip Increase	Increases Volley Gun clip size by 100%.	$740
Burstgun: Ammo Increase	Increases Burstgun reserve ammo by 50%.	$672
Repeater: Clip Increase	Increases Repeater clip size by 100%.	$449
Heater: Spread Boost	Increases Heater cone width by 20%.	$467
Hail Fire: Clip Increase	Increases Hail Fire clip size by 60%.	$399

Hold onto the Sniper Rifle a little longer. Take your time poking around Harmony Lane's abandoned homes and shops, but keep your eyes out for the occasional baton-wielding civilian. You'll find a **Voxophone** in the wine cellar on the right-hand side of the street and a piece of **Gear** upstairs inside the shop on the left.

BEYOND REDEMPTION

AUTHOR:	Lady Comstock
DATE:	December the 28th, 1894
LOCATION:	Harmony Lane

Tonight, the Prophet moved against his political enemies. He preaches mercy, but 40 souls lie tonight dead, in unmarked graves. If a man was ever unworthy of grace, it would be my husband. But when I was beyond redemption, he offered it anyway. How can I deny forgiveness to one who, with love, granted it to me?

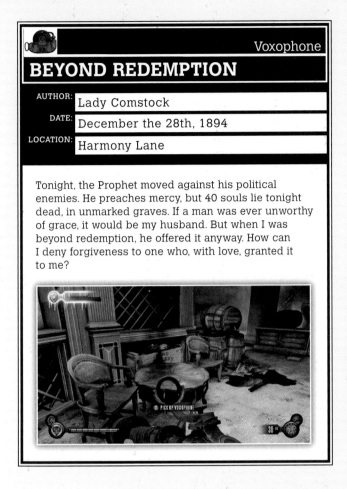

DOWNTOWN EMPORIA

The path ahead is crawling with warring groups of Founders and Vox Populi, but Elizabeth has quite a few Tears she can open to aid you in the battle. Start by opening the one for the Gun Automaton on the stone arch in the center of the street. Shoulder your Sniper Rifle and strafe up the stairs on the left for a clean shot at a few Vox Populi as they start approaching. Lay some traps down near the stairs and by the bridge to catch any who try to charge the Gun Automaton.

Don't hesitate to accept supplies from Elizabeth. The battles that follow are only going to get tougher!

Open a Tear for either of the freight hooks, then leap from it to the one of the higher attachment points so Booker can gain the balcony on either side of the street. This gives you a great vantage point for sniping and also buys time for the Gun Automaton's Tear to reactivate.

Once you reach a balcony to snipe from, reopen the Tear for the Gun Automaton.

There are no enemies in this area right now, so make your way to the far end of the downtown area and head up the stairs on the left. Be sure to explore the locked shop (three lockpicks required) across from the theater to find a **Voxophone** and a piece of **Gear**.

Z.H. COMSTOCK VICTORY SQUARE

A mighty battle had taken place on the stairs in Victory Square, leaving dozens of bodies and countless bullet holes behind. Search the corpses for cash to spend at the vending machines off to the right, then climb the steps past the statue of Lady Comstock and approach the gate. The security scanner recognizes Elizabeth for Lady Comstock by appearance, but the hand print doesn't match, so the gate won't open.

Lead Elizabeth to the gate at Comstock House.

Voxophone

THE TRUE COLOR OF MY SKIN

AUTHOR:	Zachary Hale Comstock
DATE:	December the 29th, 1908
LOCATION:	Downtown Emporia

In front of all the men, the sergeant looked at me and said, "Your family tree shelters a teepee or two, doesn't it, son?" This lie, this calumny, had followed me all my life. From that day, no man truly called me comrade. It was only when I burnt the teepees with the squaws inside, did they take me as one of their own. Only blood can redeem blood.

Voxophone

PEN PAL

AUTHOR:	Constance Field
DATE:	July the 20th, 1902
LOCATION:	Z.H. Comstock Victory Square

This is for the Miracle Child. Hello! I'm sorry your mother, Lady Comstock, is dead. (I think she is altogether better than mine.) Since you live there, can you tell me why the tower has been closed? People say it's poor weather, then the pox, then a haunting. If it is a secret, I promise not to tell a soul. — your pen friend, Constance.

FIND LADY COMSTOCK'S CRYPT

TELESCOPE

This Telescope is at the north end of Memorial Gardens, on the edge of the road closest to Z.H. Comstock Victory Square. This is one of the final Telescopes in Columbia, so enjoy the view while you can.

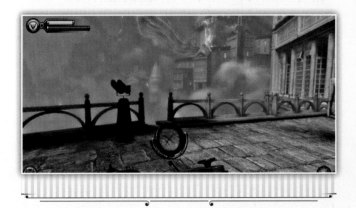

MEMORIAL GARDENS

Descend the stairs and head left toward the overhead sign for Memorial Gardens. Visit the **Telescope** on the left before locating the Kinetoscope near the blown-out storefront (if you missed it at the arcade in Battlefield Bay).

Proceed along the road until you see the entrance to the cemetery on the right, just before the fissure in the road. Continue to the right, around the perimeter of the gardens, and swap out your Sniper Rifle for the Shotgun in the Tear (if you were still carrying it). Continue to the end of the walkway and approach the gated crypt in the corner, where you can find the **Gear**. Light the torches flanking the gate with Devil's Kiss to open the puzzling lock on this gate.

Lady Comstock's final resting place is in the center of the cemetery, but don't approach it just yet. First top off your health at either of the Tears that have Medical Kits. Approach the gate to Lady Comstock's crypt and open the Tear for the lock on the gate. Elizabeth automatically picks the lock, but she'll wait for you to push the gate open. Open the coffin once Elizabeth backs away.

Cast a Devil's Kiss fireball at each of the torches on this crypt to open the gate and get the Gear.

Open the Tear for the crypt's lock, and head inside. Interact with the padlock on the coffin when appropriate.

★Siren★

MEMORIAL GARDENS SIREN'S VITALS

Health	Ranged Damage	Melee Damage	Special Damage	Special Attack
15994	N/A	985	N/A	N/A

The Ghost of Lady Comstock is what the Lutece twins would certainly call a Siren. A Siren is a spectral creature that can fly across the landscape like a wisp, only faintly visible to the naked eye, until she begins her song. That is when she is most vulnerable. The Siren sings a song that raises the dead, bringing them back to the land of the living, where they are all too anxious to attack those who attack the Siren.

Keep after the Siren, and open fire on her wherever she stops to sing. Use the Burstgun if she flies up onto one of the walkways, and employ the Shotgun if you manage to keep close by. The Siren can only deal damage with a melee strike, and she's unlikely to get too close to Booker, but the risen dead certainly pose a threat. Run for a Medical Kit from either Tear whenever you can, and stay on the ground to make getting them easier. The resurrected dead die easily, and you can keep yourself equipped with Salts if you equip the Blood to Salt Gear.

Target the Siren's body as it becomes opaque, and open fire. It's possible to damage her quickly to interrupt her raising the dead; otherwise, you'll have to fight three or four risen corpses while she flies off translucently. Unleash Murder of Crows or Bucking Bronco on the risen dead, since it makes killing them that much easier (or buys you time to ignore them and focus on the Siren). The Siren is particularly vulnerable to Devil's Kiss attacks. Try to time your attack with her reaching a crescendo in her singing. It's possible to inflict enough damage while she's singing to force her to move on without having resuscitated any more dead. The dead she has brought back instantly return to the world of the deceased upon her defeat.

FIND THE THREE TEARS

Voxophone

OUT OF THE THIN AIR

AUTHOR: Jeremiah Fink

DATE: November the 14th, 1894

LOCATION: Market District

Dear brother, these holes in the thin air continue to pay dividends. I know not which musician you borrow your notes from, but if he has half the genius of the biologist I now observe, well…then you are to be the Mozart of Columbia.

Exit the cemetery the way Booker came in. The Lutece twins then brief you on what you must do. Continue down the road in Memorial Gardens to the right, toward the building you see bobbing up and down. Loop around to the hole in Albert Fink's music store. Wait for the hole in the bobbing building to come level with the road, and leap into the structure to find a Locksmith Bag and a **Voxophone** near the piano. Continue up the road, and turn right into the Market District.

MARKET DISTRICT

Descend the stairs to the Market District, and have a look around the block. Both routes lead down to a fountain in the center of a small plaza. Take out the Vox patrolling the area, then collect the Silver Eagles and lockpicks from the small grocer's shop near the stairs.

Voxophone

A THEORY ON OUR "DEATH"

AUTHOR: Rosalind Lutece

DATE: November the 1st, 1909

LOCATION: Market District

Comstock has sabotaged our contraption. Yet, we are not dead. A theory: we are scattered amongst the possibility space. But my brother and I are together, and so, I am content. He is not. The business with the girl lies unresolved. But perhaps there is one who can finish it in our stead.

Voxophone

ON THE ENTROPY OF GENES

AUTHOR: Rosalind Lutece

DATE: July the 3rd, 1893

LOCATION: Market District

Comstock seems to have been made sterile by simple exposure to our contraption. A theory: just as sexual reproduction can de-emphasize the traits of each parent, so goes the effect of multiple realities on our own. Your traits dissipate until they become unrecognizable or cease to exist.

Follow the ghostly footprints up the steps and into the house to the left of the fountain, and head up the stairs to find an **Infusion** and the first of three **Voxophones** in the building housing Laboratory Lutece. It's on the floor near the bed. These Voxophones go a long way toward helping you understand the nature of the Lutece twins and their relation with Comstock. Open the Tear in the contraption to move one step closer to gaining entry to Comstock House. This also nets you the third Voxophone in this house.

CHILD OF SCIENCE

AUTHOR:	Rosalind Lutece
DATE:	January the 4th, 1895
LOCATION:	Market District

Lady Comstock seems to believe the child is a result of some errant act of carnality between myself and her beloved Prophet. I told the poor woman the truth: that the child was a product of our little contraption. But I think she found that less believable than her delusion.

The first of the three Tears is in the lower level of Lutece Laboratory, in the Market District.

Collect the piece of **Gear** from inside the locked store near the Lutece Lab before moving on. Continue down the stairs within the Market District, and have a look inside the bottling store on the far left corner, near the edge of the city, to find an **Infusion**. From there, follow the path around to the right as it goes past the fire. Enter Hudson's Clothier, and descend the stairs to find the Code Book for a cipher that you soon encounter in the bank.

The Code Book in the basement helps you unlock the hidden alcove in the bank later on.

Unlock the gate up ahead, beyond the fire, to return to the main area where Booker first arrived via the elevator. Approach the bank in the center slowly, as two Zealots are set to attack. Quickly knock them back with Undertow or Bucking Bronco, then unleash Devil's Kiss on them. Finish them off with your explosive weapon but know that you can flee to the safety of the Sky-Lines if you need to. The Zealots can't hurt you on the Sky-Lines. Several Vox and a Fireman attack after the Zealots; kill them if you want, or simply head inside the bank. A Tear for a Gun Automaton that wasn't present earlier can come in handy.

Two Zealots are set to attack on the stairs leading into the bank!

BANK OF THE PROPHET

Unlock the door to the bank, and head inside. The three Kinetoscopes positioned near the wall are the same as those you've encountered previously. Enter the elevator—the gate has since been ripped open, given all of the fighting taking place in this area—and press the button to descend to the main hall.

The main hall is crawling with Vox, but you have some time to set up a proper attack before they notice Booker. Run up the stairs on the left to reach the Sniper Rifle on the balcony. Hurry back down and place Devil Kiss traps on the floor, near the statues, and set to sniping the Vox in the distance. You can catch the Vox by surprise and pick off a few with the Sniper Rifle before they draw within reach.

Move to the base of the stairs,
lay down some Vigor traps, and start sniping!

Finish off the stragglers with Sky-Line Strikes
via the freight hook Tear.

"I got to get me a job in the Prophet business."

Loot the cash registers and desks in the offices flanking the main hall, then head left down the hallway in the rear, opposite the direction of the ghostly footprints. Locate the **Gear** in the room at the end of the hall, and continue on to the small office around the corner.

THE FINAL VOX CODE

You found the Code Book in the basement of Hudson's Clothier; now, it's time to put it to use. Make your way down the left-hand hall in the bank's main hall to the small office in the rear. The word "Hoarder" has been scrawled in red paint on the wall, above a series of bloody bullet holes.

Approach the desk as Elizabeth reads from the Code Book and tells you to type the word "Vox" on the typewriter. Do as she says to reveal a hidden alcove off to the right. The hideaway contains an **Infusion**, a **Voxophone**, and a Burstgun.

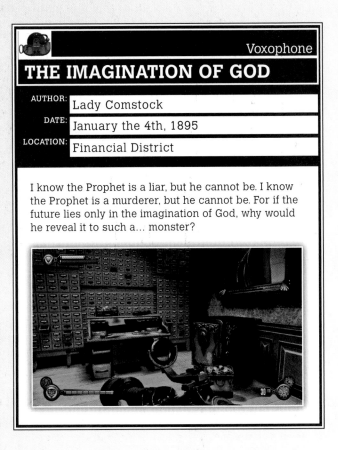

Voxophone

THE IMAGINATION OF GOD

AUTHOR: Lady Comstock

DATE: January the 4th, 1895

LOCATION: Financial District

I know the Prophet is a liar, but he cannot be. I know the Prophet is a murderer, but he cannot be. For if the future lies only in the imagination of God, why would he reveal it to such a... monster?

Continue to search the area for loot, and return the way Booker came, back to the main hall. Now, it's time to head to the right and continue to the entrance to the vault area. Pick up the piece of **Gear** in the back corner of the hallway before dropping off the edge into the vault area.

COLUMBIA SAVINGS BANK VAULT

You can see the Tear—it's right ahead of you—but you must first defeat the Zealot that attacks. Use the Burstgun to hit it if it flees to the rafters, but otherwise, keep a more potent gun like the Heater on hand. Kill the Zealot, then open the Tear in the Vault and listen closely to what is said. Collect the **Voxophone** that appears where the Tear was. Locate another **Voxophone** tucked behind the safe (three lockpicks required) in the office to the left.

Kill the Zealot, then open the Tear at the top of the steps.

 Voxophone

A BROKEN CIRCLE

AUTHOR: Zachary Hale Comstock

DATE: September the 10th, 1893

LOCATION: Financial District

The archangel tells me that Columbia will only survive so long as my line sits the throne. Yet Lady Comstock produces no child. I have done what a man can do, yet there is no child! I have asked Lutece about the matter, but even she refuses to help.

Voxophone

NO LONGER

AUTHOR: Lady Comstock

DATE: January the 5th, 1895

LOCATION: Financial District

Lutece says the bastard is a creation not of her womb, but of some unholy science. I do not know which is true. The child is no more divine than I. What says that for my husband's prophecy? He begs my silence, but I can only offer him forgiveness. But with repentance need come truth. I can suffer his lies no longer.

The large vault door swings open, revealing another Siren in the main hall. Immediately open fire with the Burstgun while casting Devil's Kiss and Murder of Crows in her direction. The Siren flies across the main hall, sometimes even moving to the upper balconies above the offices on the side, but she won't go very far. Use your Vigors to fend off the risen Vox while you continue to pepper her with Burstgun fire. Lay traps down while she's on the move to provide protection from melee assaults, then lob additional Devil's Kiss fireballs at the Siren when she begins to sing.

Cast Devil's Kiss and Murder of Crows at the Siren and her risen dead.

The Siren is most vulnerable to attacks while raising the dead. Fire!

DOWNTOWN EMPORIA

Exit the bank, and head right through the Thoroughfare and Harmony Lane, just as you had done when you first arrived in this section of Emporia. Continue up the steps to Downtown Emporia, where you find Cunningham Studios at the very top of the stairs, directly in front of you. Enter the photo studio, and open the third and final Tear to learn another piece of the puzzle and find yet another **Voxophone**.

The final Tear is located inside the photography studio.

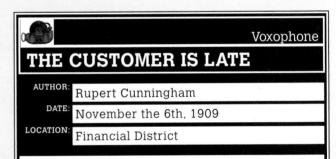

Voxophone

THE CUSTOMER IS LATE

AUTHOR: Rupert Cunningham

DATE: November the 6th, 1909

LOCATION: Financial District

Estelle: "That's insanity. What proof would you have that Mr. Fink would hurt the Luteces?"
Rupert: "The Luteces told me."
Estelle: "The Luteces? When?"
Rupert: "Yesterday. Yesterday morning."
Estelle: "Rupert... they've been dead these seven days..."

RETURN TO COMSTOCK HOUSE

Z.H. COMSTOCK VICTORY SQUARE

Fight your way back up the streets of Downtown Emporia to return to Z.H. Comstock Victory Square. Elizabeth has learned a lot by opening those Tears and takes a few moments to get some emotions off her chest near the statue of Lady Comstock. Let Elizabeth have this moment—she's earned it. Meanwhile, make sure your guns are reloaded and that you have Devil's Kiss and Murder of Crows or Bucking Bronco on hand.

Lady Comstock's Ghost reappears as a Siren one final time, but now she's got an entire army of corpses at her disposal. Immediately open the Tear for the Mosquito flying overhead, and cast Murder of Crows at the first batch of risen dead. The Mosquito's presence helps to cut down on the number of risen dead you have to deal with. Nevertheless, it still pays to cast Murder of Crows or Bucking Bronco at them to slow them down and make them more susceptible to gunfire. Focus your attention on the Siren as she floats around the stairs in front of Comstock House. She can be bested with the same tactics as earlier, although this fight does tend to go on longer because of the expansive space. Loot the corpses of the slain undead to keep your supplies topped off.

Although many of the risen dead attack with batons, Booker can easily defeat them.

Try engulfing the Siren in Devil's Kiss and Hail Fire explosions simultaneously!

The Siren's death triggers a powerful burst of energy that rips the gate to the Comstock House from its hinges. Father Comstock can't be far. Lead Elizabeth into the house; it's time for her to go home.

BLOOD IN THE STREETS

The Vox Populi have come en masse to Emporia in search of Comstock's head. Whether or not they achieved their mission remains to be seen, but you have. You not only succeeded in finding a way inside Comstock House, but you also helped a young woman come to grips with the anger she's been harboring.

FLIGHT OF THE SONGBIRD

★ COMSTOCK HOUSE ★

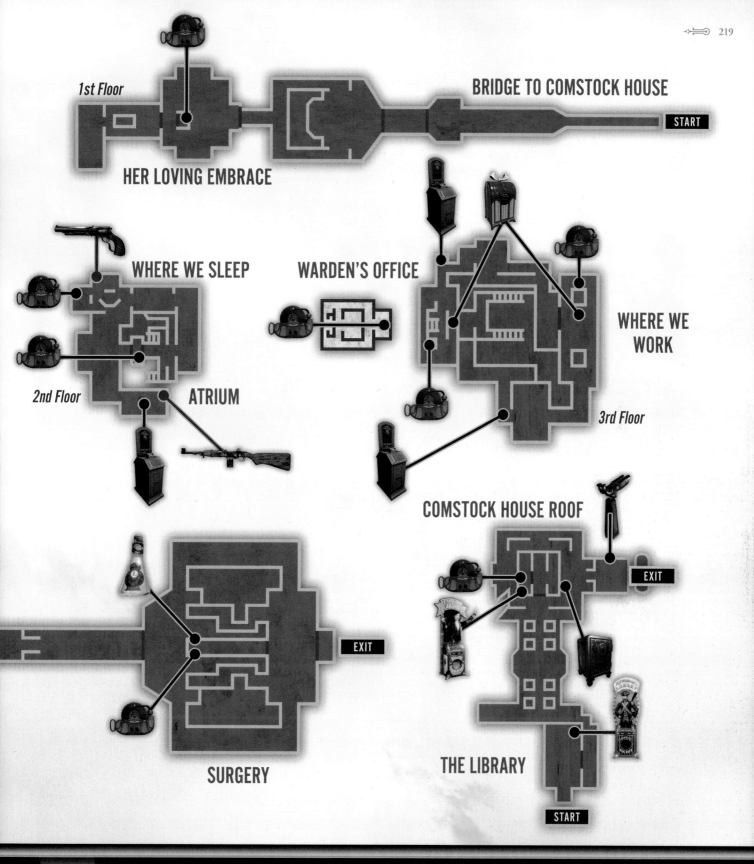

BRIDGE TO COMSTOCK HOUSE

1st Floor

START

HER LOVING EMBRACE

WHERE WE SLEEP

WARDEN'S OFFICE

WHERE WE WORK

2nd Floor

ATRIUM

3rd Floor

COMSTOCK HOUSE ROOF

EXIT

SURGERY

EXIT

THE LIBRARY

START

First Encounters

BOY OF SILENCE

Collectibles

Infusions

1

Voxophones

8

Kinectoscopes

3

Telescopes

1

Spared… for now.

BRIDGE TO COMSTOCK HOUSE

Comstock House is on its own floating island in the sky, built upon the three faces of the Founding Fathers. The island is connected to Emporia by two mighty cables from a bridge. Pull the lever at the end of the bridge, amidst the lightning storm, to reel in the house. As soon as Booker pulls the lever, Songbird arrives on the scene and throws him through the window in the belfry of the building in Victory Square, high above the hand-scan gate. Booker wakes to the sight of Elizabeth pleading with Songbird not to hurt him, and Songbird accepting her bargain.

You need to get across the bridge to Comstock House in a hurry if you're to ever see Elizabeth again. Move carefully to the hole in the wall where Songbird was, and leap to either of the freight hooks down below. From there, drop to the bridge near the lever and wait for the drawbridge to lower. Cross the bridge toward the Tear at the base of the stairs, and continue up the steps and through the doors to the home.

Booker dies if he leaps directly to the bridge below, so be sure to use either of the hooks first.

There are numerous Tears throughout Comstock House that help reveal elements of the story that you won't want to miss.

SEARCH FOR ELIZABETH

The Tears in Comstock House are Elizabeth's trail, a trail she's left just for you. Continue through the doors to the room with the large Elizabeth statue. Loop around the candlelit corridor on either side of the statue to find another Tear behind it, and continue through the door to the next area.

★Boy of Silence★

COMSTOCK HOUSE BOY OF SILENCE'S VITALS

Health	Ranged Damage	Melee Damage	Special Damage	Special Attack
N/A	N/A	N/A	N/A	N/A

The Boy of Silence is an alarm that whips the home's crazed denizens into a frenzy. There is no way to harm the Boy of Silence; all you can do is try to sneak past him without being detected. Use the available cover and monitor the flashlight-like beam of light that shines from his eyes. This light turns yellow if the Boy of Silence starts to detects your presence—immediately run and hide before it alarms the others. Shooting him, casting Possession, or making any sudden movements near the Boy of Silence immediately causes him to go on alert and vanish, but not before an army of crazed foes comes rushing forth to attack.

The wild attackers that rush forward aren't necessarily hard to kill, but there is very little ammo and even fewer Salts available in Comstock House. And Elizabeth isn't there to keep you supplied. Make your shots count, and only use Vigors that consume small quantities of Salts, such as Murder of Crows, Shock Jockey, and Bucking Bronco. The accompanying maps in this chapter reveal the locations of weapons that will almost certainly come in handy—this is no time to hold onto weapons for which you have no ammo!

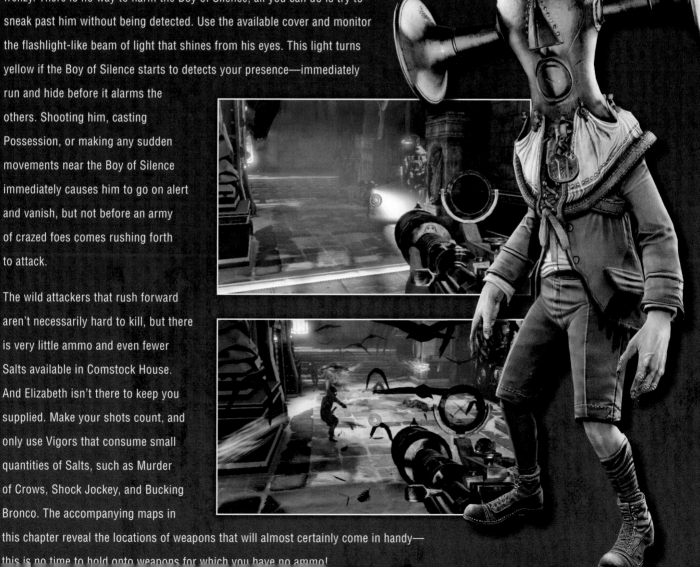

The Boy of Silence was standing watch by the door to a restricted area. Even with the Boy of Silence chased off, the door remains locked. Booker must head to the Warden's Office on the third floor to unlock the door. Use the intercom beside the door to call for the elevator.

Use the intercom near the heavy metal gate to summon a nearby elevator that can take you to the Atrium.

Voxophone

A LEASH

AUTHOR:	Elizabeth
DATE:	—
LOCATION:	Her Loving Embrace

I suppose the Siphon is a kind of leash. Yes, my father put it on me, but when the time came, neither did I remove it myself. What would happen if I took off the leash, and I found I was… as obedient as ever?

GO TO WARDEN'S OFFICE

THE ATRIUM

Exit the elevator and approach the Boy of Silence. He'll once again incite a riot among the dead and vanish into the ether if he senses your presence. Continue to use your abilities to take out the melee-fighters incited by the Boy of Silence, and search their corpses for a chance at some loot, provided you've equipped the proper Gear, since the Lunatics never have loot otherwise. A nearby Hand Cannon and Carbine will certainly come in handy.

Murder of Crows isn't the cheapest Vigor to cast, but it does a great job of stopping the rioting attackers.

From the elevator, head to the south to find a **Kinetoscope** and Carbine near another Tear, then head back and follow the "Where We Weep" and "Where We Sleep" signs around the floor in a clockwise direction to find a **Voxophone**. The room is filled with coffins, the adjacent room a furnace and crematorium with dozens of shrouded bodies waiting to be incinerated. Visit each of the Tears to hear a memory from the past.

Sunrise

Exit the elevator in the Atrium, on the second floor, and head to the dead-end on the left to find this Kinetoscope. It's located near the column by the Carbine.

Voxophone

THE VALUE OF CHOICE

AUTHOR: Elizabeth

DATE: —

LOCATION: Where We Weep

Our minds are born festering with sin. Some are so blighted, they will never find redemption. The mind must be pulled up from the roots. My children are without blame, without fault—and without choice. For what is the value of will when the spirit is found wanting?

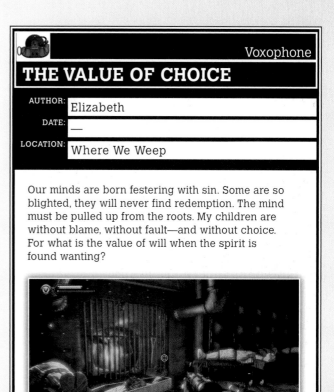

Continue through the bathing room to the dormitory, where numerous dead roam in eternal horror. A Boy of Silence stands at the rear of the room, atop a bed. You can try to sneak past his detection as he rotates in place, or you can simple open fire on him and start the battle. Defeat the crazed attackers by sticking to either end of the room to keep them all in front of you. Don't hesitate to retreat through the previous rooms if necessary. This is the longest of the Boy of Silence battles, and you may start to run low on supplies. The corpses of the attackers disappear within moments after you've killed them. The only way to search their bodies for loot is to do it within seconds of their death.

Use the Carbine to soften them up considerably as they approach, then finish them with a melee strike.

Exit the dormitory to the other side of the Atrium, at the base of the two sets of stairs that lead up to the third floor. Immediately take possession of either of the two Gun Automatons on the landing atop the stairs, and open fire on the other. Stay close to the dormitory entrance and ready yourself for battle with a Zealot. Try to keep the remaining Gun Automaton possessed to aid you, as several of the facility's orderlies are set to attack alongside the Zealot.

Loop around the third floor in a counter-clockwise direction to the **Kinetoscope** at the end of the hall near the entrance to the workshops.

Open fire on the distracted Gun Automaton, and try to keep the other one intact so it can aid you.

The workshops contain numerous handicrafts like machines for making banners, lots of paint and masks, and plaster. You'll also find a Shotgun, **Gear,** and a **Voxophone** in the area "Where We Work." Defeat the foes stirred into action by the Boy of Silence, and complete a thorough sweep of the room to find the collectibles. Depending on the upgrades you've made, the Shotgun may be capable of dropping two or more attackers with a single squeeze of the trigger—and it's always good to conserve ammo!

Enter the room with the projector and the skipping phonograph, and clamber up and over the debris to the broken observation room nearby. This isn't just "Where We Learn," but it's also home to the Columbia's final **Kinetoscope.** The Warden's Office isn't much farther.

Hummingbirds

This Kinetoscope is located on the third floor of the Atrium, down the hall from the stairs and near the entrance to the workshops. Find it in the shadows, to the right of the shop entrance.

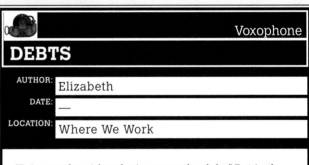

DEBTS

Voxophone

AUTHOR: Elizabeth

DATE: —

LOCATION: Where We Work

"Bring us the girl and wipe away the debt." But in the end, he is the one who'll have to pay down all of our accounts, won't he? Where does his guilt start... and mine end?

Battleship Falls

This Kinetoscope reveals a moment from Columbia's future-past, which only adds to Booker's confusion about time and space. It's on the right-hand side of the observation room, next to the room with the projector.

	Voxophone

A LAST CHANCE

AUTHOR:	Elizabeth
DATE:	—
LOCATION:	Warden's Office

As the days pass, I believe less in God and more in Lutece. My powers shrivel as my regrets blossom. All of this because my father failed me. By the time I realized how far I'd gone, it was too late to stop it. But there is still one last chance at redemption—for both of us.

WARDEN'S OFFICE

The winding path you took has led back to the room near the top of the stairs with the gun turrets, but now, you're on the other side of the bars. Check the desks in the area for items: you can loot the one in the center, at the very least. Head up the stairs toward the signs pointing to "Processing," and check the office on the left for a **Voxophone** near the projector. Continue along, proceeding around the walkway as it loops past the stairs you just came up to the Warden's Office. You'll also find a new piece of **Gear** in this area: the Rising Bloodlust hat. This hat increases weapon damage after each successive kill (up to five) and lasts for 10 seconds—a truly special item!

The Warden's Office has many searchable cabinets and represents your best chance for collecting more ammo, Salts, and money in a long time. Stock up if you can, and don't miss the **Voxophone** on the chair on the left. Approach the controls near the window and pull the lever to open access to the Restricted Area back on the first floor of the atrium. Fight your way back down the stairs to the second floor, collect the **Voxophone** in the elevator, and ride it back to the lower level.

Pull the lever in front of the computer terminal inside the Warden's Office.

SMOTHERED IN THE CRIB

AUTHOR: Elizabeth

DATE: —

LOCATION: Warden's Office

What I've done cannot be undone. I cannot stop what I have put in motion. But perhaps I can keep it from ever starting. He was my first hope, and now… he is my last.

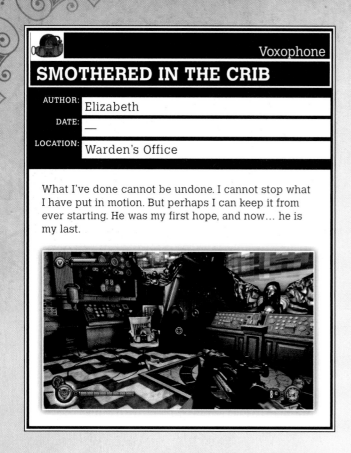

ENDING IT

AUTHOR: Elizabeth

DATE: —

LOCATION: The Atrium

Tomorrow, the leash comes off, because all of this has to end. But even if I destroy the Siphon, will I be strong enough to see all the doors, and open whichever I choose? And if I bring him here, who is to say that he would be any match for the monsters I have created?

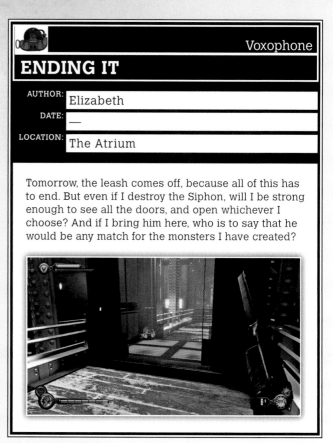

FIND ELIZABETH

Exit the elevator, and go through the recently unlocked security door. Listen to the Lutece Twins in the adjoining room, then continue up the snow-covered hallway to the silhouette in the distance. Take the card when it's offered.

Someone you've been looking for is waiting by the balcony.

SURGERY

Continue down the hall and through the doors to find Elizabeth: present-day Elizabeth, that is. Comstock is watching from his office, making sure the two doctors have Elizabeth properly strapped in and connected to the Siphon. Two more doctors supervise from elevated rooms, where they each control one of the two inhibitors needed to power the equipment. It's up to Booker to shut those inhibitors down and break Elizabeth free!

There's no way into the glass-enclosed room without first disabling the inhibitors.

Head left into the brightly lit, elegant hallway, and continue up the stairs, making sure to use Possession on the Gun Automaton in the hall as you go. Numerous Founders are stationed in the back hallway, along with two additional Gun Automatons. Use Possession and Return to Sender to stay safe, and locate the two airlocks flanking the locked door to Comstock's office.

Enter either of the airlocks and head up the stairs to the platform overlooking Elizabeth, and pull the lever to turn off the first inhibitor. You'll find a much-needed Salts Phial in each of these observation rooms housing the machine controls. A Motorized Patriot is waiting in the hallway leading back to Elizabeth after the first lever is pulled, so be ready for it.

Duck into the narrow hallway for cover, and blast away the Founders as they funnel toward you.

Shoot the scientist, grab the Salts Phial, and pull the lever to disable the machine.

Make your way back down the hall to the room where you first saw Elizabeth. With the machines turned off, she was able to open a Tear and take care of the remaining doctors herself, breaking the glass wall in the process. Climb the pile of debris serving as a ramp up to Elizabeth, and help release her from the straps. Press the corresponding button when prompted to yank the Siphon out of her back and to help tighten her corset.

Lead Elizabeth out of the operating area and up the stairs to the elevator leading to the roof. Have her first pick the lock to the small room (three lockpicks) looking out over the surgery area to find an **Infusion** and **Voxophone**. With the items in hand, have Elizabeth pick the lock on the golden gate and ride the elevator to the library.

The library has seen heavy battle. Corpses line the floor, and guns lie everywhere. Fortunately, there is a wealth of desks and cabinets to raid and corpses to loot. Load up on ammo and Salts, and use the Minuteman's Armory to purchase any extra upgrades you can afford. Pick the lock on the balcony doors, and head outside.

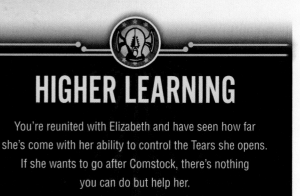

HIGHER LEARNING

You're reunited with Elizabeth and have seen how far she's come with her ability to control the Tears she opens. If she wants to go after Comstock, there's nothing you can do but help her.

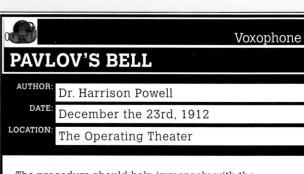

Voxophone

PAVLOV'S BELL

AUTHOR: Dr. Harrison Powell

DATE: December the 23rd, 1912

LOCATION: The Operating Theater

The procedure should help immensely with the... issues we've had with the girl. Once the device is implanted, any effort on her part to... alter the state of things will emit a most painful electric shock. Pavlov made a dog salivate. We'll make this one weep.

BOARD COMSTOCK'S FLAGSHIP

COMSTOCK HOUSE ROOF

Take the Volley Gun on the crate as the Hand of the Prophet, Comstock's zeppelin, deploys what appear to be large bombs. But they're not bombs; they're actually large pods that are intended to land safely and deploy Motorized Patriots. Dozens of human enemies have made their way onto the roof, as well, with many coming from a police barge that docks in the far right corner.

Use Possession on the first Motorized Patriot you spot, then grab the Volley Gun and run into cover.

There are numerous Tears available on the roof, including Cover, a Mosquito in the distance, and a Rocket Automaton up close on the left. Open the Tear for the police barricade first to help provide cover from the initial surge. Possess one of the early attackers so that you have someone nearby watching your back while you use the Volley Gun to lob shots at those in the distance. Keep Shock Jockey on hand whenever the Motorized Patriots come into view.

Take cover behind the barricade, and lob your Volley Gun shots at the enemies as they approach.

Alternate opening the Tears for the Mosquito and Rocket Automaton as they are destroyed, allowing you to stay in cover and save ammo.

Put down the initial crush of enemies, then open the Tear for the Mosquito in the distance to soften things up further. The Mosquito may be destroyed rather quickly, making it a prime time to open the Tear for the Rocket Automaton while the Mosquito Tear reactivates. Keep the Return to Sender Vigor on hand when chasing down any remaining Founders, especially if you have the Ammo Absorb upgrade.

Eliminate any enemies near the police barge to finish clearing the rooftop of the Founder forces, but don't board the barge just yet! First, have Elizabeth pick the lock on the door (three lockpicks required) near the flags, and go inside. The room on the right contains a safe (one lockpick needed), and the one on the left contains both a **Voxophone** and a Veni! Vidi! Vigor! Machine. Exit the interior and pay a visit to the **Telescope** on the left, the final Telescope in Columbia!

Leap onto the police barge, and pick up the Shotgun from the gun rack on the right. Pull the lever to send the gunship on its way back to the Hand of the Prophet. It's time to bring Comstock down!

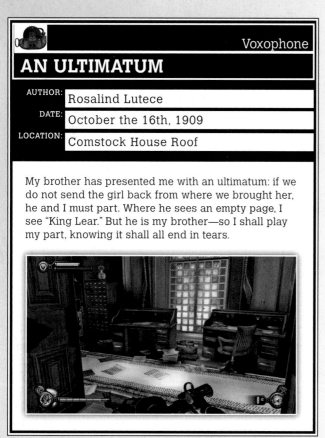

	Voxophone
	AN ULTIMATUM
AUTHOR:	Rosalind Lutece
DATE:	October the 16th, 1909
LOCATION:	Comstock House Roof

My brother has presented me with an ultimatum: if we do not send the girl back from where we brought her, he and I must part. Where he sees an empty page, I see "King Lear." But he is my brother—so I shall play my part, knowing it shall all end in tears.

TELESCOPE

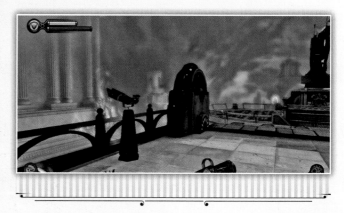

This last Telescope is located right near where the police barge docks with the roof. It's on the left-hand side and must be viewed before you get on the barge, since you won't be coming back to the roof.

REPEL THE AIRBORNE ASSAULT

The flight to the Hand of the Prophet won't be as uneventful as Booker was hoping. Another gunship soon deploys from the zeppelin and is due inbound any moment, as are several others after it. A number of Vox barges eventually join these police barges, as well.

Each ship has a couple of freight hooks that make leaping back and forth relatively safe and easy. Each gunship typically has four enemy passengers, three of which are often heavy soldiers with Machine Guns. The single best way to take them out (and unlock the "Bon Voyage" bonus) is to leap to the freight hook, perform a Sky-Line Strike on a nearby adversary to safely dismount the hook, then knock the crew off the ship with Undertow. Undertow, especially if upgraded, can knock all three or four foes overboard with a single use. Clear the deck of enemies, then leap back to your ship and deal with the Mosquitos that attack between the waves of enemy gunships. Check each gunship for Salts before disembarking.

Continue to do this until you have repelled all four barges, including the two Vox gunships. Return to your original police barge, where Elizabeth awaits, and prepare to dock with the Hand of the Prophet.

A loaded Shotgun and the Undertow Vigor
are all you need to clear the other ships.

Always use the freight hooks when leaping between ships,
even if there are two side by side.

★ HAND OF THE PROPHET ★

HANGAR BAY

The Sky-Lines strung around the perimeter of the lower decks on Comstock's ship, the Hand of the Prophet, are choked with Patriot Pods. The Sky-Lines are your only way up from one level of the ship to the next—and you begin the ascent on the lowest of five decks! You're going to have to clear those Sky-Lines to advance.

There's no reason to stop using Undertow now!

Step off the barge to the right, and quickly open the Tear for the Mosquito on the left. Continue to use Undertow to knock any enemy units right off the zeppelin, and step out toward the left-hand side of the ship and take aim at (or cast Possession) the Gun Automaton in the distance. There's a Gun Automaton on each side in identical positions and two more at the other end, near the controls.

★ HANGAR BAY ★

DECK 1

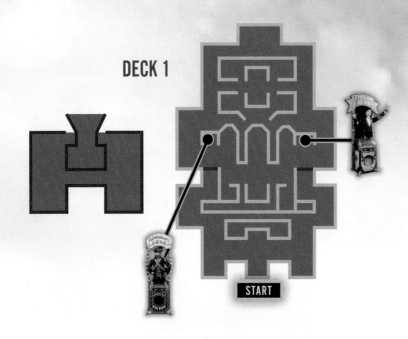

START

DECK 2

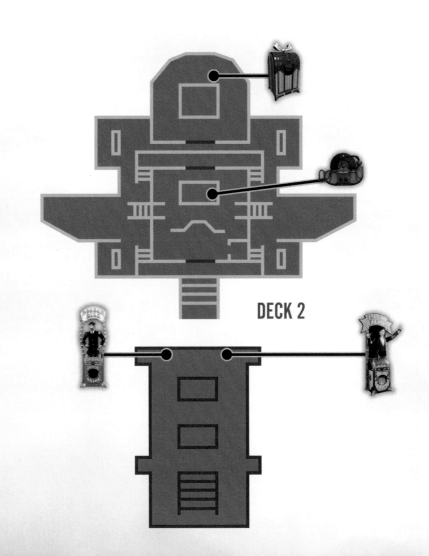

Collectibles

Infusions

-

Voxophones

3

Kinectoscopes

-

Telescopes

-

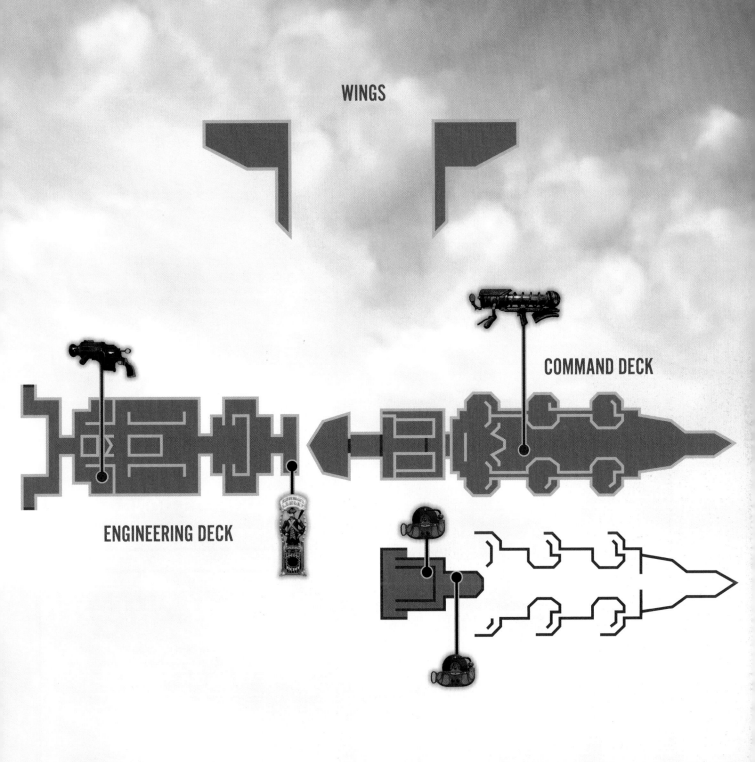

WINGS

COMMAND DECK

ENGINEERING DECK

Advance along the left-hand side of the ship to the airlock and pass through it to reach two small offices and staterooms. You can scavenge for ammo and Salts inside the belly of the ship and purchase additional weapon and Vigor upgrades from the vending machines. The interior of the lower deck is typically devoid of Founders, allowing you to explore the area without much risk. Cut across the center of the hangar bay by leaping across a docked police barge and exit on the far side. It's a good idea to sweep across the deck in a zigzag pattern, making sure to knock out each of the Gun Automatons as you go.

Press the button to deploy the Patriot Pods, then ride the Sky-Line up to the main deck.

Continue to the front of the hangar bay where a total of four Gun Automatons are located, two on the outer walkway and two on the inner. Use Shock Jockey and the Hand Cannon or Shotgun to take them out with a potent one-two combo attack! The curving walkway leads to a safer overlook if you need it, but you should be able to have Booker walk up to the controls and pull the lever to clear the Sky-Lines. This first Sky-Line clears quickly.

MAIN DECK

Travel on the Sky-Line long enough to spot a Tear for a Gun Automaton on the side of the zeppelin's second deck, and have Elizabeth open it as you leap down. Ready the Return to Sender Vigor and proceed to the center of the ship, near the stairs leading up to the controls. Use the Hand Cannon or Shotgun along with Return to Sender to take out the soldiers atop the stairs.

The center of the main deck has a series of locked rooms, several of them sealed shut with airlock doors beneath ominous red lights. Start at the south end of the ship and have Elizabeth pick the lock on the door beneath the "Secure Area" sign (and another next to an "Engineering" sign). Make your way through the interior rooms to find a **Voxophone** and a piece of **Gear**, the final one you'll find hidden in Columbia.

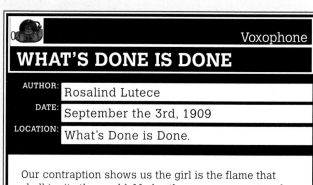

Voxophone

WHAT'S DONE IS DONE

AUTHOR: Rosalind Lutece

DATE: September the 3rd, 1909

LOCATION: What's Done is Done.

Our contraption shows us the girl is the flame that shall ignite the world. My brother says we must undo what we have done. But time is more an ocean than a river. Why try to bring in a tide that will only again go out?

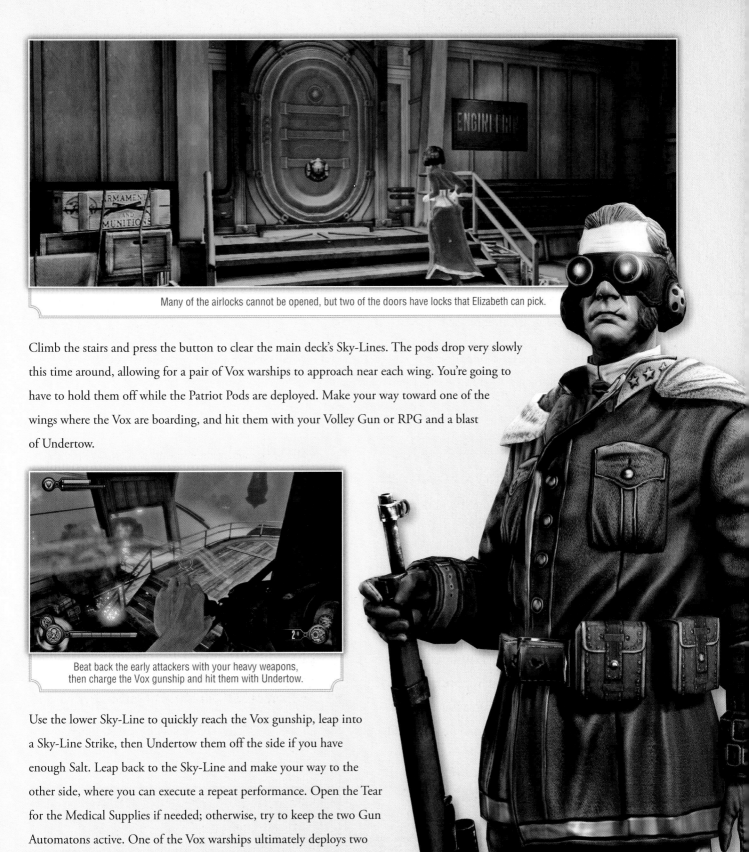

Many of the airlocks cannot be opened, but two of the doors have locks that Elizabeth can pick.

Climb the stairs and press the button to clear the main deck's Sky-Lines. The pods drop very slowly this time around, allowing for a pair of Vox warships to approach near each wing. You're going to have to hold them off while the Patriot Pods are deployed. Make your way toward one of the wings where the Vox are boarding, and hit them with your Volley Gun or RPG and a blast of Undertow.

Beat back the early attackers with your heavy weapons, then charge the Vox gunship and hit them with Undertow.

Use the lower Sky-Line to quickly reach the Vox gunship, leap into a Sky-Line Strike, then Undertow them off the side if you have enough Salt. Leap back to the Sky-Line and make your way to the other side, where you can execute a repeat performance. Open the Tear for the Medical Supplies if needed; otherwise, try to keep the two Gun Automatons active. One of the Vox warships ultimately deploys two Motorized Patriots of its own. Listen for Elizabeth's alert, and make your way over to it to put it down.

With the main deck Sky-Line cleared, it's time to head to the third level. Leap to the Sky-Line near the controls and ride it onto the upper wing as it comes into view.

ENGINEERING DECK

Dismount onto the upper wing and run up the walkway steps to the airlock door, pressing the button to go inside. Continue up the stairs and open the next door to enter the interior of the deck.

Use the supports on the wing for cover while fighting the Motorized Patriot.

The Engineering Deck is essentially comprised of two rooms. The room Booker first arrives in has a small circular Sky-Line running around it near the ceiling, whereas the second room has multiple Rocket Automatons. Pick up the Volley Gun and its ammo, and instruct Elizabeth to open the Tear for the Gun Automaton.

Ride the Sky-Line past the steps to get the Handyman's attention, but don't leave this room just yet!

Keep up the attack with Devil's Kiss while you're reloading the Volley Gun.

Leap to the Sky-Line to get the attention of the Handyman in the distance. Ride the Sky-Line in a loop while firing the Volley Gun at it. The Handyman can't help but give chase, so try to lead it back to the Gun Automaton, then leap down to avoid being electrocuted. Open fire on the Handyman's heart to kill it. Several heavily armored Founders start attacking at this time, as well. Try to stay close to the Gun Automaton and use Murder of Crows or Bucking Bronco to immobilize the enemies so the Gun Automaton can fire away without taking damage.

Dual Rocket Automatons, one on each side of the ship, guard the second section of this deck. Use Possession and the Volley Gun to destroy them one at a time, then advance past the vending machine and out onto the Sky-Line that runs along the perimeter of the ship, just below the Command Deck.

Ride the Sky-Line along the side of the zeppelin, up to Comstock's sanctuary.

CONFRONT COMSTOCK

Dismount the Sky-Line and follow Elizabeth through the door to the oasis Comstock has created for himself aboard the Hand of the Prophet. Walk with Elizabeth to the bird bath where Comstock awaits and stand by, opting only to intervene when prompted to do so. The meeting ends soon enough, and Booker and Elizabeth are then free to proceed to the exterior of the Command Deck. First things first: head up the stairs on either side of the garden and locate the final two **Voxophones**. One is on Comstock's bed, the other in the office. Equip the Shotgun hanging on the gun rack.

	Voxophone
THE PROPHET IS DYING	

AUTHOR:	Rosalind Lutece
DATE:	December the 4th, 1907
LOCATION:	The Hand of the Prophet

The Prophet is dying. The metastasis has aged him so quickly. Why does this Comstock decay, while a Comstock in another world remains fit? If genetics are destiny, what accounts for the difference? Perhaps exposure to the contraption? Hm. It merits further study.

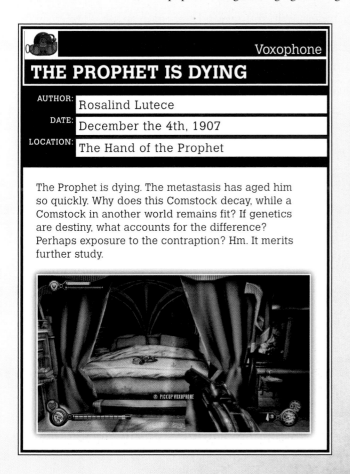

	Voxophone
THE MIRROR OF SIN	

AUTHOR:	Zachary Hale Comstock
DATE:	June the 21st, 1893
LOCATION:	The Hand of the Prophet

When a soul is born again, what happens to the one left behind in the baptismal water? Is he simply… gone? Or does he exist in some other world, alive, with sin intact?

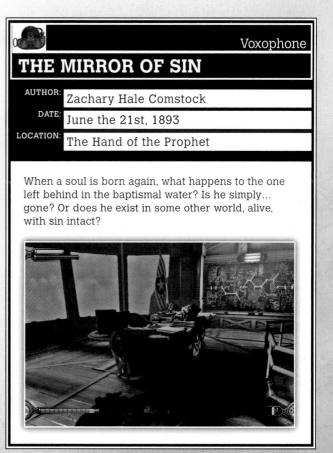

PROTECT THE ZEPPELIN

Head to the bridge and man the controls to steer the zeppelin, though you won't get very far. Fortunately, Elizabeth discovers a way to control the Songbird and entrusts Booker to use the Songbird to protect the zeppelin from an unrelenting attack by the Vox Populi.

Wait for the targeting reticle to appear,
then hold the Reload button to have the Songbird attack.

This final, epic battle takes place on the top deck of the Hand of the Prophet, an area ringed by a lengthy Sky-Line and two elevated walkways. The Sky-Line dips at the bow and rises several stories to a narrow observation deck in the stern, where you can find a Tear for a Sniper Rifle. The Vox are going to attack with an assortment of gunships and zeppelins of their own. The gunships have their own cannons, but their primary purpose is to ferry dozens of Vox Populi foot soldiers into battle atop the deck of the ship. These enemies ignore you for the most part, as their main purpose is to march across the deck and open fire on the energy core beneath the bridge. The meter in the upper right-hand corner of the screen alerts you to how much durability the zeppelin still has.

Defending the zeppelin is too hard for one person to do alone; not even Booker can do it. Fortunately, you have the Songbird. You'll be able to command the Songbird to attack any of the red targeting circles that appear. These targets appear on Vox gunships, at different areas of the zeppelin's deck, and eventually on the enemy zeppelins. Keep in mind that the Songbird has to regain its strength after each attack. The larger the target you assign it, the longer it takes to recover and be ready for another strike. Both Elizabeth and the on-screen Songbird Meter keep you apprised of the Songbird's status.

There are several Tears available on the deck, including those for Medical Kits, which you'll need. Equip Gear that boosts your capabilities while using Sky-Lines and that adds extra damage to your explosive weapons. It's also worth equipping at least one piece of Gear that offers temporary invincibility, whether from leaping off a Sky-Line or by eating a consumable. The key to successfully defending the Hand of the Prophet is to be in constant motion firing the Volley Gun or RPG at groups of enemies, using Sky-Line Strikes and Undertow to knock them off the ship, and making efficient use of the Songbird.

Ride the Sky-Line and use the Volley Gun to blast away the Vox as they target the energy core.

Instruct the Songbird to attack a gunship bearing cannons or Vox Beasts whenever it's available to strike. Try to take care of the foot soldiers on your own, saving the Songbird for larger targets. It's also worth watching the sides of the zeppelin for inbound gunships—you can save yourself a lot of trouble by having the Songbird destroy a gunship before the Vox disembark.

Order the Songbird to attack gunships that still have multiple Vox Populi on board.

You'll need to have the Songbird destroy three Vox zeppelins to survive the fight.

Do whatever it takes to protect the zeppelin's energy core, even if you have to stand directly in front of it.

Enemy zeppelins, Vox Beasts, and Motorized Patriots pose the largest threat to the Hand of the Prophet. Don't be afraid to hit the Motorized Patriots with Sky-Line Strikes and attacks from Vigors. Once you engage one of the Motorized Patriots in battle, try to either cast Possession on the other one (they almost always attack in pairs), or (at the least) focus your attention on that one. It's better to have one fully functional Motorized Patriot shooting the energy core than two half-damaged ones attacking it.

This is a lengthy, difficult battle to survive on your first try, but stick with it. Use the Sky-Lines to move about the deck quickly, and try to kill as many of the Vox as you can the moment they board the zeppelin—do not allow them to make their way all the way to the energy core! Use the brief breaks between gunships to grab a Medical Kit or Salt Phial (there are several Vigors and Salt Phials near the controls behind the energy core), and stay on the move. Switch to the RPG on the crate near the energy core if you run out of ammo for the Volley Gun, but save its limited ammo for groups of enemies. Don't be afraid to scavenge ammo and weapons from enemy corpses.

Enemies nearest the energy core are your top priority!

Join Elizabeth on the bow after staving off the Vox assault to bring this story to a conclusion. Congratulations.

ENEMIES

As he attempts to rescue Elizabeth and wipe away his own debt,

Booker encounters scores of enemies; from the ruling class Founders

to the unruly Vox Populi revolutionaries. In this chapter, you'll learn

everything you need to know about your foes—their different methods

of attack, abilities, and weaknesses.

As you advance through the game, your foes gain more health

and deal more damage. Each section of the game has a certain

"rank" of enemies.

WHERE YOU'LL FIND EACH RANK

Rank 1	Raffle Square
Rank 2	Battleship Bay
Rank 3	Finkton Docks
Rank 4	The Factory
Rank 5	Downtown Emporia

SOLDIERS—FOUNDERS AND VOX

TACTICS AND STRATEGY

Booker's most common foe comes in the form of soldiers for different factions, whether they're from the Columbia police, the Founders' army, Slate's disenfranchised troops, or the Vox Populi rebels. These soldiers have various backgrounds and a wide array of equipment, but in game terms, they all behave similarly.

HIGH POWERED FOES

It is important to note that enemies are also powered up by the difficulty level that you are playing.
Be extra careful of Rank 5 enemies in 1999 Mode!

Rank	Type	Health	Ranged Damage	Melee Damage
1	Police (Baton)	150	—	100
1	Police (Pistol)	100	25	94
2	Founder (Baton)	542	—	187
3	Founder (Baton)	705	—	225
4	Founder (Baton)	916	—	270
5	Founder (Baton)	1191	—	323
4	Vox (Baton)	916	—	270
5	Vox (Baton)	1191	—	323

The first type of enemy you'll face in Columbia is the melee-based soldier. These club-wielding assailants pursue Booker relentlessly until either he is dead or they are. When they're approaching, they'll occasionally try to sidestep your attacks, which can be especially annoying if they happen to evade a Vigor attack.

PISTOL

Rank	Type	Health	Ranged Damage	Melee Damage
2	Founder (Pistol)	295	50	187
3	Founder (Pistol)	384	60	225
4	Founder (Pistol)	499	73	270
5	Founder (Pistol)	648	87	323
4	Vox (Pistol)	499	73	270
5	Vox (Pistol)	648	87	323

When melee types are attacking, you should generally backpedal while firing to take them out before they reach you. If they get too close, slap them with the Sky-Hook to stop them from attacking, and finish them off with a Sky-Hook execution, another weapon, or a Vigor attack.

Since melee soldiers will charge at you to the ends of Columbia, they are particularly susceptible to traps. Backpedal into one, and watch as your attackers run headfirst toward their doom!

Alongside the melee enemies, there are many soldiers armed with various light weapons, such as the Pistol, Shotgun, and Machine Gun. Depending on the weapon they carry, these soldiers can be anything from a slight annoyance to a deadly threat.

Rank	Type	Health	Ranged Damage	Melee Damage
4	Founder (Hand Cannon)	499	575	270
5	Founder (Hand Cannon)	648	691	323
4	Vox (Hand Cannon)	499	575	270
5	Vox (Hand Cannon)	648	691	323

When facing armed attackers, check out what weapons they're carrying before making a decision about whom to dispatch first. Soldiers armed with a Pistol or Machine Gun are minor threats who have a hard time breaking your Shields, especially if you keep moving. These soldiers need to be set in place before attacking, so if you keep moving, they'll be unable to draw a bead on you.

MACHINE GUN

Rank	Type	Health	Ranged Damage	Melee Damage
2	Founder (Machine Gun)	354	41	187
3	Founder (Machine Gun)	460	49	225
4	Founder (Machine Gun)	598	59	270
5	Founder (Machine Gun)	777	71	323
5	Vox (Repeater)	777	156	323

When enemies are armed with a Hand Cannon or Shotgun, things get much more dangerous. Against these foes, it's absolutely imperative that you fight them while on the run, because letting them get a shot out can completely wipe away your Shields! These adversaries need to be closer than the others to attack you, so zap them with a Vigor whenever they're drawing near.

CARBINE

Rank	Type	Health	Ranged Damage	Melee Damage
3	Founder (Carbine)	460	180	225
4	Founder (Carbine)	598	216	270
5	Founder (Carbine)	777	259	323

Unfortunately for many soldiers, they're vulnerable to every Vigor, from Possession (as long as you buy the Possess Humans upgrade) to Bucking Bronco and everything in between. When possessed, enemy soldiers fight for you for a few seconds, and once it wears off (if they're still alive), they'll kill themselves, making Possession an instant kill!

SHOTGUN

Rank	Type	Health	Ranged Damage	Melee Damage
3	Founder (Shotgun)	642	625	225
4	Founder (Shotgun)	835	750	270
5	Founder (Shotgun)	1085	900	323
5	Vox (Heater)	1085	1451	323

The most effective Vigor against soldiers is often Bucking Bronco, especially after it's been upgraded. Bucking Bronco levitates soldiers for quite a while, leaving them vulnerable the entire time and allowing you to take them out at your leisure.

Rank	Type	Health	Ranged Damage	Melee Damage
3	Founder (Sniper)	460	923	225
4	Founder (Sniper)	460	923	225
5	Vox (Sniper)	777	1329	323

There is a unique breed of soldier who, although rare, is incredibly deadly—the sniper. You'll only face a handful of snipers in Columbia, but each encounter can end incredibly quickly, as a single sniper shot can drain your Shields no matter how much you've upgraded them!

BURST GUN

Rank	Type	Health	Ranged Damage	Melee Damage
4	Vox (Burstgun)	598	173	270
5	Vox (Burstgun)	777	207	323

Try to take snipers out with either a Sniper Rifle of your own or another long-range weapon like the Carbine or the RPG. Most Vigors won't reach a sniper, but you can use Undertow's alternate fire to pull them straight to you, removing their advantage and giving you the chance to take them out at close range with whatever you want!

AUTOMATONS (TURRETS)

TACTICS AND STRATEGY

All around Columbia, you'll run into many robotic emplacements built to fire upon any adversary in their line of sight. These Automatons are fairly common enemies but can be very difficult to take down due to their high defense and the constant stream of gunfire they send toward you.

The most common Automaton found in Columbia is the Machine Gun Automaton, which sprays a continuous stream of bullets at any hostile around it. While you might think you can safely avoid a turret's line of sight, it's nearly impossible—if you take a shot at them, they'll keep firing until one of you is defeated!

The easiest way to take care of a Machine Gun Automaton is to possess one—you'll create a powerful ally that will either finish off your opponents, or your opponents will finish it off for you! Machine Gun Automatons don't deal that much damage, but they do fire on you constantly. If you want to take one out with a gun, unload on it, trading damage until one of you is defeated. Unlike soldiers, turrets won't commit suicide after Possession runs out, so watch for the color of its light to change from green back to yellow to see when your ally will become your enemy again.

For fewer Salts, you can incapacitate a turret using Shock Jockey and then finish it off quickly, since this makes it both vulnerable and unable to fire on you.

The second type of turret, the Rocket Automaton, is much less common but much more dangerous, as it fires high-damage rockets at you! These turrets aren't as scary as they seem because they have a very low rate of fire, allowing you to move in and out of cover and fire at them in between shots. Much like Machine Gun Automatons, it's usually best to reduce their threat using the Possession Vigor.

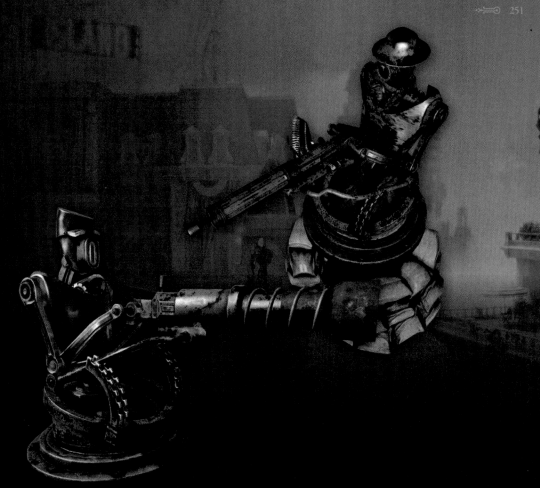

The third type of turret, the Barrage Automaton, is very rare, but it is the most deadly and sturdy of all of them. The Barrage Automaton is only found in a few spots but it is a very irritating enemy that constantly unloads rockets at you. Barrage Automatons are also completely immune to Possession, meaning you'll have to take out these beefy emplacements with other Vigors and standard weaponry.

The best strategy for these foes is to keep firing shots at them until they're defeated. There is an occasional break from their mortar fire—use this brief moment to unload on them until they start firing again! You can also use Shock Jockey to make them vulnerable and to stop their barrage for a moment, giving you a chance to take them out without fear of retribution.

Rank	Type	Health	Ranged Damage	Explosion Damage
2	Machine Gun Automaton	871	31	240
3	Machine Gun Automaton	1132	37	288
4	Machine Gun Automaton	1472	45	345
4	Rocket Automaton	1472	540	345
4	Barrage Automaton	4394	432	—
5	Machine Gun Automaton	1914	54	414
5	Rocket Automaton	1914	649	414

MOSQUITO

TACTICS AND STRATEGY

These flying Automatons behave like aerial turrets—once they see you, they'll fire on you until they are defeated! Unlike turrets, they don't fire nearly as often, making them much easier to deal with.

You won't have to fight these foes until you've earned Shock Jockey, so be sure to make use of this Vigor when engaging them. Shock Jockey renders them immobile and vulnerable, giving you plenty of time to take them out safely.

Mosquitos are also susceptible to Possession, which allows them to serve a dual purpose—not only are they your ally in battle, but all enemies will stop what they're doing and look up, allowing you to take them out while they're distracted!

Rank	Health	Ranged Damage	Explosion Damage
3	1132	37	288
4	1472	45	345
5	1914	54	414

ZEALOT OF THE LADY

TACTICS AND STRATEGY

The Zealot of the Lady is a devout follower of the deceased Lady Comstock who carries a coffin around on his back as penance for failing to stop her murder. The Zealot also worships the crow and has fully embraced the Murder of Crows Vigor.

The Zealot can be hard to pin down, since these enemies move around the area by turning into a flock of crows and teleporting to various locations. In crow form, a Zealot is completely invincible, and he can only be attacked when he materializes into human form.

After reforming into human shape, a Zealot attempts to run at you and slash with his sword. Once he turns back into a man, back away from him to avoid his melee attack, and fire at him until he turns back into a flock of crows.

Before you have Bucking Bronco or Shock Jockey, the Zealot can be a major threat, because it's impossible to stop him from teleporting around. Once you have these Vigors, blast him with them as soon as he materializes to stop him from moving, then unload on him.

Rank	Health	Melee Damage
2	2356	532
3	3062	639
4	3981	767
5	5175	921

FIREMAN

TACTICS AND STRATEGY

These heavy hitter enemies are trapped in iron maiden-like devices that are constantly burning them for their wrongdoings in life. They use the Devil's Kiss Vigor in combat, allowing them to attack you with the fire that surrounds them.

The Fireman generally attacks by throwing Devil's Kiss projectiles at you. While these fireballs are slow and easy to avoid, they explode shortly after hitting the ground, damaging anything nearby. This explosion has enormous range, so even if you dodge the initial fireball, run as fast as you can to get away from it!

If you get too close, the Fireman attacks with a close-range explosive attack. Before this attack occurs, the Fireman glows brighter and brighter before exploding. You can bait this attack by moving close to the Fireman, causing him to stop and charge up. Then, move backwards out of his range to fire at him.

To take a Fireman out, keep aiming at his head while moving from side to side to avoid the attacks he throws at you. Once you get used to his methods of attack, bait him into exploding by moving close, then backpedal while firing at him to stop him from throwing fireballs.

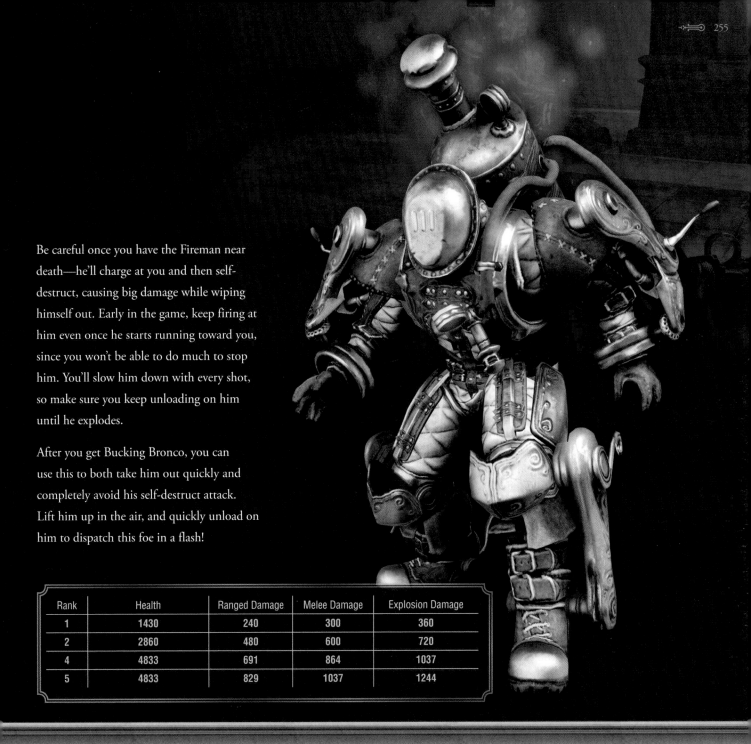

Be careful once you have the Fireman near death—he'll charge at you and then self-destruct, causing big damage while wiping himself out. Early in the game, keep firing at him even once he starts running toward you, since you won't be able to do much to stop him. You'll slow him down with every shot, so make sure you keep unloading on him until he explodes.

After you get Bucking Bronco, you can use this to both take him out quickly and completely avoid his self-destruct attack. Lift him up in the air, and quickly unload on him to dispatch this foe in a flash!

Rank	Health	Ranged Damage	Melee Damage	Explosion Damage
1	1430	240	300	360
2	2860	480	600	720
4	4833	691	864	1037
5	4833	829	1037	1244

MOTORIZED PATRIOT

TACTICS AND STRATEGY

The Motorized Patriot is an Automaton that comes in many forms, the most common of which is modeled after George Washington, America's first president and one of the key figures in Columbia's religion. There are also other models that resemble the other Founding Fathers. The Motorized Patriot is a very sturdy enemy that can be difficult to take down. These foes are a major threat in any encounter.

The Motorized Patriot carries around the Peppermill Crank Gun, which can shred your Shield in an instant and drain your health nearly as quickly. The Crank Gun has a very long start-up time, and the Patriot only fires on you if he has a guaranteed shot, so keep moving to prevent him from firing.

If you get too close, the Motorized Patriot will swing at you with his Crank Gun, which can really hurt. If you must get close, move toward the Patriot to force a melee attack, then move backwards to avoid it.

The Motorized Patriot has two weak spots—his head and the giant gears on his back. Shooting the gears deals much more damage than hitting him in the head, so try to shoot him there to take this threat out as quickly as you can.

The Patriot is extremely susceptible to Shock Jockey, which overloads him and freezes him in place. Zap him and move behind him to shoot at the gears to quickly wear the Automaton down. If you're too far away to get behind this mechanical monster, zap him with Shock Jockey, fire while moving toward him, then zap him with Shock Jockey again as soon as he can move.

Although the Patriot is an Automaton, he's not nearly as vulnerable to Possession as the turrets are. While it may seem like a huge advantage to take control of a moving, sturdy robotic ally, the Patriot shrugs Possession off rather quickly. It often isn't worth the Salts to take control of one.

Rank	Health	Ranged Damage	Melee Damage
3	5053	72	432
4	6569	86	518
5	8540	104	622

BEAST

TACTICS AND STRATEGY

The Beast is a heavily armored soldier carrying an explosive weapon. These heavy hitters are incredibly sturdy and can be very difficult to take down until you take out their armor.

You'll be able to pick the Beast out in a crowd—his armor makes him almost twice as wide as other soldiers! If you see one, you should make it your priority to remove this threat before you deal with the other enemies.

The Beast's armor causes him to take much less damage from your guns than normal soldiers. Before you can even start to deal damage, you'll need to hit the Beast with a few headshots just to take off his helmet, which lets you start dealing normal damage to him.

This foe has the same vulnerability to Vigors as normal soldiers, so make use of your Vigor arsenal to take him out faster. Bucking Bronco and Shock Jockey are especially effective, since they keep the Beast from firing while making him more vulnerable to your weapons.

Rank	Type	Health	Ranged Damage	Melee Damage
3	RPG	1743	1112	225
4	Volley Gun	1743	667	187
5	Volley Gun	3830	800	323
5	Volley Gun (Vox)	3830	1201	323
5	RPG	3830	1601	323

HANDYMAN

TACTICS AND STRATEGY

The Handyman is a robotic monstrosity that was once a man. Illness or injury has ravaged the bodies of these men to the point where they are only kept alive by having most of their body parts replaced by mechanical ones. A Handyman is an incredibly difficult enemy to defeat and is always a gigantic threat whenever one is around.

The Handyman primarily attacks by getting close and trying to punch you. These punches deal an incredible amount of damage so if you see a Handyman running toward you, run! After the Handyman swings, he'll stop and grab at his glowing heart. Use this opportunity to take some shots at him or put some distance between you.

From a distance, the Handyman can attack by throwing corpses and other objects at you. This attack has a long wind-up, and he won't be able to do it if there aren't any corpses or other objects close at hand, so look for an opportunity for him to pick something up and fire on him while moving to the side.

If the Handyman can't find an object to throw, he can shoot at you by generating electricity in his hand and turning it into a sphere before throwing it toward you. This projectile is extremely damaging and moves quickly, but it is not fast enough to catch you if you are moving.

Many Handyman encounters take place around Sky-Lines, giving you an easy route of escape if the Handyman is getting too close. Don't hang on them too long, though, since the Handyman can jump onto a Sky-Line and electrocute it, damaging you! You can use this attack to your advantage, however—hop onto a Sky-Line to goad him into grabbing hold of it, then jump down and shoot at him while he's defenseless!

The Handyman has two weak points— his head and his large glowing heart. He's much more vulnerable in his heart, so focus all your fire at it.

Since his body is powered by electricity, Shock Jockey is almost useless against him. The Undertow Vigor's normal fire typically only does a small amount of damage to the Handyman, but a charged Undertow will stun him for a few seconds, leaving his heart vulnerable while also dealing damage. The best Vigor to use against the Handyman is, surprisingly, Murder of Crows—the Handyman gets distracted by the crows, allowing you to fire at him without retribution!

After defeating the Handyman, keep an eye out because he drops a piece of Gear when he dies! This Gear can occasionally be hidden around the Handyman's massive corpse. Pay attention and make sure you don't miss out on a valuable piece of Gear!

Rank	Type	Health	Ranged Damage	Melee Damage
4	9952	1334	800	1382
5	12938	1601	960	1659

SIREN

TACTICS AND STRATEGY

The ethereal Siren is an other-dimensional form of Elizabeth's perception of who Lady Comstock was. The Siren is a very difficult enemy, and the utmost preparation and care should be taken in order to defeat her.

The biggest threat from the Siren usually isn't even from her—it's from the corpses she revives to fight you! When the Siren is reviving enemies, she'll be vulnerable, so use that time to deal some significant damage. Afterwards, it'll be difficult to find time to focus on the Siren, since you'll also have to contend with several reanimated soldiers. Try to take out the soldiers as soon as possible so you can focus on the Siren again.

In between reviving soldiers, the Siren attacks similarly to the Fireman by moving toward you and charging up a melee attack. This attack deals massive damage, so try to keep some distance away from her whenever possible.

The Siren is mostly immune to the effects of Vigors—they'll deal damage, but you won't be able to stun her. She takes more damage from Devil's Kiss, so use this Vigor on her whenever she's raising the dead. In general, you'll be better served by using your Vigors on the soldiers and your ammo on her.

"I owe you an apology… Comstock used me to bring you back… but I brought back a version of you… from the reality I had built up in my own head… He pretended to love you, as he pretends to love me."

-Elizabeth

Rank	Health	Melee Damage
5	15994	985

BOYS OF SILENCE

TACTICS AND STRATEGY

The Boys of Silence, blind from birth, are placed as security in Comstock House. With enhanced hearing, the Boys of Silence essentially function as security cameras with legs.

A Boy of Silence stands in place and swivels his head, searching for intruders. If he detects you, the light on his mask turns yellow, and if he keeps spotting you, it turns red. Then, he'll teleport away, and the minions of Comstock House will be directed to attack you.

This is not ideal, since the Comstock House minions are incredibly durable warriors that attack in large numbers, and can wipe you out in a hurry. Avoid being detected by a Boy of Silence at all costs.

Even though this foe takes a human form, he cannot be killed. If attacked, the Boy of Silence immediately spots you and raises the alarm.

Try to avoid a Boy of Silence by staying away from his area of detection. He surveys the area in a predetermined pattern—watch his pattern and move past him whenever he starts scanning in a different direction. As long as you carefully monitor his pattern of detection, avoiding him should be no problem.

> You cannot kill Boys of Silence.

ACHIEVEMENTS AND TROPHIES

Bioshock Infinite contains a total of 50 Xbox 360 Achievements equaling a total of 1000 Gamerscore. There are 50 Trophies for the PS3, including one Gold Trophy.

SPOILER WARNING

The following pages reference some events and locations in the game that may be considered to be mild spoilers. Read on at your own risk if you haven't completed the game.

★ STORY ACHIEVEMENTS ★

The following nine challenges each unlock as you progress through the story. They're included here for completion's sake, but this guide withholds comments or descriptions to avoid potential spoilers. Follow along with the walkthrough portion of this guide for assistance in unlocking them.

Icon	Title	Gamer Points	PS3 Trophy
	Written in the Clouds	5	Bronze
	Welcome to Monument Island	10	Bronze
	Shock Tactics	10	Bronze
	First Class Ticket	10	Bronze
	Armed Revolt	10	Bronze
	Working Class Hero	25	Bronze
	Blood in the Streets	25	Bronze
	Higher Learning	25	Bronze
	The Bird or The Cage	25	Bronze

DIFFICULTY MODES

Bioshock Infinite contains four difficulty modes ranging from "Easy" to "1999 Mode." Completing the game on any one difficulty unlocks the Achievement or Trophy for all lower difficulties simultaneously. 1999 Mode is unlocked only after completing the game on Hard difficulty. Consult the Detective Training portion of the guide for specific differences between each of the difficulty settings and for tips and suggestions concerning 1999 Mode.

Icon	Title	Description	Gamer Points	PS3 Trophy
	Tin Soldier	Complete the game on Easy difficulty or above.	10	Bronze
	Saw the Elephant	Complete the game on Normal difficulty or above.	25	Bronze
	Stone Cold Pinkerton	Complete the game on Hard difficulty or above.	50	Silver
	Auld Lang Syne	Complete the game in 1999 mode.	75	Silver
	Should Auld Acquaintance…	Unlock 1999 Mode.	10	Bronze
	Scavenger Hunt	Complete 1999 Mode without purchasing anything from a Dollar Bill vending machine.	75	Gold

★ COMBAT ACHIEVEMENTS ★
FOUNDER WEAPONRY

Each of the 11 Founder weapons (including the Sky-Hook) has a corresponding bonus. Use these weapons as Booker engages in combat with the Founders and Vox Populi to rack up enough kills to meet the criteria for each. You'll likely be tempted to swap out the Broadsider Pistol for the Founder China Broom at your first opportunity. This is fine. Just make sure to periodically use the Pistol later on in your journey to unlock the Achievement/ Trophy. Note that only the Vox Hail Fire counts toward your progress on these challenges, as each of the other Vox guns (the Burstgun and Repeater) differs significantly from its Founder counterpart. Consult the table on the next page for the Achievement/Trophy details.

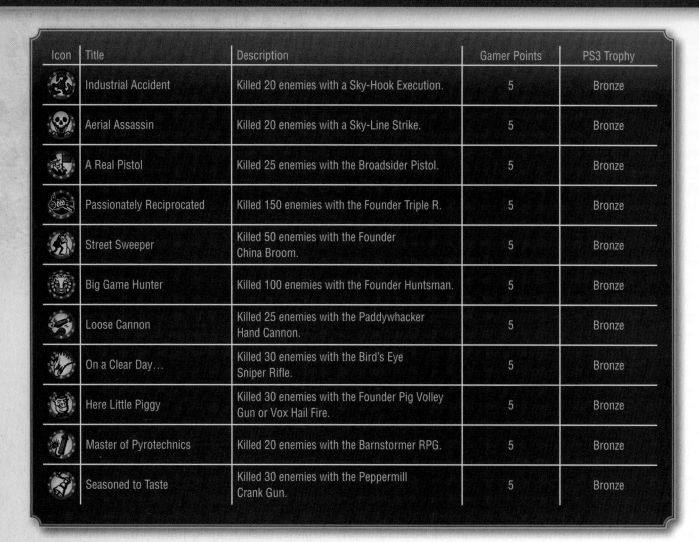

Icon	Title	Description	Gamer Points	PS3 Trophy
	Industrial Accident	Killed 20 enemies with a Sky-Hook Execution.	5	Bronze
	Aerial Assassin	Killed 20 enemies with a Sky-Line Strike.	5	Bronze
	A Real Pistol	Killed 25 enemies with the Broadsider Pistol.	5	Bronze
	Passionately Reciprocated	Killed 150 enemies with the Founder Triple R.	5	Bronze
	Street Sweeper	Killed 50 enemies with the Founder China Broom.	5	Bronze
	Big Game Hunter	Killed 100 enemies with the Founder Huntsman.	5	Bronze
	Loose Cannon	Killed 25 enemies with the Paddywhacker Hand Cannon.	5	Bronze
	On a Clear Day…	Killed 30 enemies with the Bird's Eye Sniper Rifle.	5	Bronze
	Here Little Piggy	Killed 30 enemies with the Founder Pig Volley Gun or Vox Hail Fire.	5	Bronze
	Master of Pyrotechnics	Killed 20 enemies with the Barnstormer RPG.	5	Bronze
	Seasoned to Taste	Killed 30 enemies with the Peppermill Crank Gun.	5	Bronze

VIGORS AND TEARS

WELL ROUNDED

Gamer Points: 10   PS3 Trophy: Bronze

Used all eight Vigors against enemies.

There are eight Vigors available for you to find in Columbia. Unlock this bonus by testing out each newfound Vigor against at least one enemy. The Vigor must make contact with an adversary to count toward this challenge.

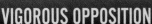

VIGOROUS OPPOSITION

Gamer Points: 50   PS3 Trophy: Silver

Killed 75 enemies with a Vigor or while the enemy is under the effects of a Vigor.

This may sound like a lot of Vigor-based kills, but you're bound to meet this total in a single playthrough (likely while in Emporia) as long as you make frequent use of attacks like Devil's Kiss, Shock Jockey, and Murder of Crows. These three Vigors have a relatively low Salts cost and lengthy duration of effect. Gunning down an opponent suffering the effects of a Vigor also counts toward this challenge.

TEAR 'EM A NEW ONE

Gamer Points: 25   PS3 Trophy: Bronze

Opened 30 Tears.

You won't gain the ability to direct Elizabeth in opening a Tear until you're making your way through the Hall of Heroes, but they become invaluable aids in combat. You can rush this bonus by repeatedly opening the same two or three Tears back and forth (there is a 10-second cooldown on most Tears), or you can just let it unlock naturally through the course of gameplay.

MORE FOR YOUR MONEY

Gamer Points: 25   PS3 Trophy: Silver

Lured three enemies into a single Vigor trap five times.

The walkthrough portion of this guide calls attention to several instances where a "surprise" ambush is about to happen. Get the jump on the opposition by laying traps down in front of the door they'll be exiting. Traps also work especially well in the exhibits at the Hall of Heroes, during the battle with Slate's men, and against the risen dead in Memorial Gardens. It's rare to have many Salts available, but you can snare multiple enemies in Vigor traps wherever a Boy of Silence lurks.

- DEVIL'S KISS AND MURDER OF CROWS
- DEVIL'S KISS AND BUCKING BRONCO
- DEVIL'S KISS AND CHARGE
- DEVIL'S KISS AND POSSESSION
- SHOCK JOCKEY AND MURDER OF CROWS
- SHOCK JOCKEY AND UNDERTOW
- SHOCK JOCKEY AND POSSESSIONCHARGE AND BUCKING BRONCO

STRANGE BEDFELLOWS

Gamer Points: 10   PS3 Trophy: Silver

Kill 20 enemies using allies brought in through a Tear.

This bonus is unlocked by opening Tears for Mosquitoes, Gun Automatons, Rocket Automatons, and Motorized Patriots. There are several battles in particular where continued reliance on Tear-based Mosquitoes is recommended. As long as you don't wait too long to open the Tears or manage to kill the same enemies that your ally is targeting, you shouldn't have much trouble unlocking this bonus during the normal course of gameplay.

MIND OVER MATTER

Gamer Points: 10   PS3 Trophy: Silver

Killed 20 enemies using Possessed machines.

Taking using Possession on a Gun Automaton, Mosquito, or Rocket Automaton is one of the best uses for the Possession Vigor. The effects aren't terribly long-lasting, but a machine under the influence of Possession can quickly rack up multiple kills on your behalf. Make a point of casting Possession on every machine you see, even after you've unlocked this bonus.

SKY-LINES

ON THE FLY

Gamer Points: 10	PS3 Trophy: Bronze

Killed 30 enemies while riding a Sky-Line.

Depending on your personal style of play, this could be a tricky Achievement/Trophy to unlock without making a concerted effort. Weapons like the RPG and Volley Gun are easier to use while riding a Sky-Line, since they require far less precision and can eliminate multiple foes at once. It's advisable to equip pieces of Gear that aid your combat abilities on the Sky-Lines. Consider equipping both the Sky-Line Accuracy and Death From Above items. Three of the places where you can really rack up a lot of kills from a Sky-Line are: Soldier's Field (second visit), the Thoroughfare in Emporia, and aboard the Hand of the Prophet's upper deck.

BOLT FROM THE BLUE

Gamer Points: 25	PS3 Trophy: Silver

Killed five enemies with a headshot while riding a Sky-Line.

This is for the true sharpshooters out there, but this challenge doesn't have to be as hard as it sounds. Equip the Throttle Control, Sky-Line Accuracy, and Winter Shield pieces of Gear, and load up the Carbine Rifle. Find an area with at least a couple of enemies, and leap to the Sky-Line. Slow down as much as possible, and use the Carbine to get as many headshots as you can. You don't actually have to be sliding along the Sky-Line to get this to count; you just need to be hanging from it. Watch the reticle turn red over an enemy's head, and fire!

GENERAL COMBAT

HAZARD PAY

Gamer Points: 25	PS3 Trophy: Silver

Killed 10 enemies by using environmental hazards.

Keep your eyes peeled for fireworks barrels, oil slicks, puddles of water, and other environmental hazards because you can use them to kill unsuspecting Vox and Founders. While Booker can detonate some hazards simply by shooting at them, like the barrels of fireworks at Raffle Park, others require use in conjunction with a Vigor. Send a bolt of Shock Jockey at water puddles to electrocute enemies standing in the water. Cast a firebomb from Devil's Kiss at an oil slick to create an instant inferno. Some hazards can be brought into the world via a Tear, particularly at Emporia. Tesla coils and oil slicks brought in by a Tear also count toward the total.

SKEET SHOOT

Gamer Points: 25	PS3 Trophy: Silver

Kill five enemies while they are falling.

It's possible to earn this bonus by killing enemies as they leap from Sky-Lines, but it's much easier to simply target them as the effects of Bucking Bronco wear off. Hit a group of adversaries with Bucking Bronco, fire a couple of rounds with the Machine Gun to soften them up, then really open fire as they start to drop. Bucking Bronco lasts roughly five seconds (minus upgrades). One way to all but guarantee a quick completion of this Achievement/Trophy is to have the RPG ready. Fire a rocket at the ground beneath a group of enemies just as the effects of Bucking Bronco wear off. The splash damage should take care of them.

BON VOYAGE

Gamer Points: 25	PS3 Trophy: Silver

Killed 20 enemies by knocking them off Columbia.

The easiest way to knock enemies off Columbia is with the Undertow Vigor, and the best place to do this is on the roof of Finkton Factory and on the barges leading to the Hand of the Prophet. Aim Undertow at a group of foes, and bowl them over with Undertow's powerful stream of water. One dose of Undertow can knock multiple enemies backwards. Purchase upgrades for this Vigor to extend its reach and effectiveness!

LOST WEEKEND

Gamer Points: 10	PS3 Trophy: Silver

Killed five enemies while you are drunk.

This is one of the trickier bonuses to unlock because Booker must quickly guzzle at least three alcoholic beverages while engaging enemies in a fight. Vision becomes severely blurred after quickly drinking the booze, and his balance and ability to aim are hindered. Alcoholic beverages drain Salts, so make sure to start with a full Salt Meter to ensure you can still cast a Vigor or two while drunk. Unleash a dose of Murder of Crows or Bucking Bronco, then spray-and-pray with the Machine Gun or Repeater to hopefully hit the weakened foes.

HEARTBREAKER

| Gamer Points: 50 | PS3 Trophy: Bronze |

Killed a Handyman by only shooting his heart.

This is arguably the most difficult challenge in the game, next to "Auld Lang Syne" and "Scavenger Hunt." The Handyman moves quickly, and it's rare that you can line up an attack that he doesn't see coming. Equip precision weapons like the Pistol, Carbine, or Burstgun, and only fire when you have a clean shot at the Handyman's heart. It's also possible to use a charged-up Undertow attack to pull the Handyman towards you. This disables him for several seconds, leaving him weak and his heart vulnerable. Another option is to lure him up onto a nearby Sky-Line, then leap off when he begins his electrify attack. He'll be stuck motionless on the Sky-Line as he uses his energy to electrocute the rails. This is your best chance at lining up a shot at a temporarily stationary Handyman. Make it count!

DAVID & GOLIATH

| Gamer Points: 10 | PS3 Trophy: Bronze |

Killed 20 "Heavy Hitter" enemies.

This Achievement/Trophy will unlock during the course of the game. The following enemy types count toward this bonus: Fireman, Zealot, Handyman, Motorized Patriot, and Siren.

★ UPGRADES AND COLLECTIBLES ★

This final group of Achievements/Trophies tests your commitment to exploration. Unlock these bonuses by searching all containers, spending money in the vending machines, and leaving no stone unturned. Follow along with the walkthrough portion of this guide—paying special attention to the maps—to uncover every hidden collectible in Columbia. This guide details the whereabouts of every Telescope, Kinetoscope, and Voxophone and includes the location of each and every safe, Infusion, and piece of Gear on the maps.

Icon	Title	Description	Gamer Points	PS3 Trophy
	Dress for Success	Equip a piece of Gear in all four slots.	5	Silver
	Kitted Out	Fully upgraded one weapon and one Vigor.	10	Bronze
	Raising the Bar	Upgraded one attribute (Health, Shield, or Salts) to its maximum level.	10	Bronze
	Infused With Greatness	Collected every Infusion upgrade in a single game.	25	Bronze
	Sightseer	Looked through every telescope and watched every Kinetoscope film (Lifetime tally).	50	Bronze
	The Roguish Type	Used Elizabeth to pick 30 locks (Lifetime tally).	25	Silver
	Eavesdropped	Collected every Voxophone (Lifetime tally).	50	Silver
	Grand Largesse	Spent $10,000 at the vending machines of Columbia (Lifetime tally).	10	Bronze
	Coins in the Cushion	Loot 200 containers (Lifetime tally).	10	Silver

OFFICIAL STRATEGY GUIDE

Written by Doug Walsh and Logan Sharp

DK/BradyGames, a division of Penguin Group (USA) Inc.
800 East 96th Street, 3rd Floor
Indianapolis, IN 46240

ISBN 13 EAN: 978-0-7440-1385-6

Printing Code: The rightmost double-digit number is the year of the book's printing; the rightmost single-digit number is the number of the book's printing. For example, 13-1 shows that the first printing of the book occurred in 2013.

16 15 14 13   4 3 2 1

Printed in the USA.

BRADYGAMES STAFF

PUBLISHER
Mike Degler

EDITOR-IN-CHIEF
H. Leigh Davis

LICENSING MANAGER
Christian Sumner

MARKETING DIRECTOR
Katie Hemlock

OPERATIONS MANAGER
Stacey Beheler

CREDITS

SENIOR DEVELOPMENT EDITOR
Chris Hausermann

DEVELOPMENT EDITOR
Jennifer Sims

MANUSCRIPT EDITOR
Matt Buchanan

COPY EDITOR
Angie Lawler

SENIOR BOOK DESIGNERS
Keith Lowe
Brent Gann

SUPPORTING DESIGNERS
Dan Caparo
Carol Stamile

PRODUCTION DESIGNER
Wil Cruz

ACKNOWLEDGMENTS

BRADYGAMES
BradyGames would like to thank the following individuals at Irrational Games and 2K Games for their hard work and help in creating this book.

PRODUCTION
Sophie Mackey
Don Roy
Elena Siegman
Sarah Rosa
Ashlee Flagg

ART
Scott Sinclair
Gavin Goulden
Jorge Lacera
Adam Bolton
Mauricio Tejerina
Calen Brait
Laura Zimmerman
Paul Presley
Chad King
Robb Waters
Shawn Robertson

NARRATIVE
Ken Levine
Drew Holmes
Kristina Drzaic
Drew Mitchell
Joe Fielder

QA
Robert Tzong
Amanda Cosmos
Charles Dworetz
Amy Keating
Tyler Caraway
Adam Cohen
Chris Fidalgo
Glenn Palmer
Raymond Corsetti

SYSTEMS
Adrian Balanon
Steve McNally
Sean Madigan
John Abercrombie

MARKETING
Leonie Manshanden
Zoe Brookes

Melissa Miller
Nico Bihary
Michael Kelly
Ben Holschuh
Josh Viloria
Nik Karlsson
Shawn Watson
Peter Welch

DOUG WALSH
Authoring the strategy guides for the *BioShock* series has been one of the true highlights of my career. So it was with great surprise and dismay that I learned a scheduling conflict might prevent me from working on the book for *BioShock Infinite*. Fortunately, my pleas for reconsideration were heard and within weeks I was racing Hurricane Sandy across New England to lay eyes on the most anticipated game of 2013. Now, several months and numerous visits to Columbia later, I can say it was all worth it. Not only was I just as mesmerized by the sights and sounds of Columbia as I was the underwater horrors of Rapture, but I got to meet some great people at Irrational Games as well. This book could not have been possible without the tremendous support of Sophie Mackey. Thank you so much for all of your support and assistance! I'd also like to thank Nico Bihary from 2K Games and everyone at Irrational Games who helped answer our questions and make us feel at home. To Logan, thanks for all the hard work! I want to thank my long-time editor Chris Hausermann for the enthusiasm, support, and encouragement on this book and so many others. Lastly, I want to give special thanks to Leigh Davis and Mike Degler of BradyGames for their continued support. Thank you both so much!

LOGAN SHARP
I would like to thank Chris Hausermann and the BradyGames team, Nico Bihary at 2K, Sophie Mackey and everyone else at Irrational Games for helping us with our ridiculous requests in the creation of this guide. I also want to thank Vanessa for understanding the ridiculous things I told her